MW01610734

1999
SIGNED

Fur Trade *Wars*

The Founding of Western Canada

To Bunty — Len
with regards from the
author

by J.M. Bumsted

GREAT PLAINS
PUBLICATIONS

© Copyright 1999 J.M. Bumsted

Great Plains Publications
3 - 161 Stafford Street
Winnipeg, Manitoba
R3M 2X9

All rights reserved. No part of this book may be reproduced in any form without the prior written consent of the publisher.

Design & Typography by Bill Stewart

Printed in Canada by Friesens

The publisher acknowledges the support of The Canada Council and the Manitoba Arts Council in the production of this book.

CANADIAN CATALOGUING IN PUBLICATION DATA

Bumsted, J.M., 1938-

    Fur trade wars

    Includes bibliographical references and index
    ISBN 1-894283-03-1

1. Fur trade--Canada--History.   2. Hudson's Bay Company--History.   3. North West Company--History.
4. Northwest, Canadian--History--To 1870.*   I. Title

FC3212.B84 1999   971.2'01   C99-920098-4
F1060.7.B84 1999

For Siân and Michael

Table of Contents

Thomas Douglas, Earl of Selkirk

Prologue

The place was Hudson's Bay House in Fenchurch Street, London, the headquarters of the venerable North American fur trading company, the Hudson's Bay Company. The date was 30 May 1811. A General Court meeting of shareholders was in progress. In attendance at the meeting were twenty-one primary shareholders, by far the largest number in years. Significantly, some of those present were not London businessmen, but individuals active in the HBC's Montreal-based rival, the North West Company.

The disparate group had assembled to deal with a controversial proposed land grant by the Company to Thomas Douglas, Fifth Earl of Selkirk, "within the Territories of the Hudson's Bay Company." This grant, huge in size and historical implication, would become the basis for European settlement of the Canadian Prairie. At the time, however, it was regarded more as a complex business deal, rife with intrigue and submerged violence.

The grant had been first mentioned by the Company's committee of management on 6 February 1811. It was discussed again on 13 February, tentatively approved a week later, subject to revisions and to the ratification of the Company's shareholders meeting in General Court. No business was concluded on that 22nd of May. The opponents of the grant forced a week's delay, giving those present time to examine the proposals in detail.

According to an anxious Miles Macdonell — the prospective governor of the new colony to be settled on the grant — there had been angry words inside the meeting room. Sir Alexander Mackenzie, the retired partner of the North West Company who had made such a reputation as an explorer in North America, had evidently stormed out of the Court. He insisted to anyone who would listen that one disaffected Canadian could set the natives of the region against the settlers at any time.

The General Court assembled again on 30 May. The meeting was heavily attended. A memorial prepared by six dissident shareholders, including Nor'Westers Edward Ellice and Alexander Mackenzie, was read to those assembled. The memorialists doubtless realized that they lacked the votes to stop approval of the grant to Selkirk — several of them had not held stock long enough to even vote on the matter — but they were going on the record. They complained of lack of time to prepare proper objections.

The memorial made eight points, four concentrating on the procedures involved in making the grant and four on Selkirk's motives. It concluded, "Your Memorialists cannot perceive for the said grant, any other motive than to secure to the posterity of the said Earl at the Expense of the Stockholders of the said Company an immensely valuable landed estate." This ad hominem accusation did not necessarily reflect the reasoning behind the grant, as doubtless the memorialists recognized. They could hardly admit, of course, that the Selkirk grant might well destroy their profitable trade in the interior of the continent.

The critics noted briefly the difficulty of populating a wilderness 2,000 miles from a seaport (obviously thinking of Montreal rather than of York Factory) and asserting that the inhabitants of the settlement would compete with the Company while gravitating to the Americans. "It has been found," they maintained, "that Colonisation is at all times unfavourable to the Fur Trade." Such valuable territory should be sold at auction, said these dissenters. The Earl of Selkirk might have been forgiven a sense of relief at this weak performance, which scarcely did justice to the issues involved.

The reading of the arrangements for the Selkirk grant, which followed the minority memorial, was anticlimactic. Probably only Alexander Mackenzie among those present had any real conception of the vastness of the 116,000 square miles of territory which was being transferred to Selkirk. The land was on both sides of the present Canadian-American border, and included much of the present province of Manitoba as well as large parts of Minnesota and the Dakotas. Selkirk was to pay a nominal rent and provide some services to the Company, chiefly in recruiting up to 200 effective servants annually for ten years.

After desultory discussion, the matter was put to the vote. Exactly £29,937 worth of shares voted in the affirmative and £14,832 in the negative. It is worth noting that Selkirk and his family voted only £8,561.13.4 worth of stock, and the largest single voting shareholder — William Thwaytes with £9,233.68 — voted against the grant. The Selkirk family had no controlling interest in the

Company in 1811, although they dominated its council chambers. With this vote, however, the great wars for the control of the Canadian fur trade began. The wars would last for 10 years, involve much destruction of property and loss of life, and would end only with the merger of the two fur trading companies in 1821.

The wealth-producing items for which all contended were mainly furs. On one level, the contention was mainly between the two fur-trading companies, with the Earl of Selkirk, who sought to establish a settlement at Red River, as a wild-card player. Other organized elements involved more peripherally in the struggle, however, included a number of American fur trading firms, and various levels of government. Within the British Empire, those governments included the British government represented by the War and the Colonial Office, and the colonial governments of Upper and Lower Canada. In the United States, the government at Washington was an occasional participant.

At another level, however, the conflict involved a variety of peoples who were already resident in the fur trade region or were soon to be introduced to the region as settlers. These included the First Nations; the European employees of the fur trading companies; Selkirk's settlers, who were mainly from the Highlands of Scotland; and the mixed-bloods, the sons and daughters of the fur traders and their aboriginal wives.

The fur trade wars of the early 1800s were by no means a simple conflict between two groups of European fur traders at Red River. The number of participants was many, their geographic extent enormous, and their ambitions complex. Attempting to untangle those ambitions and to tell the story of those contending interests across half a continent is what this book is about.

CLERICAL.
(Eighteenth Century)

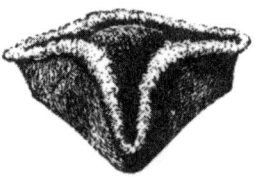

"CONTINENTAL"
COCKED HAT.
(1776)

(THE WELLINGTON.)
(1812)

(THE PARIS BEAU.)
(1815)

NAVY"
COCKED HAT.
(1800)

ARMY. (1837)

(THE D'ORSAY.)
(1820)

(THE REGENT.)
(1825)

~1~

Of Companies, Colonizers and Governments

From the beginning of Europe's intrusion into the Americas, the principal incentive was the extraction of exploitable wealth. The Europeans stumbled upon rich civilizations and large quantities of precious metals in Central and South America. In the northern regions of North America, however, they found a different kind of riches — fish and furs. Fish could be harvested directly from the sea, but furs required a trade with the First Nations of the continent, who were adept at trapping the fur-bearing animals (particularly the beaver) and processing the skins into a usable commodity. Europe had a species of beaver, but it was not as large and its skins not as attractive.

The North American beaver (*Castor canadensis kuhl*) was the continent's largest rodent, weighing from 30 to 60 pounds. Its amphibious body was covered with a soft felt-like underfur, one inch thick, protected with an overlayer of coarse guard hairs roughly two inches in length. The beavers lived in the forested regions of lakes and rivers, constructing dams for their lodges in the watered areas — usually slow-moving streams — and gathering construction materials from the adjacent woodlands. One family (two adults and young) inhabited a lodge, although the lodges often gathered together in colonies. The thickness of the beaver's fur depended on the length and coldness of the winter, and the number of beaver depended on the richness of the habitat. This meant that the furs got thicker and the number of beaver greater as one headed north and west across the continent, with the greatest centre for these fur-bearing rodents in the drainage basin of the Mackenzie River — the so-called "Athabasca country." Because the beaver lodges were so substantial, the beaver was not a migratory animal and was easily trapped. The pressure of trapping upon any local beaver population was severe, and thus the need for new supply drove the fur traders constantly west into the northern regions, where they found the skins superior.

From the very outset, the European intruders discovered that native practice with beaver skins provided an element of processing that made the skins especially desirable in Europe. The natives not only skinned their catch and sun-dried the beaver skins, but they then stitched a number of skins into a robe which they constantly wore, often immediately next to their body. Beaver skin was not only warm, but water resistant. The act of rubbing the skin against an oily human body over long periods had the useful effect of eliminating its guard hairs and reducing the skin to its felt component. It was possible to get rid of the guard hairs in other ways, but they were not quite as efficient or satisfactory. *Castor gras* (greasy beaver), or coat beaver, was always the most valued commodity in the fur trade. Skins that had merely been sun-dried (parchment beaver) were acceptable but not as valuable.

Initially the furs were made into coats, but Europeans soon discovered that North American beaver felt could be processed into hats. These became the principal end-product of the beaver trade. Fashion in hats came and went, although the beaver always provided the preferred felt because of its thickness and water-shedding capacity. In the seventeenth century, French policy drove the hatters (who were mainly Protestant craftsmen) out of that country. They settled in London, where the best furs were soon being auctioned. By the end of the 18th century, the felt stovepipe or "top" hat was assuming prominence. It consumed a fair bit of felt. Most beaver skins (or pelts) had to be stripped of their guard-hair and turned into felt in European factories, employing a complex process of combing and beating and shellacking and dying. The use of intoxicating chemicals (chiefly mercury) in this process affected the minds of those involved; hence the phrase, "mad as a hatter."

Other commodities could also be traded with the First Nations and collected off the land by the fur traders. There was some market in Europe for the skins of fur-bearing animals such as marten and lynx. Down feathers (for pillows and coat linings) from ducks, geese, and even swans, were also shipped to Europe in some quantity. The skins of the buffalo (or bison) did not become an important trade item until later in the nineteenth century. As for the wool of the buffalo, to the chagrin of the later settlers of Red River, it turned out that the buffalo wool was quite impervious to bleaching and dying. One could have it in any colour, as long as it was black.

The chief value of the bison before the later nineteenth century, when it was killed for buffalo robes, was as food. When cut into strips, cooked, pounded into flakes, mixed with berries, and packed into 90-pound bales, it was turned into a high-energy easily portable ration called pemmican. This ration served as a basic food of the voyageurs on their canoe journeys. One trader described it as tasting like dried blood. Whatever its taste, pemmican along with beaver fuelled the conflict among the great trading companies of the northern half of the continent.

1. The Hudson's Bay Company:

T his venerable trading company had originally been chartered in 1670 by Charles II at the behest of his cousin, Prince Rupert. It sought to take advantage of the rich fur trading territory uncovered by the Frenchmen Pierre Radisson and the Sieur des Groseilliers a few years earlier. The founding of the HBC followed the arrival in London of a rich cargo of beaver skins landed by the trading ship *Nonsuch* in 1669. The charter was in many ways a fairly typical document of imperial commerce of the seventeenth century. Beyond its grant of a trading monopoly, it also made the Company "the true and absolute Lordes and Proprietors" of a huge territory described as "all the Landes Countryes and Territoryes upon the Coastes and Confynes of the Seas" of Hudson Bay and the river systems that drained into it. This clause would allow the Company to create colonies and governments at will, although nothing of the sort was done at the outset.

From the beginning, employees of the Company located themselves in trading forts or 'factories' on the Bay with their manufactured goods brought from England, and traded with First Nations who canoed with their furs to the coast in the summer. The trade was easily and frequently disrupted by the French, who challenged the English militarily for control of the Hudson Bay region until 1713, when the Treaty of Utrecht restored the Bay to the HBC. No dividends were paid by the Company between 1690 and 1718, and the preservation of the charter increasingly became dependent on the vagaries of British politics.

Things were not going much better in Canada. An expedition to explore the inland territory and uncover the Northwest Passage led by Governor James Knight turned into a terrible disaster in 1719. After that date it would be many years before the Company's servants on the Bay became adventurous again. Their lack of initiative led an Irish Member of Parliament, Arthur Dobbs, to mount a campaign against the Company's privileges on the grounds of its persistent colonial inactivity while making enormous profits. Parliament refused to interfere. A book published in 1752, Joseph Robson's *An Account of Six Years Residence in Hudson's Bay*, provided further fuel for the controversy, charging that "The Company have for eighty years slept at the edge of a frozen sea." The Company was forced to undertake some inland exploration, but established few trading posts except along the Bay, where it had factories at York, Albany, Churchill and Moose, as well as posts at Eastmain, Henley House, and Severn.

No sooner had the trade settled into a somewhat profitable pattern than the Company became once again involved in an open competition. After the fall of Quebec to the British in 1759, new (mainly Scots-Canadian) traders based in Montreal took over the trading routes of the French voyageurs. They continued to utilize the labour of the French, as well as their aboriginal connections, but they added access to the British world of business. Thus they became much greater threats to the HBC.

The brash Canadians paid absolutely no attention to the chartered monopoly the Company thought it enjoyed. They expanded up the western rivers toward the Bay, meeting the natives on location and trading aggressively. The Company found competition expensive, not only involving the need to pay higher prices for furs but also to increase salaries for more servants to protect its ever-decreasing share of the market. Efforts to get its servants to move inland to meet their rivals directly were not very successful. Intimidation and even violence were used against Company traders who dared to contest the inland territory. The HBC men were placed at a distinct disadvantage in such encounters by Company orders to avoid conflict. They suspected (probably quite correctly) that the Montrealers had no great concern for the renewability of the fur resource or the future of the native peoples with whom they traded.

With its share of the North American fur trade reduced to perhaps one-quarter, the HBC in 1805 attempted to come to terms with the North West Company "to concert arrangements for the better regulating of the Indian Trade in America." The Nor'Westers demanded access to the transit route through Hudson Bay but offered nothing in return except a partitioning of the territory described in the charter. In several respects, therefore, the charter would have been openly breached without real gains. The Company instinctively balked at such an arrangement, recognizing that despite the decline in their share of the trade, the charter privileges still held from the British Crown were a valuable asset — if they could be enforced — not to be squandered lightly. It ended negotiations early in 1806, explaining a determination "not to procrastinate a negotiation which we thought could not be completed and which in the end would be ruining ourselves without a doubt or a remedy."

The *coup de grace* for the Company's profit sheets did not occur in North America but in Europe. When Napoleon closed the Baltic to trade in 1807, he shut off the principal market for furs. The Company had suspended auction sales rather than risk low prices. It relied heavily on its credit standing with London bankers to continue operating in North America. The British Treasury failed to respond to requests for "temporary Assistance which we cannot ask at any other hands."

With dividends suspended and the value of Company stock lowered, Sir Alexander Mackenzie became involved in the acquisition of stock in 1808. Mackenzie had long entertained a vision of expanding overland into the lucrative fur trade of the Pacific Slope — his famous explorations of the area had helped make such a venture possible — but he had been unable to reach a satisfactory business arrangement with his Canadian colleagues. He thus decided to try to harness the beleaguered and stodgy HBC to his ends.

Mackenzie, like the Nor'Westers of 1805, saw the Company less as a competitor than as the possessor of certain legal advantages through the charter, as well as holding a potentially better route to both the interior and the Pacific Coast than the lengthy one of the canoe brigades. He enlisted the Earl of Selkirk in his stock acquisition scheme, evidently so that the Mackenzie name would not be associated with the operation and drive up prices. Mackenzie had not contemplated that Selkirk—an aristocrat and a social activist — would become actively involved with the affairs of the Company. Part of his frustration with subsequent developments was a quite unwarranted sense of having been betrayed by the man he was attempting to exploit.

2. The Earl of Selkirk:

Alexander Mackenzie may have been a great explorer, but in his efforts to manipulate the Earl of Selkirk he demonstrated that he was not much of a judge of men. Thomas Douglas, Fifth Earl of Selkirk, had been born in Kirkcudbright, Scotland in 1771, the youngest son of Dunbar Douglas, Fourth Earl of Selkirk, and Helen Hamilton. His father was a relatively obscure Scottish nobleman whose "True Whig" political proclivities isolated him from his fellow peers. A Scottish nationalist, Dunbar and his eldest son Lord Daer had fought for the independence of the Scottish peerage from English control and had opposed the American War of 1775-1783. As a fifth son, Thomas was not expected to inherit the title. He was educated at a Unitarian dissenting academy and then sent to the University of Edinburgh, where he studied law with the young Walter Scott. Leaving the university without a degree, he spent some years in revolutionary France while his brother Lord Daer became increasingly involved in radical political agitation.

The deaths in rapid succession of his four elder brothers unexpectedly brought Thomas Douglas to the title in May of 1799. As Lord Selkirk he had political ambitions, but realized that he would have to overcome the family stigma of political radicalism to become successful. He thus turned to North American colonization as a field of activity, at least partly on the grounds that it was relatively innocuous. Beginning in 1802, Selkirk presented a series of proposals to the British government to lead dispossessed Irish and Highland Scots to resettlement in North America. One of his proposed locations was at the forks of the Red and Assiniboine Rivers, but he first concentrated in 1803 on Upper Canada and Prince Edward Island. His entrance into the Highland emigration business brought him to Scottish prominence. He was often excoriated by the ruling classes of the Highlands. Selkirk sent more than eight hundred Highlanders to Prince Edward Island in 1803 and another one hundred to Upper Canada in 1804, accompanying the Island party to North America and touring the continent for the better part of a year.

Upon his return to Britain Selkirk began writing the manuscript that would become *Observations on the Present State of the Highlands of Scotland*, his major contribution to political economy. The critical acclaim he received for this book in 1805 — although there was much criticism of it in Scotland — helped Selkirk in December 1806 to gain election to the House of Lords as a representative Scottish peer, loosely associated with the Reform Whigs. He managed to gain the support of the Tory government for re-election in 1807, but he did not enjoy the confidence of the ministry. He was appointed Lord Lieutenant of Kirkcudbright, but despite this and his membership in the House of Lords, he was not really utilizing his considerable talents.

In 1807 Selkirk married Miss Jean Wedderburn Colvile. The marriage gained him as a brother-in-law the shrewd and successful London sugar merchant Andrew Wedderburn (he later changed his name to Wedderburn-Colvile). If Selkirk was a visionary, Wedderburn was a hard-nosed businessman. His most notorious maxim was: "No man has a right to complain of hardship when he gets a bargain of his own making." Alerted to the opportunities in the HBC by his brother-in-law, Wedderburn quickly grasped the implications of the Mackenzie-Selkirk stock dealings. If Alexander Mackenzie could hope to gain control of the HBC through a relatively small investment in devalued stock, so could others. And while the famous Canadian explorer was chiefly concerned to acquire the Company's privileges, a few enquiries in the City told Wedderburn that the Company had been very conservatively managed for generations, and might easily be turned around by new and aggressive policies. In short, the HBC was ripe for a takeover bid.

Selkirk and his relations, including another brother-in-law, John Halkett, began acquiring stock and proxy support on their own behalf in 1809. Very early in the process Selkirk realized that the Company offered him another opportunity for North American colonization, and he was quite prepared to seize it. Selkirk made his first appearance at the Company's General Court in November of 1809, having purchased £2,000 of stock from a Mrs. Merry the previous March.

Although neither he nor his relations at this point actively intervened in Company affairs, Selkirk was already thinking in terms of a Red River settlement. On 6 December 1809 he wrote to Captain John MacDonald of Prince Edward Island about a proposed military expedition in connection with a colonization venture that he hoped MacDonald would lead. That same day he also wrote to Miles Macdonell in Upper Canada: "I have lately heard . . . of an agency, which will probably suit you, not in the regular army, but in a service which would be attended with permanent advantages. The employment to which I allude, having been mentioned to me confidentially, I am precluded from entering into an explanation at present, further than to express my conviction, that if I can succeed in obtaining it for you, it would be more advantageous than that which you were desirous of obtaining last year." Macdonell was to remain in readiness for a summons to London when and if the plans matured.

The Company had already begun deliberations on proposals from fur traders William Auld and Colin Robertson to reinvigorate its trade when Andrew Wedderburn on 3 January 1810 purchased the stock of Thomas Neave. Auld and Robertson wanted to move inland into direct competition with the Montreal-based Canadians in the rich Athabasca territory. Wedderburn announced his intention of standing for election to the committee of management not long after obtaining his stock. He was quickly accepted.

The committee had already decided before his election on a new policy, although not the one recommended by the two traders. No longer would the HBC attempt to compete directly with the

Canadians, but instead it would serve as an agent supplying goods to inland traders who would operate on their own account; the major Company initiative would be put into the supposedly lucrative timber trade. This shift in policy, associated with long-time director Anthony Wollaston, quickly became known as "Wollaston's Plan." It was not only unpopular with Robertson and Auld, but met little favour from the Earl of Selkirk, who commented both upon it and a better arrangement in papers written in February of 1810. At about the same time, the earl was writing to Miles Macdonell that while his proposals had "not yet taken such shape as to leave me at liberty to enter into fuller explanations," they had matured sufficiently to make Macdonell's presence in London essential.

The Wollaston Plan, Selkirk argued, would lead the inland traders to detach themselves from the Company, either decamping to the United States with the trade goods or entering into competition with one another. Because the right of the Company to exclusive navigation of the Bay was legally suspect, a single successful lawsuit by an independent trader might open it to all. Only the continued trading presence by the Company maintained the monopoly, and under active management it could outbid interlopers such as the Canadians operating from Montreal.

Referring to the earlier struggle between Sir Alexander Mackenzie's XY Company and the North West Company, Selkirk observed it was a "contest of Capital — the question was which had the heaviest purse." He continued, "Such is the Contest, for which the Company must be prepared, when they determine to make a vigorous & effectual effort to obtain a footing in Athabasca." This view of the fur trade as a simple business competition in which the winner would be the party with the greatest access to capital was incomplete. As Selkirk would subsequently discover, in the wilderness of western North America, far removed from the law to which he was accustomed in Britain, commercial competition often included sudden and harsh violence. Human capital in the form of soldiers, as well as financial capital, would inevitably be involved in the fray. A more telling analogy would have been not to commercial rivalry, but to war.

For the moment, Selkirk saw better ways of opening the interior than the plan suggested by Wollaston. He expanded on these in another memorandum which became part of Andrew Wedderburn's counterproposal, the "Retrenching System" or "New System" submitted to the committee on 7 March 1810. Even before unveiling his detailed proposals, Wedderburn had suggested the recruitment of personnel from the western islands of Scotland to introduce some backbone into the Company's struggle with the Canadians. The HBC had already moved away from hiring Londoners, who were regarded as soft and prone to alcoholism. Orkneymen and Scottish Highlanders, hardy survivors of a difficult climate, were regarded as ideal 'Bay men' and excellent stock for settlement. Wedderburn was authorized to recruit such men and to offer them land in Red River upon the expiration of their contracts. Like Wedderburn's proposed system itself, these arrangements suggest the fertile and inventive brain of Selkirk rather than the cautious business tactics of the merchant. While it is impossible to assign responsibility, it makes good sense to see the Earl of Selkirk at the centre of the new policy.

Combining features of the Wollaston Plan and the Auld/Robertson proposals with a vigorous prosecution of policy, the new scheme had Selkirk's mark stamped all over it. His brother-in-law contributed the insistence on sound business and accounting practices. The main thrust of the new system was the acceptance of profit-sharing with the Company's servants, combined with a vigorous inland expansion. Colin Robertson's scheme to compete with the North West Company by recruiting Canadians (mainly French-speaking voyageurs) was set aside, and the Company would attempt, for the next half-decade, to use Europeans inexperienced in the North American wilderness as its 'shock troops'. The scheme wedded the re-invigoration of the Company (which was what interested Wedderburn) with the encouragement of Highland emigration (which was what excited Selkirk).

In the short run, the Retrenching System offered little new or useful to the Company's servants forced to deal with Canadian competition. It was often criticised for its sublime ignorance of the realities of the fur trade, operating as though saving money would somehow improve the Company's dealings with the First Nations. But what Wedderburn and Selkirk envisioned was a long-term reorganization of the Company's activities in the West, based upon the advantages granted in the Charter of 1670, which was the Company's major asset. As Selkirk himself explained in an undated memorandum written at Fort William over the winter of 1816-17, "If the trade had come to a stand, the Indians would have been left completely at the mercy of the North West Company, and the influence of that unprincipled association would have been so completely confirmed that the Hudson's Bay territorial rights would not only have become a mere dead letter, but it would have become utterly impracticable ever at any time to recover them."

Reorganization could not take place overnight, and what would transpire demonstrated that more cautious building, combined with innovation, was what was really required. The opposition certainly caught the whiff of a new spirit afoot in HBC ranks, and began another round of negotiations in November of 1810. Again the Canadians offered to partition the territory and divide the trade. Again the HBC declined to accept such an arrangement.

While Andrew Wedderburn, with the somewhat perverse assistance of the HBC's Northern Department Superintendent William Auld, succeeded in cutting Company expenses to the bone, the Selkirk interests were quietly preparing a bombshell — which burst upon the London-based committee of management on 6 February 1811. Substantial amounts of geographical information about the territories claimed by the Hudson's Bay Company were by this time available to anyone willing to seek it out, not least in the mounds of records accumulated over the years by the Company itself. Selkirk would have been acting out of character in not doing considerable homework in advance. He read the records and talked to retired Company servants. His conclusion was that the southern portion of the HBC territories had considerable agricultural potential. The minutes of the meeting of 6 February recorded: "Resolved that Mr. Wedderburn be desired to request Lord Selkirk to lay before the Committee the Terms on which he would accept a Grant of Land, within the Territories of the Hudson's Bay Company, and specifying what restrictions he is at present prepared to consent to be imposed on the Settlers: And what Security he sees fit to offer the Company, against any Injury that may eventually arise to the Trade of the Company or any of their Rights & Privileges." This was the grant that would be ratified by the General Court a few months later.

Back in the colonization business, Selkirk plunged himself headlong into the affairs of the Company. In April 1811 he was negotiating with Christie & Co. of Birmingham for a new ten horsepower steam-driven sawmill. That same month saw the appearance of an advertisement in the *Inverness Journal* calling for a "few young active stout men" to join the employ of the Hudson's Bay Company, chiefly for a settlement "The Company have resolved to encourage . . . in a part of their territories, which enjoys a good climate, and favourable soil and situation." The advertisement did not mention Selkirk's name, and its confusion of Company service and Selkirk's settlement began a pattern which persisted for many years.

While he had succeeded in the establishment of small settlements in Prince Edward Island and Upper Canada, the earlier ventures were mere child's play compared to the audacity of Selkirk's new vision. He was proposing, with the HBC's reluctant co-operation, to plant a British colony in the middle of the vast, largely unexplored North American continent, nearly 1,000 miles beyond the normal communication and transportation facilities of the Company. The settlement

Andrew Wedderburn

John Halkett

Most of Lord Selkirk's first colonists were
Highlander victims of landlord clearances.

would be along the inland canoe route established by the HBC's Canadian rivals. Because only one passage per year to Hudson Bay was undertaken by the Company — leaving normally in June — it was necessary to begin recruiting for it before the final approval had been given by the General Court to the arrangement with Selkirk. Selkirk's usual impatience, combined with an effort to catch the NWC enemy off guard, accounted for the haste. Miles Macdonell was in London eager to begin his new assignment, and William Auld had made clear the need for reinforcements if open conflict with the Canadians were to be joined.

3. The North West Company:

The fur trading enterprise with which the HBC was proposing to compete was an operation in almost every sense antithetical to the traditions of the old chartered company. The North West Company was initially founded in 1779 as a joint stock company by a number of independent trading partnerships active in the western fur trade. Its intent was to provide an organization for raising capital, as well as providing a lobbying presence with the government of Quebec. From the outset, the strength of the company was in the hands of its traders and the voyageurs who manned the canoes that headed west every spring for the *pays d'en haut*. The traders were, for the most part, Highland Scots. The voyageurs were French-Canadians. The NWC flourished because of its flexible organization and the ambitious exploring thrusts of some of its intrepid partners. It also flourished because its traders could be absolutely ruthless when the situation required. Eventually the company became overextended, both in terms of investment and geography, which led it to seek some sort of understanding with the HBC to avoid unnecessary competition.

The leading French traders who had been in the West during the French Regime were rapidly replaced after 1763 by Americans and especially by Scots Highlanders, many of whom had spent some years in America. Highlanders proved adaptable to the fur trade. One aspect of Highland culture that suited them to the fur trade was their clannishness, which led them in the wilds of North America to work together, reinforce one another, and recruit kinsmen. The second feature of Highland culture that made these Highlanders successful fur traders (and explorers) was their familiarity with hunting, the bush, and rough living. The men who ran the NWC were not sons of crofters, but sons of Highland tacksmen who had entered the

British army as officers serving in North America or who had immigrated to America because of the disruptions to the clan system after Bonnie Prince Charlie's defeat by the English. For such men, the wilderness of western Canada was not intimidating. Most were surprisingly well educated and multilingual. They soon added native languages to their arsenal, introducing some aspects of Gaelic into fur trade patois in the process. Those who made careers in the West took native wives and, like the French, began raising families in the country. Most were "wintering partners," who remained among the native peoples for years on end. Bold, adventurous, utterly ruthless, the Highlanders soon totally dominated their competition.

Clannishness was both an advantage and a disadvantage to the NWC, which was increasingly dominated by the McTavish and McGillivray families. After 1800 no less than fourteen members of these two families were involved in the NWC. On the one hand, such family dominance helped provide solidarity of direction. On the other hand, it made innovation difficult. The NWC in 1811 was headed — as it had been since 1804 — by William McGillivray, a native of Dunlichty in Scotland and a nephew of Simon McTavish, one of the early spirits in the Montreal fur trade. The company's Thunder Bay depot had been named Fort William after him in 1807. McGillivray operated out of Montreal, was a member of the Scotch Presbyterian Church, and had important political links to the government of Lower Canada (Quebec). In 1814 he would be appointed to the Legislative Council of Lower Canada, which meant that he had the ear of the governor of the colony. McGillivray was responsible for putting his brother, Simon McGillivray, in charge of McTavish, McGillivray and Company, the London agents for the NWC.

The NWC was able to flourish because of its flexible organization and the local initiative of its partners. Over the period between 1779 and 1811, a number of Montreal-based firms provided short-term competition in the western fur trade. Almost without exception, they were first opposed and then swiftly incorporated into the NWC partnership. Competition from the so-called XY Company, which broke away from the NWC in 1798, lasted the longest, for about six years. Equally important, inland exploration was actually encouraged by the company, on the grounds that it would eventually lead to new sources for furs and to the potential riches of the Pacific Coast.

As early as 1792, the NWC had engaged in trans-Pacific commerce, initially through American merchant firms. The company found the cost of shipment through the East India Company to be prohibitive and the trade permitted by the EIC quite restricted. As a result, it proved less expensive to ship its furs to an east coast American port and have them transshipped in an American ship to Canton than to ship around the Horn with the East India Company. The shipments averaged 36,822 pelts per year between 1792 and 1796, and over 20,000 per year between 1804 and 1808. The NWC was anxious to be able to ship West Coast beaver directly to China, although the Oregon furs were not prime and would have to be used for felt rather than as coats.

Prime beaver came chiefly from the Athabasca. Dealing with the Athabasca region via a canoe route of several thousand miles was inefficient and expensive. The Athabasca was believed to be close to the Pacific, and it theoretically could be supplied with less expense from a coastal depot. This same thinking led the NWC to attempt its negotiations with the HBC to gain access to its coastal outlet. Thus, in a series of daring expeditions, Alexander Mackenzie explored first the Mackenzie River to its entry into the Arctic Ocean, then the Peace River, and finally reached the Pacific Slope overland. In 1808, Simon Fraser successfully completed the navigation of the treacherous Fraser River to its mouth at the Gulf of Georgia. David Thompson, who left the HBC for the NWC in 1797, explored the headwaters of the Mississippi and in 1811 ascended the Columbia River to its source, then traversed it to its mouth at Fort Astoria.

In 1811, the NWC petitioned the British government for a charter giving it exclusive rights in the region between the Rockies and the Pacific slope. The NWC did not limit its expansion to the West. In 1802 the partners had purchased the stock of the King's Domains (the Tadoussac Posts) originally held as a monopoly by the King of France in the Saguenay River country of what is now Quebec and continued by the British conquerors. The monopoly was leased for twenty years. The effects of the relentless expansion of the territory in which the NWC traded were, in the short run, overextended supply routes, which required great organization and coordination (as well as large amounts of capital) to support. But the overall effect of the system of partnership was an active competition among the partners themselves for success, one which the Hudson's Bay Company could only hope to emulate.

Without doubt the NWC could be extremely ruthless, in dealing with its own employees, with competition, or with unco-operative natives. In 1816 Lord Selkirk devoted his book *A Sketch of the British Fur Trade in North America* to cataloguing the excesses of the company. Selkirk observed that the absence of any institutions of law and order encouraged disorder, because the traders believed "the commission of almost any crime would pass with impunity." Selkirk also insisted that most of the intimidation was effected through the agency of the aboriginals and mixed-bloods, whose role in the violence was distinctly misunderstood in Europe.

William Coltman, who prepared a report on the fur trade wars for the British government in 1817, agreed with Selkirk that the business activities of the NWC were rooted in violence and intimidation. The company did not always treat its own employees generously. Much hostility prevailed between the winterers and the Montreal merchants who supplied them. One winterer in 1809 wrote that "whatever arrangements the A[gen]ts adduce to vindicate injustice oppression & corrupt practices will be fully as convincing as that of the Irishman who Being accused of smelling inoffensively in company wishes to prove the contrary by showing his Backside." The company certainly dispensed summary justice to Indians who were judged guilty of bad behaviour. It reserved its roughest treatment, of course, for its competitors, particularly the Hudson's Bay Company.

By 1811 the NWC was on the brink of its maximum extension, for in 1812 it would actually take over the administration of the fur trade on the Pacific Coast. It had formally schemed for this extension since early 1810, when it requested from Whitehall a 21-year monopoly on trade in those parts of the British West not claimed by the HBC. It also asked for permission from the East India Company to export furs straight to Canton. An NWC agent in London arranged a meeting in March 1810 with the secretary of state for war and colonies, Lord Liverpool, who failed to respond to the request. The British government eventually sent word to its ambassador in London to investigate the American plans for the Northwest. In November of 1810 Simon McGillivray wrote to Lord Liverpool calling for a British warship to be sent to the Columbia to prevent an American takeover of the region. McGillivray insisted that what was at stake was "the ultimate right of Possession of the whole Northwest coast of America." In the summer of 1811, the NWC decided to act unilaterally, voting at Fort William to send a brigade of sixty men west to the Columbia to compete with the Americans.

The NWC expansion to the Pacific would be a very mixed blessing. Extended transportation lines stretching virtually across the continent required the use of more extensive personnel simply to maintain communications. These men had to be paid and supplied. Along with them came larger numbers in dependent entourages. In 1806 the company at its annual meeting at Kaministiquia (Fort William) discussed the proposition that "the number of women and Children in the country was a heavy burthen to the concern." It attempted to reduce the number of women maintained by the NWC, particularly at various provisioning posts established along the lengthy route into the lucrative trading region of the Athabasca. One of the principal provisioning regions was at the junction of the Red and Assiniboine Rivers, the very site at which Lord Selkirk hoped to plant his colony.

Extended transportation lines also meant that it took years for the capital invested in an "outfit" of trading goods sent west to return east in the form of furs to be sold in the European markets. While all commerce in this period took long periods for investment to come to fruition, the five to seven years delay the NWC incurred seemed excessive by anybody's standards. Certainly the NWC went constantly deeper in debt to London bankers, a problem that would eventually help sink the company.

4. Other Fur-trading Companies:

Aggressive and expansionistic, the North West Company and the Canadian fur traders competed for furs in many places in North America besides the territory of the Hudson's Bay Company. In order to operate the southwest trade in the region south of the Great Lakes and in the Mississippi Valley, a number of Montreal fur traders had in 1806 — after the Americans purchased Louisiana — reorganized the Michilimackinac Company, with headquarters in Montreal. The Michilimackinac Company had originally been founded in 1784 by Canadian traders to do business in the territory ceded the United States under the peace treaty of 1783. The leading figures here included Forsyth, Richardson, and the McGill family. A large percentage of the furs shipped from Montreal actually came from the United States. Within a few years, the Michilimackinac Company faced increasing competition from the Americans, led by John Jacob Astor, who sought to control the American fur trade.

Astor (1763-1848) was born in Germany and had emigrated to the United States after the American Revolution. He soon became involved in the fur business, and he chafed at having to buy in Montreal and London furs that had originally been obtained in the United States. A ruthless and aggressive man, he had the same instincts to monopoly as the Nor'Westers. In 1808 Astor created the American Fur Company with the assistance of experienced American traders and a number of politicians. Almost immediately he offered to buy the Michilimackinac Company, but he and the Montrealers could not come to terms on a price. In 1810 Astor took advantage of an earlier business opportunity to supply the Russian settlements in Alaska by creating the Pacific Fur Company. As he emphasized to American politicians, this was an opportunity for the United States to "extend its dominion over a most interesting part of the opposite coast of the American continent, and perhaps open communications of no small moment with Japan and the East Coast of Asia."

Astor feared destructive opposition from the NWC. Before he organized the Pacific Fur Company he offered to cut a deal with the NWC which was in spirit similar to the arrangement the Montrealers had offered the HBC in 1805. The Canadians were being asked to share ongoing operations with a relative newcomer who had not yet actually entered the field. Astor offered the NWC the opportunity to acquire through investment a one-third share of the Pacific trade. In return, he would buy half of the Michilimackinac Company. The offer seemed unreasonable at the time, and the NWC initially rejected it. International developments, particularly trading embargoes by the United States, subsequently appeared to threaten the American trade with Montreal. Fearing "utter ruin", William McGillivray and John Richardson went to New York in early 1810 to accept Astor's terms. Conditions were put on the arrangement which the Nor'Westers could not possibly meet. The Canadians insisted that the deal would have to be agreed to by both the Montreal fur traders and the wintering partners of the NWC. Astor countered that the arrangement must be settled by May 1810 or it would be null and void. The wintering partners could not meet at Fort William until early July. Nevertheless, McGillivray and Richardson agreed to the terms and apparently did not think Astor would stick by his deadline. They brought the American arrangement with Astor to the Fort William meeting, which approved it reluctantly.

Meanwhile, having heard nothing from the NWC, Astor created the Pacific Fur Company on 23 June 1810. This company would establish a trading depot at the mouth of the Columbia River. Yankee traders had for years sailed to the Northwest Coast to obtain sea otter furs, which were then traded to Asia. This new operation would clearly muscle into that trade. Astor himself furnished all the capital for the new venture. He recruited in Montreal a number of disgruntled (and retired) NWC partners as associates. For five years Astor would supply all the money and take all the financial risks. Wilson Price Hunt, a businessman from New Jersey without fur trade experience was to be Astor's representative. The deputy-agent was Duncan McDougall, an old Nor'Wester. A number of young men were taken on as clerical employees, including Alexander Ross, Gabriel Franchère, and (later) Ross Cox. All three of these men would subsequently provide first-hand accounts of the venture, which was thus one of the best documented of all fur trade ventures. On 2 July 1810, Wilson Price Hunt led a small party from Lachine. It headed by canoe through the great inland water system for St. Louis, where Hunt recruited a "motley crowd" to strengthen his party. After spending a year collecting information, Hunt would set off for the West Coast from Dakota in the summer of 1811. Astor also acquired a ship, the *Tonquin*, which set sail from New York for the West Coast on 6 September 1810. There were 22 sailors and 33 passengers on board.

Like most lengthy voyages around the southern tip of South America, that of the *Tonquin* had its problems. The fur traders could not get on with the ship's captain, who like many such men was an imperious sadist. The vessel met violent gales, first off the Falkland Islands and then east of the Sandwich Islands. All the livestock acquired in the Sandwich Islands was lost in the latter storms. The *Tonquin* departed the Sandwich Islands on 1 March 1811 and arrived at the Columbia River on 22 March. An exploratory boat was dispatched, into rough seas, which was never heard from again. The party carried on and eventually picked a site in early May. They called it Astoria.

On 11 January 1811, William McGillivray and John Jacob Astor had signed an agreement at New York that produced the South West Company. The agreement stipulated that the NWC could buy into the enterprise by obtaining some of the half-interest acquired by McTavish, McGillivray and Company, and Forsyth, Richardson and Company. This organization continued an earlier practice of the division of fur trading territory, in this case agreeing that the NWC would surrender all trading posts and trading interests within the territorial limits of the United States. Many of the wintering partners of the NWC, led by Pierre de Rocheblave, were highly critical of this arrangement, which seemingly surrendered posts without getting anything in return. The same meeting at Fort William which agreed to the Pacific Fur Company/Michilimackinac Company deal also voted on this one. McGillivray defended the agreement by pointing out that Astor and the American government which seemed to countenance him would not hesitate to invoke trade sanctions. He also insisted that the understanding had no application west of the Rocky Mountains or on the North West Coast. Rocheblave was silenced by his appointment as manager of the South West Company.

5. The British Colonial Office:

The department of the British government that administered the colonies after 1801 had been created as part of the domain of the secretary of state in 1794. Previously colonial affairs had been run under the auspices of the Home Secretary. After the loss of the United States, colonial affairs suffered a fairly lengthy period of administrative neglect. The government of the old empire was allowed in most respects to continue by default. The eventual official establishment of a new office to run the colonies, which occurred in 1795, produced a remarkably compact operation.

The British Empire, while not as vast as it would later become in the nineteenth century, was still substantial in area and population. It was run by a single secretary of state, an under-secretary or two, and a handful of clerks. Ingoing and outgoing correspondence was filed in large ledger volumes on a colony-by-colony basis; these volumes can still be consulted by scholars at the Public Record Office at Kew Gardens in London. The administration of the Empire was very much a hands-on business for the secretary of state in charge. He made virtually all decisions, both major and minor, although details were often left to his under-secretary or sometimes to clerks, to be transmitted to the individuals involved. The volume of business was obviously fairly limited. Not surprisingly, the Colonial Office had real mastery over the dynamics of few of the territories it administered. Both the small size of the bureaucracy and the problems of transoceanic communication meant that the wheels at the colonial office revolved very slowly. Paper was never turned around swiftly. Months if not years passed before important decisions were made and transmitted to the relevant colonial authorities.

While turnover at the top was common in British politics and government, there was a remarkable stability at the Colonial Office during most of the period of the conflict involving the HBC and the NWC in the second decade of the nineteenth century. From 10 June 1812 to 30 April 1827, Henry, third Earl Bathurst, was secretary of state for the colonies. Bathurst did not have much of a public profile, but he was a minister who managed to maintain a fairly consistent, if conservative, policy in operation. Bathurst was not good on details, but he did manage to keep the big picture in view. From 4 August 1812 to 11 December 1821, his principal undersecretary was Henry Goulburn, a man of enormous industry. Goulburn was the perfect subordinate, capable of supervising the day-to-day operation of an extensive enterprise. Record-keeping, particularly of the means by which decisions were taken, was fairly primitive. Much business was done by personal interview and consultation that was never minuted.

Until 1815, the affairs of the Colonial Office — and indeed of the British Empire — were largely controlled by the war against Napoleon. Indeed, for much of the period of the War of 1812, the offices of the War Department and the Colonial Office were combined under one secretary for War and Colonies, Lord Bathurst. The end of that war at

Waterloo would liberate both the Colonial Office — and everyone concerned with colonies. Not until after the war would Lord Selkirk be able to respond personally to the situation in Red River, for example. When he and the HBC did respond, they found themselves operating at several disadvantages with the Colonial Office. As has already been observed, neither Bathurst nor Goulburn were innovators. They tended to prefer the status quo to the unknown, and in the North American fur trade, the dominant position of the NWC represented the status quo. This position was enhanced by the support the NWC received from the colonial governors of the Canadas, especially the governor of Lower Canada.

The HBC and Selkirk had at Red River established a new colony without any authorization from the Colonial Office, which had a normal bureaucratic reluctance to allow itself to be controlled by actions beyond its ken. Moreover, the HBC itself, as well as the territories it claimed under its charter, was well outside the administrative orbit of the Colonial Office. Parliament had legislated for these territories in 1803 to provide some minimum amount of law and order, but neither the HBC nor Red River had its own ledger books at the Colonial Office. Finally, both Lord Bathurst and Henry Goulburn appear to have inherited some vestigial dislike of Lord Selkirk, whose family had been radical Whig and who had joined the Tories only in 1807. Goulburn was active in the same evangelical circles as Selkirk, but there was no guarantee that this had made the two men congenial. Bathurst had supported Selkirk's efforts to organize a Highland Regiment in 1813, and had perhaps been burned in the process. In any event, Bathurst and Goulburn obviously preferred to view Selkirk as an upstart troublemaker. Thus, despite the HBC's august Royal Charter and long history of operations, the Colonial Office did not automatically perceive NWC as the interloper.

6. The Colonial Governments:

Given the importance of the fur trade to the commerce of Lower Canada, it is not surprising that the Montreal-based NWC should have great influence in the province. "That body took the lead in all assemblies, clubs, and other circles of society: their name influenced the tone of public opinion, within as well as without the city," wrote one commentator. The Nor'Westers also had great influence with the colony's government. The NWC also had some support from individuals within Upper Canada, although that colony was never as intimately involved with the business end of the trade. A succession of colonial governors visited the Beaver Club in Montreal and generally paid attention when men like William McGillivray (who became an executive councillor of Lower Canada in 1814) commented on fur trade affairs. "The Tartars never held the Grand Lama in higher estimation than the Canadians did the North Westers in those days," recalled Alexander Ross. Neither Lord Selkirk nor the HBC could expect any more support from the Canadian governments than they received from the Colonial Office

Although the vast territory of the West was not regarded administratively as part of the Canadas, parliamentary legislation in 1803 had provided an element of Canadian involvement in the West's administration of justice. 43 George III, c. 138, entitled "An Act for extending the jurisdiction of the Courts of Justice in the Provinces of Lower and Upper Canada to the trial and punishment of persons guilty of crimes and offences within certain parts of North America adjoining to the said Provinces", was passed by Parliament in response to increasing evidence of legal impotence in the fur trading country. A number of capital crimes were reported to London, several involving private vendettas and mock trials. Aboriginal peoples were both instigators and victims. The legislation declared that all criminal offences committed in the West were to be treated as if they had been committed in the provinces of Lower or Upper Canada. It further authorized the governor of Lower Canada to appoint civil magistrates and justices of the peace for the western territories. These officers were to apprehend culprits and convey them to Canada to be dealt with according to law. Some offences could also be tried in Upper Canada, although the law was somewhat confusing on this point. The legislation was not made operational before the War of 1812, but it would subsequently become a bone of enormous contention between the contending parties, all of whom had Canadian justices of the peace on their payrolls.

7. The American Government in Washington:

The American government was concerned with the fur trade in several respects. In the Great Lakes area, of course, the British authorities had failed to evacuate all of their military posts and give up their paternal supervision of the First Nations. British influence with the aboriginals was regarded by the Americans as extremely threatening to westward settlement in the region. Beyond the areas of settlement, American nationals such as those employed by John

Jacob Astor were themselves involved in the fur trade and engaged in active competition with the Canadian traders. Men like Astor had the ear of the authorities in Washington, always pitching their message in terms of an anti-British manifest destiny on the North American continent. On the Pacific slope, the British opening of the sea otter trade had soon seen that trade taken over by Americans, sailing to the region in American-registered vessels and taking them laden with furs directly into the Asian markets. The United States recognized its vested interest in both the Pacific Coast and the China trade, although it regarded itself as powerless to intervene actively in either.

The Americans did not declare war on Great Britain in 1812 because of the direct importance of the fur trade. But the United States' declaration of war was greatly influenced by its objection to British policy with the First Nations in the Great Lakes area. One of the byproducts of aboriginal policy was, of course, the fur trade.

The fur trade wars, especially during the decade 1811-1821, were never simply a commercial confrontation between two competing trading companies. It was a struggle that bit deeply into the fabric of society and government in North America, especially in the British colonies. There were many players and a variety of different interests to be taken into account. The fur trade wars were also far more than a mere competition carried out in the unorganized Red River district of what would become Manitoba. It was an international contest, conducted across the width and length of North America and involving a number of governments. The conduct of the conflict, as well as its eventual outcome, would have a profound effect on the development of western Canada.

~2~

People of the Fur Trade

he fur trade did not consist solely of the fur trade companies and a handful of European traders supported by their governments. A substantial population of local residents was also involved in the trade. The makeup of that population was constantly changing over time and was very dynamic.

Initially the fur trade country had been populated solely by members of the First Nations. With the introduction of the fur trade, company employees were soon living year-round in the country. Some traded, but many more supported the infrastructure of the fur trade, serving in such capacities as mariners, craftsmen, and canoe paddlers. By the eighteenth century, the HBC recruited most of its employees in the outlying islands of Scotland, especially in the Shetland and Orkney Islands. The NWC obtained most of its employees from among the Francophone inhabitants of Lower Canada.

Originally these employees, as well as the leading fur traders, were all temporary sojourners who returned to their homes after a tour of duty in the fur trade country. Over the course of time, however, the traders and company employees established regular relationships with aboriginal women and began to raise families of mixedbloods. Family ties encouraged some employees, especially those from Lower Canada, to remain in the region after their contractual connections with the fur trading companies were completed. They became known as "freemen" because their service was not formally contracted. The liaisons with aboriginal women also gradually produced a new group of people in the mixed-bloods, sometimes called Métis, whose claims to a separate identity were emerging just as, in 1812, Lord Selkirk began introducing European-born settlers into the region around Red River.

1. The First Nations South of the Bay:

The fur trade in Canada would have been impossible to operate without the people of the First Nations. They were, after all, the principal gatherers of the furs. The relationship was symbiotic but, as time went on, some tribes became dependent on the trade with the Europeans for their weapons and other commodities. They gradually spent more and more of their energy trapping furs and supplying fur traders with food, chiefly meat. But while their relationship with the fur traders profoundly changed the First Nations, it had begun as a natural extension of their traditional way of life and was not immediately destructive. So long as the First Nations were able to control the trade to some extent, they could utilize it for their own purposes. The process of change was not evenly distributed across the West nor among various First Nations tribes and bands. Instead, it was closely related to the duration and extent of contact between aboriginals and Europeans. Since such contact spread westward over time, so too did the dependency and destruction. Those First Nations in the regions closest to the Bay were the first affected.

The principal inhabitants of the region south of Hudson Bay now comprising Manitoba and eastern Saskatchewan were the Assiniboine and the Western Cree peoples. The Assiniboine spoke Sioux and the Cree spoke Algonquian. Both were relatively late arrivals to the region, having migrated westward from the lakes region of what is now western Ontario and Minnesota around the time of the first arrival of Europeans in North America. By the end of the seventeenth century, the Assiniboine had clearly separated themselves from their Sioux relatives to the south, with whom they had come to contend militarily. At about the same time, the newly arriving Cree in the region allied themselves with the Assiniboine against the Sioux. With the arrival of the HBC on Hudson Bay in the 1670s, both Assiniboine and Cree were drawn northward for trade with the newcomers, receiving firearms which provided at least an initial military advantage over the Sioux.

By the middle of the eighteenth century, the pattern of trade between the Bay posts and their aboriginal trappers had settled into its own routine with its own customs and traditions. Fleets of First Nations canoes would be led to the Bay by a "captain" who expected to receive ceremonially a red-coated British uniform and other gifts from the Company. The captain supervised the subsequent trading to make sure that "good measure" was given. Good measure meant not only proper pricing, but goods of proper quality. An extra profit for the local traders resulted from the difference between official exchange rates and what could be managed by reducing that rate, often by watering alcohol or giving short measure. This difference was called the "overplus" by HBC traders. Although an important middleman in the fur trade, the captain was probably not a traditional chief, but an individual who assumed the role for a season or more.

Native consumer demand for trade goods was relatively inelastic, limited by needs and an itinerant way of life which made possessions an encumbrance. Guns and ammunition, knives, cooking pots and blankets were the goods desired by the First Nations, and there were limits to demand. When these limits were reached, the traders were often tempted to move into non-material addictive consumer goods, particularly alcohol and tobacco. Before the 1770s, there was not much competition for the HBC. The French under the La Vérendryes had penetrated into what is now southern Manitoba and Saskatchewan, but did not much affect the tribes who traded at the Bay.

The arrival of the "pedlars from Quebec" — precursors to the Nor'Westers — after the conquest of Quebec by the British greatly increased competition, both at the Bay and in the interior. The HBC men had become accustomed to waiting at the Bay for the canoes; the newcomers went directly to the source of the furs, in effect intercepting the furs before they could be carried by the middlemen to the Bay. Because they eliminated the middleman, the Montrealers were able to offer better prices.

Competition among fur traders ultimately moved the prices for furs upwards, but also increased the temptation to trade in the easily consumable and addictive substances. The HBC opposed the use of credit, but local factors sometimes extended it, especially in competitive situations. The NWC found credit to be a powerful weapon in the constant struggle for furs. First Nations trappers or hunters indebted to a fur trading company found themselves committed to trade exclusively with that company. One of the regions in which competition between the HBC and NWC was strongest was along the western parts of the Assiniboine River and the adjoining Saskatchewan River, where by the end of the eighteenth century both companies had competing forts. The use of ammunition, cloth, liquor, and tobacco as trading goods was substantially higher in the competitive posts of the HBC in this region than elsewhere in the HBC trading sphere.

By the eighteenth century, every fur trading post began collecting a group of First Nations families who lived more or less permanently in the shadow of its walls. These families supplied meat to the posts, and preformed a variety of other tasks, such as guiding and mail-carrying. The HBC posts were the first to acquire these "Home Guards," because their residents were usually less experienced in living off the land than the Canadians of the NWC. But as the relationship between the Home Guards and the fur traders gradually became more complex, the posts of both companies were affected. The young women among the Home Guards were the obvious candidates for liaisons with the fur traders, because of their proximity to the posts. The children of these liaisons usually lived with their mothers. Only occasionally did such children attain non-aboriginal status because of their fathers. In some cases, particularly among the NWC, families living near the post consisted almost entirely of wives and children of fur traders. Not all of the traders were necessarily in residence within the walls of the post. A trader who died, for example, often left his family dependent upon the post for its survival.

Both because of the increasing dependence of the families on the fur traders and because of the obligations felt by the fur traders themselves for constantly larger numbers of their children among those immediately outside the fort, the Home Guards (the term was an HBC one) became set apart from other First Nations groups in the West. Gradually some of the mixed-bloods would themselves begin to emerge as a distinct people, but most continued to be part of the aboriginal community, usually among the "post Indians." Such people were often sadly deficient in both cultural roots and natural identity.

The presence of Europeans in the West drew aboriginal peoples into varying degrees of dependence. Some First Nations bands could easily become reliant upon European trade goods, particularly if they had regular access to competitive trading in them. In 1801 Daniel Harmon reported from Bird Mountain, Saskatchewan — in a zone of heavy competition among the fur traders — that "The Indians in this quarters have been so long accustomed to use European goods that it would be with difficulty that they could now obtain a livelihood without them." But dependence was not the only way in which Europeans altered the balance. Pressure of hunting, trapping, and fishing upon a non-cultivated resource base could rapidly exhaust it.

One of the most obvious effects of contact was in the introduction of disease which could reach epidemic proportions among First Nations lacking centuries of immunity. Epidemic, even occasional pandemic, disease had accompanied the arrival of Europeans everywhere in the Americas. In the regions south of the Bay, smallpox, measles, and whooping cough took a devastating toll in the latter years of the eighteenth century, with many reports among the fur traders of local epidemics. Both the exhaustion of resources and disease helped in the depopulation of Cree and Assiniboine from the areas of the Red River Valley, the lower Assiniboine River, and the

Interlake region of Manitoba. By 1800, the Cree and Assiniboine were being replaced by Ojibwa from the east.

The flux in the areas around the Red River meant that it was difficult for those in Europe to gain any adequate picture of the numbers and state of the resident population in the region. By 1811, for example, the principal band of First Nations inhabiting the lower Red River Valley were Saulteaux, often known as Plains Ojibwa. They lived along Netley Creek, about halfway between the Forks and Lake Winnipeg. Led by a chief named Peguis, these Saulteaux had moved into the temporarily uninhabited Red River region from further east around the turn of the century. Peguis had lost his nose in a fracas, and was often known as "Cutnose." His band consisted of about sixty males, who farmed along the river banks and hunted buffalo on horseback further inland. Like most of the bands resident in the region at the time, the Saulteaux led by Peguis were not particularly warlike. Conscious of their precarious position as recent arrivals relatively small in numbers, they were fearful of the far more militant and numerous Sioux to their south. The possibility of making arrangements with incoming Europeans to legitimate their land claims and provide protection against their enemies was attractive. A few were loyal to the NWC, but like many native leaders, Chief Peguis was not much enamoured of the treatment he received from the NWC, which had controlled the Red River before the arrival of the Selkirk settlers. Not finding the Saulteaux particularly useful, the Nor'Westers acted with disdain towards them. This would later lead to an unexpected benefit for Selkirk's settlers.

2. The Athabasca Region:

By the 1780s, the fur trade had moved westward and northward. The traders had come to recognize that the best furs — in both numbers and quality — came from the basin of the Mackenzie River — the "Athabasca" — a region described by the NWC in 1802 as situated 55 degrees north latitude to 66 degrees north latitude and 110 degrees west longitude to 120 degrees west longitude. This district encompassed the Peace River, Athabasca River, Slave River, and Mackenzie River systems — much of modern-day Northwest Territories, as well as northern Alberta and Saskatchewan. Most of it was subarctic in nature. Its native inhabitants were chiefly Chipewyan — which is Cree for "pointed skins" — who called themselves Dene ("people"). The Dene spoke a variation of northeastern Athapaskan.

They were part of those who inhabited and hunted for caribou in the entire subarctic north from Hudson Bay to the Coppermine River. They had probably begun moving towards the western parts of the barrens because of pressures from the Cree. The Dene, who were not natural canoemen, found the journey to the Bay both exhausting and dangerous, and much preferred to trade closer to home.

The American Peter Pond was the first trader to reach the Athabasca, in 1778. He returned with 140 packs of prime furs, and reportedly left as many behind for want of transportation facilities to bring them out. From the outset, transportation and provisioning were major problems for the Athabasca fur traders. The establishment of fur trading posts (or "forts"), chiefly by the Nor'Westers beginning in the 1780s, attracted many Dene into trapping. Before long the Dene were divided by the fur traders into two categories: the Trappers and the Caribou Eaters. The latter were considerably less affected by the fur trade.

The trapping Dene were regarded, especially by the Montrealers, as a very timid people. As a result, brutality and intimidation became an integral part of the fur trade in this region, especially in competitive situations. Much of the competition before 1805 did not involve the HBC, but rather rival groups of Montreal-based traders. Trading with the competition was often punished with physical violence. Such abusive behaviour was frequently justified in terms of the indebtedness of the aboriginals to the one company or another. The traders encouraged permanent indebtedness as a deliberate strategy for keeping the First Nations people dependent, although gradually debt loads became heavy and both the debts and the credit system would have to be cancelled. In the absence of legal institutions, the fur traders could do as they pleased. Aboriginals could be and were summarily executed, often when they responded with violence to fur trader intimidation.

As elsewhere in the fur trade, demand for European goods among the Dene was relatively inelastic. Increased prices during periods of intense competition simply reduced the number of furs offered for trade. Peter Fidler reported in 1804 that the First Nations "have very little occasion to work as they are liberally supplied betwixt those two Companies [the NWC and the XY Company] with Goods at a meere nothing." The expedients employed by the fur traders to expand the supply of furs included intimidation and an increasing use of the addictive substances, tobacco and alcohol, as part of the subtle manipulation of aboriginal customs such as gift exchanges. To their surprise, the traders found that the Dene were not much attracted by liquor, although they could be encouraged by ammunition. Another surprise was the shrewdness native traders frequently exhibited after arriving

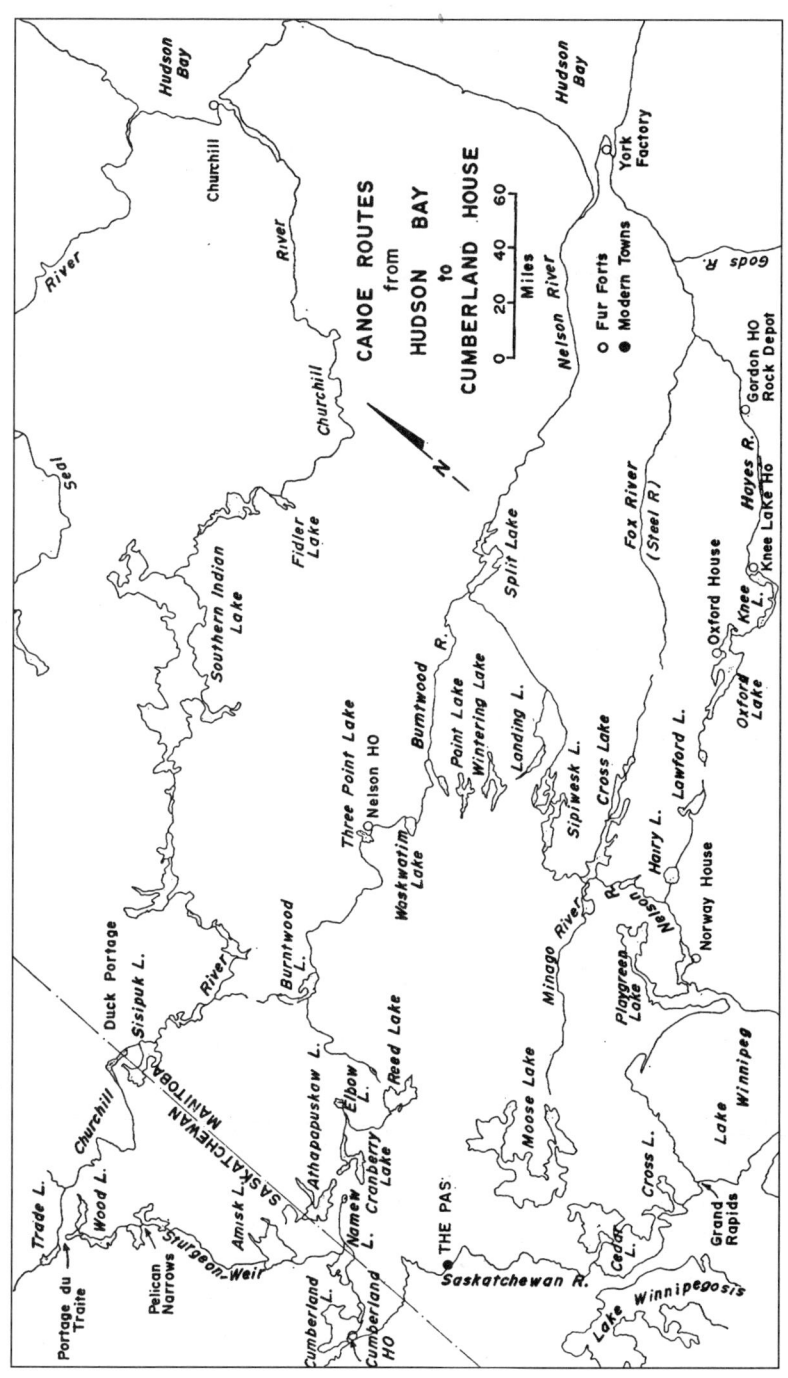

CANOE ROUTES
from
HUDSON BAY
to
CUMBERLAND HOUSE

Miles
0 20 40 60

○ Fur Forts
● Modern Towns

at the fort. The Europeans complained bitterly when the Dene sought to take advantage of competitive conditions by demanding higher prices. One trader wrote, "These damned Rascals delight in nothing more than in changing forts and in getting Goods for nothing at every place they go."

3. First Nations West of the Rockies:

Recorded European contact along the Pacific Coast did not begin until Captain James Cook landed at Nootka in 1778. What Cook found were semi-sedentary people who, despite the absence of agriculture, enjoyed a rich economic base centred on salmon and the cedar trees common to the region. He was greatly impressed by their trading acumen, although others would be more fascinated by the furs they were offering for trade, particularly the pelts of the sea otter. The northern groups — the Tlingit, Haida, and Tsimshian — had more highly developed social organizations than southern tribes. The Kwakiutl, Bella Colla, and Nootka in the south were still cultures in process of becoming. Nevertheless, all these coastal peoples had a very hierarchical society, with divisions into nobles, commoners, and slaves. Like their eastern aboriginal cousins, they also had complex social systems based on kinship and centred on clans - something Scots fur traders could easily relate to.

For all the Pacific Coast First Nations, fish, sea mammals, and shellfish were available in relative abundance, and could be supplemented by berries and other natural vegetation. These people lived well and were active traders. They had no need to farm. They resided in villages in large houses built of cedar, and travelled the coastal waters in big dugout canoes. Their prosperity encouraged a concept of material wealth, and their houses and villages displayed evidence of a strong aesthetic sensibility, expressed in intricately carved house joists and in totem poles depicting ancestral symbols.

Despite the lateness of the European contact, and the distance from both Europe and eastern North America, the sea otter quickly drew many traders in the wake of Captain Cook. They arrived by ship, and sailed with the furs straight to Asia. Many of the early sea captains were Americans, sailing in American vessels. The Americans came to dominate the early sea otter trade. John Jacob Astor established Astoria to try to confirm a resident trading presence on the coast, and the NWC was eager to break into the trade as well.

From the outset, the traders were persuaded that the coastal First Nations were extremely warlike. Most trade took place on shipboard, and treating the natives with both suspicion and intolerance could be costly. The First Nations did retaliate for violence done to them and were quite capable of aggression for their own purposes, often to maintain control over the trade. An attack on the American vessel *Boston* in 1803 ended with one crewman, John Jewitt, taken captive and held as a slave. A first-person account of his captivity was subsequently published as *A Journal Kept at Nootka Sound* in 1807. This popular "captivity narrative" introduced a generation of readers to one man's view of the Nootka. which was not always flattering. Although the contact with Europeans would eventually undermine the First Nations society of the region, in the period of the fur trade wars before 1821 — which was also the period of the dominance of the sea otter pelts — the natives were still very much in control of the coastal trading relationship and experienced little cultural disruption. Astoria (aka Fort George) was the only trading post built on the Pacific Coast before the 1820s.

The situation was different further inland in the region west of the Rockies. The NWC had begun establishing trading posts in the mountains as early as 1805, when Simon Fraser established one at McLeod Lake. The Nor'Westers quickly realized that, apart from the sea otter pelts, most of the furs offered for trade on the coast had come from the interior region. They could thus intercept the furs here, much as they had done with the Hudson Bay trade, by moving on site.

The peoples of the northern interior — Interior Salish, Kootenay, Chilcotan, Okanagan — were mainly Athapaskan speakers whose society and culture shared attributes of both the West Coast and further east. In their social organization, the inland tribes were divided into clans and hierarchies, but in their economies they were a semi-migratory folk dependent on hunting, fishing, and trapping. South of the 49th parallel, the Nez Percé had adapted to the horse after 1720 and were a highly militant people who did not trap and were hostile to trapping on their land. At its maximum extent before 1821, the NWC operation in this region consisted of ten posts and several hundred men. Considerably more warlike than the Dene, the First Nations of the Rockies forced the Nor'Westers to operate with much more circumspection than in the Athabasca. The accounts of early fur traders like Ross Cox and Alexander Ross contain many stories of violent confrontations with war parties. The fur traders had to trap their own furs in this region.

4. Employees:

Both the NWC and the HBC had hierarchical organizational structures, with enormous gaps between the various ranks. At the top were the merchants. In the HBC, these men were the stockholders who sat on the London-based Committee of Management. In the NWC, the merchants owned and operated the firms that supplied the fur trade. In both companies the men at the top tended to be British, although this was more true for the HBC than the NWC, which operated to a great extent out of Montreal. In the fur trading country itself, those at the top were the wintering partners of the NWC and the chief factors and chief traders of the HBC, both groups largely made up of Scotsmen.

Another substantial gap prevailed between these "gentlemen," who did the actual trading with the First Nations, and the ordinary employees of the companies, who did all the menial work, ranging from bookkeeping to operating boats to paddling canoes. In 1786 there were 51 "servants" at York Factory, representing nearly 20 designated occupations, including bricklayer and armourer. Because of the extended supply lines of the NWC, before 1811 a greater proportion of NWC employees were involved in the east-west transportation of goods, which was a full-time occupation for hundreds of individuals. Almost all of those in the fur trade brigades were from Lower Canada and were of habitant, Catholic, and Francophone origin. While both companies were hierarchical and status-conscious, there was always some mobility possible through the ranks. Indeed, in the eighteenth and early nineteenth centuries, it is likely that the HBC was actually more open to men of talent than was the NWC. This was particularly true given the disabilities placed upon illiterate Francophones by the fur trading system.

The HBC had recruited most of its employees in Scotland as early as the late seventeenth century. By the eighteenth century, it had shifted its recruitment patterns from the Lowlands of Scotland to the western and northern Islands, particularly the Orkney Islands. Despite their location, the Orkneys were not really part of Highland Scotland. Instead, their inhabitants combined rural poverty with a strong Norse inheritance of maritime activities. Orkneymen tended to be relatively literate and numerate, able to keep records and journals. They were able to tolerate the climate and the geographical disadvantages of the Bay — including the short daylight hours in the winter — and they were easily satisfied economically. Many were able to save enough money through service to retire comfortably at home. Orkneymen were also regarded as being more difficult to debauch than their southern compatriots, although this was obviously a relative matter. By the end of the eighteenth century, many HBC servants had aboriginal wives and families — who usually lived outside the walls of the forts — and alcohol abuse was common.

Despite the strict vertical integration between traders and servants at any HBC post, Orkneymen were relatively easily able to advance in the service of the HBC. Young labourers with no training recruited for seven years had two distinct routes to improvement. One was through the acquisition of skills of utility in the fur trading country. A second was by agreeing to serve in the interior in a position of greater responsibility. Best of all, the two routes could be combined. An ambitious young man could learn an aboriginal language and become a trader. The biggest complaint about the Orkneymen was that they lacked ambition and imagination. Many refused to take responsibility even when it was offered them. Edward Umfreville described the Orkneymen in 1790 as "a close prudent quiet people, strictly faithful to their employers, and sordidly avaricious."

The underlying foundation of the NWC was the accumulated wilderness expertise which the French-Canadian people had acquired over the course of nearly two centuries of fur acquisition in North America. While the wintering partners — the actual traders — were almost exclusively Highland Scots, the lower-level workers were Canadians, carrying on the techniques of the French fur trade. Only a handful of Canadian employees ever made it into the ranks of the partnership. Travel into the interior of the continent was engaged by the use of the birchbark canoe portaged from one river system to another, beginning with the St. Lawrence.

Canadian employees of the Montreal-based fur companies were of two types. One was the winterer (or *hivernant*), who contracted for a specified number of years which he spent in the West. Many winterers took aboriginal or mixed-blood wives, who lived with their children outside the forts. They paddled the canoes from Fort William loaded with provisions to their destination and brought back the packs of furs. Increasing numbers of winterers decided to remain with their families in the West after the expiration of their contracts, swelling the ranks of the "freemen" who operated around the fringes of every NWC post. The other type of employee was the voyageur or *mangeur du lard*, hired seasonally and usually for a single return journey from Montreal or Lachine to Fort William. These seasonal emplyees wintered in Lower Canada with their families. Because of the shortness of the season, it was possible to get only to Fort William and back in one summer. Thus the canoe brigades were manned by different people east and west of Fort William.

All these Canadians were accustomed to monotonous diets and to heavy labour over extended periods of time. Not only did they paddle heavily-laden canoes, but they hauled both them and their cargoes overland whenever necessary, often carrying several hundred pounds of provisions on their backs. Most such men were recruited as youngsters from within the ranks of the French-Canadian habitants from a relative handful of parishes, such as Sorel. They tended to be of limited educational accomplishments; many were quite illiterate and innumerate. The NWC understood perfectly well that its initial strength came from "experienced Guides, expert Canoe men and able interpreters," as well as from "the facility of procuring Birch Canoes and the knowledge which our traders have of the various articles necessary for the many Indian nations."

5. Settlers:

Although the preference of Highlanders for emigration to British North America had been theoretically arrested — by the government legislation of 1803, by the various schemes of Highland improvement set under way, and by the resumption of war with France — in truth the Highlands still remained a region ripe for emigration which Lord Selkirk hoped to exploit. Government action had little effect on the underlying causes of emigration, which were a combination of overpopulation (in terms of exploitable resources) and dislocation caused by the modernization activities of the great landlords. While earlier emigrations had come mainly from the kelping districts of the western Highlands and Islands and had not been the consequence of the notorious clearances for sheep, that latter "improvement" was clearly on its way in the central districts of the region.

Particularly susceptible was the huge estate belonging to the Sutherland family headed by the Duchess of Sutherland (also the Marchioness of Stafford). This estate consisted of a number of distinct holdings which together virtually covered the entire north-central area of the Highlands, and which included the entire county of Sutherlandshire. It had been the centre of recruitment for several Highland regiments in the eighteenth and early nineteenth centuries, including the Sutherland Fencibles, the 93rd Sutherland Highlanders, and the abortive Canadian Regiment of 1803.

The Sutherlands first became truly sympathetic to sheep-farming in 1799, the year in which recruiting had been carried out for the 93rd Sutherland Highlanders. Before the end of the eighteenth century, the estate had not become much involved in sheep-farming. Difficulty was experienced in raising the 93rd, despite the Sutherland continuation of traditional landholding practices — particularly the letting of land to small tenants in return for service. Although the family let substantial amounts of property for lengthy periods in order to obtain recruits in 1799, it became persuaded that the old Highland military spirit was dead. A long-term continuation of the old clan arrangements was no longer advisable. Over the next few years sheep-farms made slow progress on Sutherland land, but a number of new managerial appointments were made to the estate, all of which pointed in the direction of a major new emphasis upon "improvement" as estate policy.

At the beginning, the managers sought to modernize while retaining as much as possible of the existing population by such strategies as removing them to planned villages. In 1809, William Young and Patrick Sellar made their initial appearance on the Sutherland scene as agricultural tenants for one of the larger holdings on the estate. Young particularly believed in the need for planning, advocating a package that included the creation of harbours for fishing, reclamation of waste lands, new villages, and consolidated farms. He became an unofficial advisor for the family on improvement, and carried out a successful consolidation on a farm at Skelbo which displaced and resettled twenty tenants. In 1810, Young, with Sellar as assistant, was offered the management of the entire estate. The two assumed control in the early days of 1811. For the next few years, Young pursued a policy of consolidating tenancies, removing small tenants, as well as creating sheep-farms and muir settlements. He substantially increased expenditure on the estate in the process, as well as dislocating many tenants.

In any event, by 1811 everyone in the Highlands (and many interested parties beyond) knew that vast changes over the next few years were afoot for Sutherlandshire. This information fit perfectly with Lord Selkirk's renewed interest in North American colonization at the Red River and with the HBC's scheme to reinforce its servants with more militant Highlanders. The process of improvement on the Sutherland estates was bound to provide discontented and even dislocated tenants who might be signed up for service either with the HBC or the Red River colony. Selkirk did not for a moment doubt that he could fill his rosters with men who had traditionally been molded into some of the finest soldiers in the Empire, especially when commanded by their traditional clan leaders.

The problem was that such people did not necessarily make for the best settlers in an unorganized wilderness, or even the best military force to do battle with the warriors of the NWC. The Sutherlander at Red River was not led by his traditional leaders, but by men with which he had no easy familiarity and in which he had no particular confidence. Moreover, whatever else the ordinary Highlander was, he was not really a farmer but rather more a herdsman, not of sheep but of black cattle, which were the principal export of Sutherlandshire before 1810. Selkirk's settlers had difficulty in finding farm implements to use, but in truth, the hoe and the spade were as unfamiliar to them as were ocean voyages and the climate of North America. The typical Selkirk settler was, from the time of leaving home to his arrival at Red River, in a state of cultural shock from which he never really recovered.

6. The Mixed-Bloods:

Probably more numerous than the full-blooded aboriginal inhabitants of the region around Red River was a growing mixed-blood or Métis population, the products of liaisons (both long and short-term) between fur traders and native women. Because of the complexities of both the relationships between traders and First Nations women and of the fur trade itself, the progeny were not easy to categorize. As William Coltman explained in 1818, some of the mixed-bloods were extremely well educated, others were "scarcely removed from the savage state," and the bulk lived in a continuum somewhere between the two extremes.

By 1811 the liaisons had been going on long enough so that there were a fair number of mixed-blood women available. The first mixed-bloods in the West probably appeared shortly after the French had first moved into the area in the middle of the eighteenth century. Mixed-bloods grew among the "Home Guard Cree" clustered around the HBC trading posts of York Factory, Fort Albany, Moose Factory, and Churchill River. Many of these eventually became employed by the HBC, if mainly in menial occupations not usually associated with technical training requiring long apprenticeships. A few, mainly the sons of chief factors and chief traders, rose to some local prominence. Charles Price Isham, son of chief factor James Isham and a First Nations woman, was educated in Europe in the 1760s and rose through the ranks to become a postmaster.

By the end of the eighteenth century, the HBC was becoming aware of the need to educate its mixed-blood children, and the first schoolmasters were sent out to the Bay in 1808. By the end of the eighteenth century as well, it was becoming possible to be a mixed-blood associated with neither the British nor the aboriginals, but simply described as a "native of the country." Much of the lower-level personnel employed by the HBC were such "natives".

Most of the mixed-blood children at the Bay had Orkney fathers and Cree mothers. Those who emerged from the villages of the Home Guard Cree were usually the progeny of the more prominent traders. The situation was even more complex in NWC circles, where power also meant ethnic differentiation. Here too, sons of the prominent traders could be pulled out of the First Nations villages and given some special attention, often in the form of eastern Canadian or European education. The prominent traders were almost without exception Scots Highlanders, and their children a distinct minority. The young men specially treated usually were employed as clerks by the NWC, and they would become the leaders of the mixed-blood horsemen during the fur trade wars. Cuthbert Grant, for example, was the son of Nor'Wester Cuthbert Grant and a Métisse woman born at Fort Tremblante on the Saskatchewan River in 1793. His father died when he was six, but left instructions for the education of his son. William McGillivray himself supervised it. Cuthbert was educated in Scotland and returned to Canada a young gentleman.

Cuthbert Grant was not a typical mixed-blood. The bulk of the mixed-bloods growing up around NWC posts in Saskatchewan and Manitoba were the children of Francophone Canadians at the occupational bottom of the fur trade. Most of these children were absorbed into the tribes among which they were born, although some recognized their Canadian heritage. By and large, however, the offspring of Francophone fur traders and voyageurs received little parental support. They were uneducated and unfamiliar with the teachings of the Church into which their fathers had been baptized. By the beginning of the nineteenth century, there was some substantial number of mixed-bloods west of the Lakehead, probably many thousands, as neither the HBC nor NWC had been able to prevent their employees from becoming involved with the local women. Some mixed-bloods had moved into the western region away from the more settled East, where they were clearly regarded as outcasts.

Most of the HBC mixed-bloods, who often referred to themselves as halfbreeds, continued to reside in the North. A number of the largely Francophone mixed-bloods associated with the NWC, however, ended up around the Forks of the Red and Assiniboine Rivers or further up the Red River, drawn chiefly by the opportunities to sell produce (mainly meat) to the NWC to be manufactured into pemmican for the fur brigades. Some of them were actually employed by the NWC in various capacities ranging from clerk to hunter. They were joined by a smaller number of French-Canadian renegades (usually called "freemen") who were no longer under contract to the fur trading companies but continued to prefer to live on the plains. The freeman best known to later historians, of course, was Jean-Baptiste Lagimodière, who returned from Lower Canada to the Red River with a European wife in 1806. More commonly, a freeman's decision to remain or return was conditioned by the family he had sired in the region.

The mixed-bloods (also known as "bois brûlés", "métifs" and later Métis) were a highly volatile population, simultaneously aggressive and marginalized. If they could be convinced that they too had aboriginal land claims to and other "rights" in the Red River territory, they would make powerful enemies. If the mixed-bloods of the Red River region drew in their kinsmen associated with more distant trading posts, the resultant numbers could be quite considerable.

Lord Selkirk's research into the Red River region had established the existence of the aboriginal groups, which most HBC observers in the region regarded as fairly docile and pliable. Aboriginal title would have to be recognized and the land obtained from them by some sort of treaty. But there was little evidence that they would make trouble for a colony. Selkirk and his associates thus tended not to take very seriously the threats of the NWC of "Indian" attacks against a settlement. The HBC forces did not appreciate that the NWC was not simply talking about mobilizing Peguis's Saulteaux, but rather the mixed-bloods, who did not appear at all in any of the early calculations of Selkirk or his advisors. As late as 1815, when Selkirk drafted *A Sketch of the British Fur Trade*, the mixed-bloods remained totally unrecognized in Selkirk's thinking. This lack of awareness would soon become an extremely serious problem.

The decision-makers in the fur trade wars had at best a limited and incomplete notion of the other corporate players. But for the most part, they had no conception of and even less concern for the resident people in the fur trade region. As is usually the case, the failure to take into account the interests of all the players in a volatile situation helped produce disastrous consequences.

~3~

Preparations For Conflict

By 1811 all the inevitable ingredients for conflict were in place. The Hudson's Bay Company had been reinvigorated, the North West Company was recalcitrant and Lord Selkirk's controversial colony had been added to the mix. The HBC's chief aim was to defend its charter and monopoly from the NWC. In turn, the NWC sought to maintain its dominant position in the Hudson Bay drainage basin and Athabasca regions, as well as to compete successfully with American rivals for the control of the fur trade on the Pacific Slope.

The ensuing struggle thus covered much of the western part of the continent. It is not clear at what point the participants first understood that they were involved in a war. By early 1815, however, Nor'Wester Alexander Greenfield Macdonell would write from the interior, "We in this quarter assault the Colony in the rear, and to make safe work, we intend to draw some of their own men to our side, when have got a sufficient number we will then make them face about and fight the Battle. I intend to make myself their General." Around the same time, another Nor'Wester — Duncan Cameron — wrote to a Francophone employee: "I wish that some of your Pilleurs who are fond of mischief and plunder would come and pay a hostile visit to these sons of Gunpowder and riot."

Military metaphors became increasingly common on both sides. The wars took a variety of forms, and the fur trade country was not to settle down until 1821, when the major combatants finally merged. While the conflict was technically between two fur trading companies — the North West Company and the Hudson's Bay Company — almost everyone saw Lord Selkirk and his settlement as a key to the struggle. In this sense, the Scottish context was very important. In Scottish terms, the major combatants were Highland Scots on the Nor'Wester side and a Lowland Scottish laird with Highland and Irish connections on the other. Other simplified oppositions were those between England and Canada, between London and Montreal, or between a maritime supply route and an overland one. The conflict between French and English speakers — especially amongst the Métis — was not yet a major issue.

Contemporary perceptions, while important, were never entirely accurate. A tendency to oversimplify the issues prevailed on both sides, particularly in the press wars of the time. Through sympathetic newspapers, the NWC charged that Selkirk, the HBC and the Red River settlement were all part of the same conspiracy to destroy the NWC.

For his part, Selkirk insisted that he was not identical with the Hudson's Bay Company. While there was considerable overlap between the two, his point has much validity. The interests of Selkirk's settlement were not the same as those of the HBC, and Selkirk certainly faced the wrath of government quite independently of his fur trading colleagues. On the other side, the HBC and Selkirk always treated the Nor'Westers and the Métis as a single conspiracy, although there was considerable evidence that the company and its military arm often operated separately of one another. Moreover, everybody outside the Indian Territories tended to be unable to distinguish the Métis from the native tribes. Appreciating the complexity of the relationships among the antagonists is a key feature of understanding the conflict.

1. The Affair at Stornoway:

The North West Company always claimed, and has been credited with, the mounting of a persistent opposition to the fledgling colony at Red River from its inception. For their part, Lord Selkirk and his HBC associates were always ready to blame all disasters upon the interference of the Nor'Westers. In truth, in the first few years of the fur trade wars, little real antagonism on the part of the North West Company to either the HBC or the colony was in evidence. From 1811 to 1813, the attitude of the Nor'Westers to the colony was mainly one of patient forbearance, mixed at times with generous assistance. Most of the early difficulties experienced by Selkirk and the HBC were more the product of attempts to mount hastily and prematurely a vast transatlantic enterprise. Less Nor'Wester malevolence than HBC (and Selkirk) incompetence was involved in the early disasters of Company and colony. Indeed, in the years 1811 and 1812 the

NWC was probably more concerned with the American competition of the Pacific Fur Company on the Pacific Coast or the American Fur Company in the Great Lakes region than it was with the HBC.

While everyone was waiting for the General Court of the Hudson's Bay Company to approve the land grant to Lord Selkirk at the end of May 1811, the HBC had begun the process of recruiting young Highlanders for service in Hudson Bay. On 19 April 1811, Charles McLean of Coll and Donald Mackenzie of Stornoway advertised in the Inverness Journal for "A FEW YOUNG, ACTIVE, STOUT MEN for the service of the Hudson's Bay Company, at their Factories and Settlements in America."

This advertisement was part of the new HBC "Retrenching Scheme," calling for the recruitment of more aggressive Company servants from the Highlands and western islands of Scotland, as well as the establishment of a colony at Red River. McLean had been appointed Hudson's Bay Company agent in the Western Highlands to engage men for service in 1810, as had Captain Roderick McDonald for the Glasgow region. No evidence exists to suggest that Lord Selkirk had anything to do with either of these appointments, or that of Colin Robertson to recruit in the Orkneys. The Company secretary, Alexander Lean, corresponded with McLean and informed him that "the Company have resolved to encourage a Settlement at a part of their Territories which enjoys a good climate & is of a favorable soil & situation in other respects." Lean suggested that the hundred or more recruits McLean was being asked to provide could acquire land in the settlement at the completion of their engagements.

McLean reproduced Lean's words virtually verbatim in his advertisement. He then added some rhetorical flourishes of his own, to the effect that the climate was the same as at Montreal, Nova Scotia or Prince Edward Island — all familiar places to the Highlanders from past emigrations — and that wheat, oats, barley, Indian corn, potatoes, hemp, flax and tobacco would thrive on the soil. These remarks were intended by the recruiting agent to assure prospective recruits that the settlement would be in country little different from that already known to Highlanders. They were part of a long series of rhetorical overstatements by emigration agents of North American advantages. In truth, McLean had no real notion where the proposed settlement would be or what its climate was really like, later admitting that he had placed the advertisement as a routine matter "without consulting my employers."

To the surprise of Selkirk and his supporters, stockholders from the North West Company forced a delay in the formal vote on the land grant until the end of May. While the manoevering went on, the

Company's agents were busy collecting recruits in the north of Scotland and Ireland. They would have to be ready to depart in early June if they were to sail to Hudson Bay with the annual supply ships. Captain Miles Macdonell, who had responded to Selkirk's invitation to lead the party, was cooling his heels in London awaiting formal approval of the grant. He had not yet even met his recruits. The collection of Irish labourers was entirely in the hands of B.H. Everard of Sligo, again chosen by the Company rather than by Selkirk, although the earl was privy to the activities of the Board of Directors. But until his grant was formally approved on 30 May 1811, he had not taken an active role in recruiting either in the Highlands or in Ireland. Selkirk's involvement with recruitment of Company personnel would begin only with the 1812 season.

Immediately after the final approval of the grant Selkirk wrote to Alexander MacDonald of Dalilia asking him to take charge of his Highland recruiting operations, suggesting that he himself had not been close to the earlier recruitment. Selkirk noted that the men would be led to Hudson Bay by Miles Macdonell (who was Selkirk's choice) and the Irishman William Hillier (a military man who was apparently the Company's selection). The recruits had been obtained under Company orders. Selkirk's intention in 1811 was merely to detach a few labourers from the Company party to begin the lengthy process of preparing the settlement for subsequent emigration.

Even after the favourable vote on 30 May, Miles Macdonell and the Company ships (the *Eddystone*, the *Prince of Wales*, and the *Edward & Anne*, the last chartered for the voyage at a cost of £2,500 and intended to carry the new recruits) had difficulty in getting north. They did not weigh anchor from the south of England until late June, having been delayed waiting for convoy and by contrary winds. The vessels therefore did not manage to arrive at Stornoway until 17 July, by which time the recruits, most of whom had been awaiting passage since early June, were understandably restive. The tiny Highland village of Stornoway was not exactly well equipped to accommodate more than a hundred vigorous young men. There was little to do except drink and grumble. An account by an anonymous "Highlander" in the *Inverness Journal*, writing of the terrible climate in Hudson Bay, the distance of the region from the remainder of Canada, and of the dangers from hostile Indians, thus reached receptive eyes. Even without such information and veiled threats, Miles Macdonell would have experienced a great deal of difficulty in successfully embarking the waiting men, who had been hastily gathered by a number of recruiters under varying terms and conditions.

Particularly disruptive were the terms under which Captain Roderick McDonald had collected men at Glasgow, including a number of young "writers" (or clerks), intended for the HBC's service. These men were by definition better educated and more status conscious than were the labourers who made up the bulk of the prospective party. They had not only demanded and received promises of high wages at an annually augmented scale, but claimed they had been guaranteed treatment as cabin passengers on the voyage. They further complained that they had not been given copies of their indentures. Captain McDonald later insisted he had not promised cabin accommodation, but merely offered "a cabin, or apartment in the ships entirely separate from the men, but what that cabin was he could not describe." The writers had also been promised mattresses and blankets before departure. Such luxuries simply were not available for purchase in Stornoway. Failure to provide them confirmed a suspicion that the Glaswegians would not, on shipboard, be treated in a style befitting their self-perceived station.

The entire recruitment procedure was called into question when the clerks were informed by Miles Macdonell that the Glasgow agent had exceeded his authority regarding the augmentation of salaries. There would be no annual increments. As for the twenty labourers collected at Glasgow, ten had been promised salaries higher than their fellows and the labourers recruited in Ireland and the Orkneys. Although Macdonell had endeavoured to persuade them to take land in lieu of extra salary, they refused and naturally regarded the effort as insidious. As Macdonell explained to his employer, "it is an unfortunate circumstance that they were engaged different from the others, which will always be a source of grievance and discontent." The Glasgow contingent was clearly restless and unhappy. Regrettably for Macdonell, he was unable to sail swiftly enough to prevent the discontent from becoming serious. The vessels were held up by customs clearance.

Miles Macdonell and Selkirk always regarded the bureaucratic delays in embarkation brought about by the Stornoway customs officers as part of the Nor'Wester plot against the settlement. Such an interpretation is belied by the customs records of Stornoway, which still survive in the Scottish Record Office in Edinburgh. The port's collectors were legally bound, in clearing passengers for North America, to do so in terms of the "Ship's Passenger Act" (43 George III, c. 56). This legislation, which strictly regulated the conditions of passage, had been passed by Parliament in 1803 to prevent Highlanders departing for North America. Lord Selkirk always opposed the act as inequitable restriction (and he would in 1813 win its amendment by Parliament to exclude Company vessels from its provisions), but he had no real reason to assume that it was not operative in 1811 or that its application was directed specifically against his venture.

The Stornoway officials were consistent in their enforcement of the act whenever emigrant vessels cleared their port. Indeed, only a few weeks before the arrival of the HBC vessels, the collectors had learned of a "very daring and Criminal deception" which had been practiced against them the previous year. One of the chief provisions of 43 George III, c. 56 was that every vessel carrying emigrants should have a qualified surgeon on board, and in 1810 a ship headed for Prince Edward Island had cleared Stornoway with a "surgeon" using another man's credentials. Having only recently been deceived, it was quite understandable that the customs officers should be strict in processing the HBC's papers. According to the collectors, and there is much evidence to substantiate their position, they were in the end forced to bypass many of the regulations in order to process the ships as quickly as they did. Unable to obtain stamped paper, they were obliged to take bonds on ordinary paper. Moreover, the surgeons on board the *Prince of Wales* and the *Edward & Anne* could not produce their credentials. Considerable dispute ensued over whether the HBC had authority to export oatmeal and bulled barley to Hudson Bay; Secretary Lean later apologized for the confusion over the meal.

Given the general officiousness of customs collectors in Scottish outports, the wonder was the willingness of the Stornoway collectors to overlook many technicalities they could have applied. Here the relevant fact was not Collector John Reid's alleged relationship by marriage to Sir Alexander Mackenzie, but the documentable close connection between his colleague James Robertson and the HBC. Robertson had been appointed Company agent at Stornoway on 30 May 1811, charged with "all the Men engaged for the Service who are addressed to your care." Miles Macdonell testified to Robertson's assistance, writing to Selkirk, "He has been indefatigable to forward our affairs & has rendered important services in every manner in his power." Macdonell added, "Without his assistance we should not have succeeded so well as we have done." It was Robertson, after all, who housed and fed a hundred men for over a month — at "enormous outlays" of money, of course — and kept the party together until the tardy arrival of the transports. Probably the knowledge that Robertson was "one of ours" contributed to the suspicion that John Reid's lack of enthusiasm was a result of his being "one of theirs," although there exists no evidence except Macdonell's assertion to substantiate the charge. Of the two collectors, Reid was clearly the stickler for regulations, but given the circumstances this attitude was understandable. Reid unquestionably was opposed to Robertson, partly because Robertson was overly solicitous for the HBC welfare and partly because he had superseded a member of Reid's family as HBC agent in Stornoway.

While the Company's captains were struggling with the formalities of customs clearance, a certain "Captain McKenzie" appeared. Very likely the Donald Mackenzie who had advertised with Charles McLean in April, he attempted to recruit for the army among the employees, going so far as to give the King's shilling to some of the men. Little is known of Mackenzie, who was later described as "shabbily dressed and dirty," with "not at all the appearance of a Gentleman." Miles Macdonell claimed that Mackenzie was a son-in-law of Collector Reid, adding that the Captain had been formerly HBC agent in Stornoway. Having been replaced by James Robertson only a few months earlier, Mackenzie had no reason to feel well disposed to the Company. If his livelihood were being gained by military crimping, he would have been a fool not to take advantage of one hundred unattached, able-bodied, and discontented men landed fortuitously at his doorstep. The latest war with Napoleon was now eight years old, and eligible recruits were in short supply everywhere in the Highlands. The HBC, after all, was competing with the government for manpower. Those involved in military recruiting were traditionally mortal enemies of any emigration to North America. With his own positive interests added to his grievances, Mackenzie's actions require no reference to a London-based conspiracy of the NWC for explanation.

Mackenzie's chief target for recruiting became the *Edward & Anne*, anchored in the harbour with many of the new employees on board. The vessel itself was not up to Company standards, being old and badly fitted. Miles Macdonell had assigned most of the Glasgow writers to this ship. He had fitted up a place between the decks, where they were to lodge and mess among themselves. According to the subsequent testimony of the chief dissident among the clerks, this space was separated from the other passengers — Scots and Irish labourers — only by a sail fastened as a curtain from one side of the ship to the other. It was totally dark, and there were no mattresses or bedding. Even hammocks were unavailable. The clerks were most displeased with this accommodation, remonstrating unsuccessfully with Macdonell about the promises made to them of cabin facilities.

On 25 July, James Robertson and a clerk toured the ships to check the final muster of passengers, as they were obliged to do by the legislation of 1803. They ran into no difficulties with the *Eddystone* and *Prince of Wales*, but the *Edward & Anne* was a different matter. Captain Mackenzie was circling the vessel in a boat loudly proclaiming that it was harbouring deserters from His Majesty's forces, while on board the Glasgow clerks were seething with self-righteous indignation. On the deck of the *Edward & Anne*, Robertson assembled the passengers and read the muster amidst a chorus of complaints about conditions. He explained the terms of the parliamentary legislation governing provisions (which had been made deliberately generous in order to frustrate emigration). More voices were raised in complaint about treatment.

At this point, Mr. Robertson quite properly announced that nobody was legally obliged to depart for Canada against his will, whatever contracts had been signed with the HBC. Pandemonium then broke out, and many went over the sides of the vessel into Captain Mackenzie's waiting boat. Others rowed away in the ship's boat. One man jumped into the sea and tried to swim for shore; he was fished out by Mackenzie. More men disappeared into Robertson's own boat, as the collector scurried to escape the melee. According to stories later told in Red River, a sailor on board the *Edward & Anne* eventually scuttled Mackenzie by dropping a nine-pound shot into his vessel and making a huge hole in its bottom. Contrary to subsequent impressions given by Miles Macdonell and Selkirk in various accounts of this scene, however, the customs collector involved in the melee was James Robertson, the Company's own agent, rather than John Reid.

Many of those absconding were ultimately recovered on the beach and returned to the ship. It later was charged their treatment was less than tender. But the sailor in charge of the little flotilla, Captain Hanwell, decided he had experienced enough problems. "Captain Mackenzie" had already challenged Hanwell to a duel. The HBC captain weighed anchor for the Bay early the next morning, without consulting further with the customs officials. Collector Robertson managed to catch the departing vessels in his own boat to return two more of the missing men. One of the Glasgow clerks who got away, a young man named Moncreiff Blair, ultimately made his way to London. With the eager assistance of the friends of the NWC, he instituted legal action against the HBC for breach of contract. The result was more controversy in the *Inverness Journal*, which reprinted a lengthy affidavit from Blair and answering affidavits from HBC people, especially the officers of the *Edward & Anne*. This exchange demonstrated that Blair had not been particularly badly treated, despite not being given the cabin accommodations and other amenities he claimed he had been promised.

News of the troubles over the Stornoway departure spread rapidly throughout the Highlands, thanks no doubt to assiduous efforts of the Nor'Westers. It was, as Miles Macdonell confessed to his employer, "a most unfortunate business." But although the fur trading enemies of the HBC were pleased afterwards to publicize the affair, it would be wrong to attribute to them very much responsibility for its occurrence. Circumstances rather than conspiracies were at the root of the problem. Mounting a major recruitment and transport of men across the Atlantic was never an easy business in the early nineteenth century. To do so in wartime was especially difficult. To attempt to do so on extremely short notice, with inadequate planning, was the height of folly.

The affair at Stornoway epitomized everything that was wrong with the early efforts of Selkirk and the HBC to mount an opposition to the NWC by setting a new colony in operation. Given the distances and difficulties of communication between Britain and Red River, it was fatuous to think that ill-conceived and hastily-executed plans could possibly unfold smoothly. Neither money nor force of will were sufficient to overcome the obstacles of time and space, a point Lord Selkirk never seemed to appreciate. Instead, Murphy's Law was only encouraged by this sort of operation.

Moreover, Miles Macdonell had not demonstrated any great qualities of leadership in the affair. He proved incapable of successful improvisation to respond to difficulties not of his own making, a failure that would curse the enterprise over the next few years. The specific folly of Stornoway would compound over the next few months, and the general folly of attempting to build on a timetable that allowed no room for error remained a problem for years. As was so frequently the case in Selkirk's projects, little room was left for the sorts of mishaps which were bound to occur in such a complex business conducted so far from normal channels of operation.

2. David Thompson and the Columbia:

In mid-April 1811, at about the same time that Charles McLean began advertising for strong young Highlanders for HBC service, David Thompson was breaking winter camp to make a final push to the mouth of the Columbia River. Thompson had joined the NWC in 1804, and had chafed as a typical wintering partner until 1806, when news of the American overland expedition of Lewis and Clark to the Pacific coast had reopened the possibility of a similar Canadian thrust. The NWC expected him to explore the feasibility of using the

Columbia River as the entree from the mountains to the sea, and for the next three years he surveyed and explored south of the junction of the Kootenay River and the Columbia. There seemed little evidence of urgency in Thompson's activities. He got no further west than Saleesh House at present-day Thompson, Montana, where he wintered over 1809-10. Then in the spring of 1810 he headed east for Montreal, apparently hoping to take a long-postponed furlough.

At Rainy Lake (now in Ontario), Thompson on 22 July 1810 got new orders from the annual meeting of the Nor'Wester wintering partners at Fort William. He turned around immediately and headed back across the mountains. What he was instructed to do is a matter of considerable controversy for which there is no direct evidence. There are two possibilities. One was that Thompson was ordered to descend the Columbia in order to guarantee the one-third share in the Pacific Fur Company the NWC partners had just voted to accept. In this scenario the partners paid no attention to Astor's timetable, and thus saw little need to put much pressure on Thompson to produce. The other possibility was that Thompson was instructed to head west with all possible speed to pre-empt the Americans at the mouth of the Columbia. If this latter were the case, Thompson obviously failed to respond, for he took nearly a year to complete his journey.

In fairness to Thompson, his earlier activities had stirred up the resident First Nations, especially the Peigans, and he had to tread carefully through the Kootenay region. But caution was clearly the watchword, in contrast to the boldness of fellow explorers Mackenzie and Fraser. Thompson's delays made it necessary for him to cross the Rockies in mid-winter, most of his men deserted, and he ended up making winter camp with only three companions in a snowbound hut on the Columbia not far from the Canoe River in present British Columbia. In his last entry of the winter, on 26 January 1811 he recorded, "We have ab't 35 lbs of Pemmican, 25 lbs. of Flour & a little of the other Provisions, & trust in the Mercy of King Providence to preserve us & find us food."

Thompson kept no daily journal of his peregrinations from late January to early July, 1811. Having broken camp in April he headed by a circuitous route overland to Spokane House, where he built a canoe. On 3 July he was actually canoeing down the Columbia with five voyageurs, two Iroquois, and two Simpoil Indians, "to explore this River, in order to open out a Passage for the Interiour Trade with the Pacific Ocean." The little party camped with a band of Simpoil, and was not underway until noon the following day, still obviously not pushing very hard. On 8 July, Thompson engaged in the symbolic gesture of discovery. He erected at the junction of a tributary river with the Columbia a pole with a half sheet of paper tied to it. The paper said: "Know hereby that this Country is claimed by Great Britain as part of it's Territories and that the NW Company of Merchants from Canada, finding the Factory for this People inconvenient for them, do hereby intend to erect a Factory in this Place for the Commerce of the Country around. D. Thompson. Junction of the Shawpatin River with the Columbia, July 8th, 1811." On 10 July Thompson closed his daily journal entry with the laconic, "Heard news of the American Ship's arrival." This was the first sign that he knew that the Pacific Fur Company had beaten the NWC to the mouth of the Columbia River. If he thought it mattered, he made no sign.

On Monday, 15 July 1811, a canoe made a final portage over a spit of land and, with British flag flying, arrived at "the House of Mr Astors Company." A well-dressed man leapt ashore and introduced himself as David Thompson, a partner in the North West Company of Montreal. The visiting party was received politely by the American leaders — Duncan McDougall, David and Robert Stuart. Thompson obviously intended to rest there for several days. Alexander Ross would later complain that Thompson "had access everywhere, saw and examined everything, and got whatever he asked for, as if he had been one of our selves." There was much to see. Construction work on the new buildings continued even as the Canadian explorer was being greeted.

Within days of the arrival of the *Tonquin* on 15 April 1811, enough land had been cleared to make a start on a 25 by 60 foot warehouse, complete with a root cellar and stone foundation. Huts for the men to sleep in had also been begun. Much of the work was done by labourers who had been collected in the Sandwich Islands. They found the local foliage difficult to work with, particularly when thick sap dulled the edges of saws and the blades of axes. Four Sandwich Islanders had begun planting a garden almost immediately. Indian corn, potatoes, turnips, cucumbers and radishes were put into the ground. The gardens had been fenced the first week in July, mainly to protect the crops from the livestock (pigs, sheep, chickens, goats) also brought from the Sandwich Islands.

The Americans had been expecting Thompson. They knew that there was to be a fierce competition between the Nor'Westers and themselves for control of the Pacific fur trade. A false alarm had come on 30 April when a native reported that a large party of men, presumably Nor'Westers, was building near The Dalles. An expedition from Astoria sent upriver returned in mid-May to report there was nothing to the rumour. In June, Indians brought a letter written 5 April 1811, from an NWC trader at Spokane House, addressed to John Stuart at "Fort Estekatadene." The contents of this letter are unknown, but the native bearers doubtless provided information about the inland activities of the NWC.

The news Thompson brought may have been surprising. He showed the Americans a copy of a letter from John Jacob Astor to William McGillivray outlining the arrangements for a joint venture. Thompson on his arrival also handed Duncan McDougall a letter he himself had written earlier in the day. It welcomed the Pacific Fur Company to the Columbia, reported that the NWC had accepted the one-third offer of Mr. Astor, and added: "I have only to hope that the respective parties at Montreal may finally settle the arrangements between the two Companies which in my opinion will be to our mutual Interest." The letter suggests that Thompson's instructions had been to establish a relationship with the Astorians rather than to open a competition. But it might have been merely bluff on the Nor'Wester's part. In any event, the Americans were bound to be confused. When they had sailed from New York the previous September, the word was that the deal with the NWC had fallen through. To be on the safe side, the Americans wrote a formal letter of reply, acknowledging Thompson's note and its "pleasant intelligence" and offering every assistance to the visiting Nor'Wester.

In private conversation Thompson may well have suggested a division of the West, with the NWC abandoning posts west of the mountains and the Americans not inferring in NWC ones to the east of that barrier. At least so Gabriel Franchère, one of the Astoria clerks, reported in his journal. But Alexander Ross was suspicious of Thompson, regarding him as a man full of "duplicity and diplomatic craft." In any event, the Astorians had no intention of ceasing the expansion of their operation. In what may have been their own version of double-bluff, they sent Thompson on his way with a packet of letters for Astor. The packet included one to Astor himself expressing pleasure at the partnership. However, the writers probably expected Thompson to read the material in the parcel as soon as he was on his own. Such solitude would not come instantly, as Thompson left for the interior on 22 July in company with two canoes from Fort Astoria. The Americans, led by David Stuart, intended to build a factory up the Columbia River. The Nor'Westers and Astorians would travel together to The Dalles. Neither party truly believed that a fur trade war in the Pacific could be avoided.

3. Wilson Price Hunt and the Overland Passage to Astoria:

While David Thompson was visiting at Astoria, on 18 July 1811 a large American overland party left the villages of the Arikara Indians on the Missouri River to strike out for the mouth of the Columbia. This expedition was led by Wilson Price Hunt, who had spent considerable effort in obtaining up-to-date geographic information before setting under way. His plan was to head across the plains in a southwesterly direction, cross the Rockies via some sort of pass, and then follow rivers into the Columbia. He was fully supplied with experienced voyageurs and mountain hunters, as well as equipment, although not with horses. The group also contained the wife of one of the traders and two children. Most of the party would have to walk on moccasins not designed for rocky ground. Hunt set out for the Grand River, but in the first week his group made only nine miles a day. Fortunately, he met up with Cheyenne Indians who were prepared to supply more horses, and there was now a mount for every two persons in the party. Average daily travel picked up to twenty miles per day. The party crossed the Little Missouri on 13 August, and could soon see the first mountains ahead.

Even the foothills of the Powder River Mountains proved more than this inexperienced party could handle. It turned south into Thunder Basin, where the hunting was good. To the west the travellers could see the Bighorn Mountains. They followed a native trail to the foot of these mountains, where they stopped to prepare provisions. Soon after, they came across a band of Crow, who provided them with fresh horses and new information about a pass over the Bighorns. On the other side of the mountains they met other aboriginals who supplied further intelligence about the route ahead. Hunt led the party along the Wind River. On 15 September the expedition headed due west for the Great Divide, much evidence of snow all around.

Having successfully crossed the Divide, Hunt discovered that nobody was quite sure where to go next. At this point he expected to find a river. There was one (the Snake), but no suitable material for building canoes. Finally Hunt learned about Teton Pass and crossed it in the early days of October, soon coming upon an abandoned fur trading post — Henry's Fort — which had been the first American post west of the Divide. Finding this site meant that, for the moment, the group knew where it was. The Snake River beckoned. The Canadian voyageurs in the party began constructing canoes out of abundant material.

Hunt now made his most crucial — and erroneous — decision. His understanding from his research was that that there were water routes west of the Divide that led to the Columbia. Unfortunately, the fact that Hunt and his company needed such easily navigable routes in order to make the overland journey a success led him to be far too sanguine about their existence. In any event, at this point in mid-October, he decided to abandon his horses and make the remainder of the journey by canoe. The Snake was far less easily traversable than Hunt had anticipated. The river was nothing but a series of terrible rapids between perpendicular mountain sides. Several canoes were upset and one engagé lost his life. Hunt paused just short of the worst rapids to reconnoiter. He was forced to press on, with only a few days supply of food and little real knowledge of the route ahead.

His scouts told him in early November that the Snake could not be managed with canoes. Hunt now determined to break up the expedition, with each of the Pacific Fur Company partners taking a small group overland in search of horses, supplies, and fresh information. Hunt led the remainder of the party on foot along the Snake, where they encountered occasional camps of Shoshoni who traded fish to the hungry explorers. Fresh advice from the Shoshoni offered a shortcut to the Boise River. On this route the men found no water, however, and were reduced to consuming their own urine. The Boise was reached on 21 November, but no natives could be found who knew the way to the Columbia. The one horse that Hunt had obtained was now eaten. The party rejoined the Snake at the end of November and continued north along the river.

On 6 December 1811, Hunt's party stumbled across one of the little groups, led by Ramsay Crooks, that had been hived off from the main expedition. Crooks and his men were fatigued and provisionless. They told of a canyon ahead — it is now called Hells Canyon — which was particularly frightening. So Hunt searched aimlessly for days for an alternative. He finally found Shoshoni willing to guide the party back towards navigable water. On Christmas Eve Hunt reported in his journal that his expedition "now consisted of thirty-two whites, a woman more than eight months pregnant, her two children, and three Indians. We had only five wretched horses for our food during the passage of the mountains." Christmas went uncelebrated that year, although the voyageurs subsequently insisted on paying homage to the New Year.

On 8 January 1812, Hunt and his group came upon, near modern Pendleton, Oregon, a large camp of Indians with food and thousands of horses. As was so often the case, the aboriginals were hospitable and helpful. They provided horses, provisions, and information,

Pacific tribes attack the *Tonquin*.

John Jacob Astor

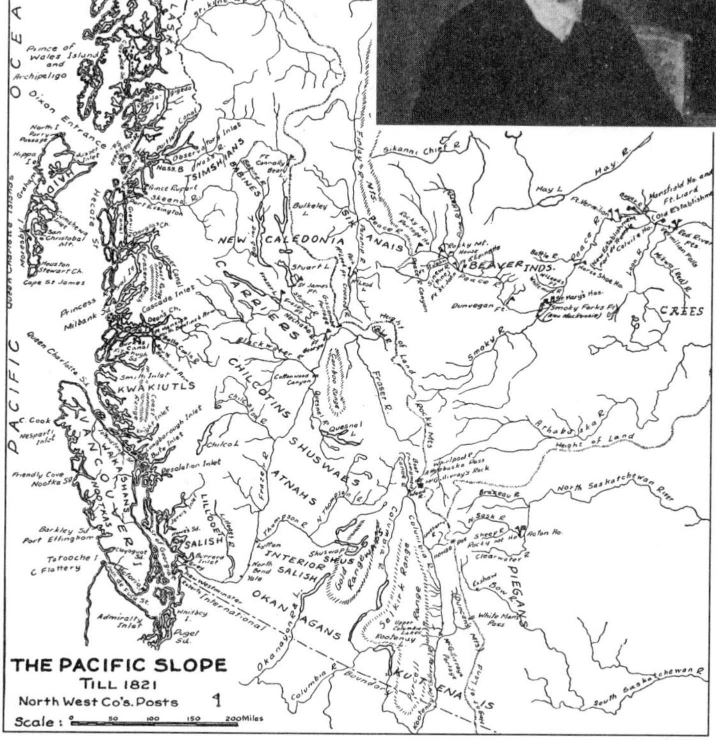

THE PACIFIC SLOPE
TILL 1821
North West Co's. Posts
Scale:

which Hunt was able to meld with what Lewis and Clark had earlier reported. On 19 January, 1812, one of the subparties detached by Hunt the previous November reached Fort Astoria. As for Hunt himself, his group was now able to follow the Umatilla Trail to the Columbia. From there the passage in six canoes was relatively easy. Astoria was sighted through the rain and fog on the afternoon of 15 February. "It was a very real pleasure," Hunt recorded, "for travellers harrassed by fatigue to rest in quiet and be surrounded by friends after so long a journey in the midst of savages of whom it is always prudent to be wary." Even in triumph Hunt could not manage to express appropriate gratitude to the native peoples who had so many times saved his life.

The Hunt expedition had ultimately surmounted bad geography, the winter climate in the mountains, and a series of wrong (if understandable) decisions to reach its goal. At least it had reached its physical target — Fort Astoria. The real goal, of course, had been to find an overland route to the west that would parallel the Canadian one. What was needed was a largely water route that could carry supplies west and furs east. Such a route Wilson Price Hunt had most definitely not uncovered. Instead, at the cost of lives and material goods he had accomplished a one-off feat of collective heroism which nobody would ever want to repeat.

4. Meanwhile, Back at Fort Astoria:

The period between the arrival at Fort Astoria of David Thompson in July 1811 and Wilson Price Hunt in February 1812 had seen many developments, not all of them positive. Food was in short supply over the first winter, although thanks to the availability of dried salmon, there was no threat of starvation. Short rations and lack of variety were a problem, exacerbated by an inability to range far afield for replenishment. The residents of Fort Astoria were left stranded by the outstanding event of the first year, the disappearance of the *Tonquin*. The vessel had left for Vancouver Island with a crew and several company partners on 1 June 1811. The plan was to trade for furs, stop briefly at Astoria on the way south, and then head off for Asia before returning to New York. Rumours of the destruction of the ship began circulating along the coast in July of 1811, although they were not confirmed until May of 1812.

Much has been written about the loss of the *Tonquin*. An eyewitness account of the final hours was later given to Astoria by Indian interpreter Jack Ramsay. It has been repeated by the various record keepers present at the time: Franchère, Ross, and Cox. According to Ramsay, Captain Jonathan Thorn was careless about protecting against attack, and he continued with the natives the same brutal behaviour he had earlier exhibited on the voyage around South America. The result was trouble. Armed Indians came on board the ship and proceeded to massacre the crew and fur traders. Only Ramsay escaped, subsequently returning to the vessel to touch off its powder magazine.

This incident was not the end of the Pacific Fur Company's immediate problems. Members of a party carrying dispatches to Astor became involved in a contretemps with Wishram Indians up the Columbia. The dispatch box was lost and the Astorians retreated back to their fort. When they returned, they found the American three-masted vessel the *Beaver* at the wharf. That vessel was on its way to China. A meeting of available partners was called, which planned a substantial expansion of trading activities and a challenge to the NWC at Spokane through the construction of a new post on the Spokane River. As part of the aggressive policy, Wilson Hunt determined to accompany the *Beaver* to visit the Russian-American Company's fur-trading posts to the north. He left Astoria in charge of Duncan McDougall, and would not return until February 1815. Hunt departed for the North at just about the time the War of 1812 began in the East. He managed to return only after all the damage had been done at Fort Astoria.

The American fur traders at Astoria were convinced that the real problems of the venture were connected with John Jacob Astor, who combined a magnificent breadth of entrepreneurial vision with a cheeseparing mentality for daily trading. Alexander Ross insisted that the trade goods he supplied were inadequate. "Instead of guns," Ross later argued, "we got old metal pots and gridirons; instead of beads and trinkets, we got white linen; and instead of blankets, molasses. In short, all the useless trash and unsaleable articles which Astor had been accumulating in his shops and stores for half a century past, were swept together to fill his Columbia ships." Moreover, claimed Ross, Astor's principal interest was in supplying the Russians, and he sent "the mere refuse" of his goods to Astoria. The resident partners agreed almost from the beginning that Astor's "underhanded policy" had jeopardized the venture.

5. The Tribulations of Selkirk's Recruits:

Delay piled on delay at Stornoway meant that the new recruits for the Bay were not actually on their way until the end of July, 1811. This made it virtually certain that they would have to winter at York Factory rather than work their way down to the more moderate site of the proposed settlement at Red River. While the rival companies engaged in fruitless negotiation over the summer of 1811, Miles Macdonell and William Hillier (who had been chosen to head the party of roving shock troops intended to stiffen local HBC resistance to the NWC) sailed with 105 men for York Factory.

The voyage to the Bay, having gotten off to its delayed start, was "the longest ever known & the latest to H Bay," reported Macdonell. The ships did not arrive until 24 September. Although Miles did not say so, there was a relationship between the lateness of the departure and the amount of time at sea. The flotilla had lost the favourable winds of the earlier part of the summer which might have shortened the voyage. Despite 61 days at sea with little to do, none of the young men had made any progress in learning Gaelic and Irish — Selkirk hoped the ancient tongues would unify the colonists and insulate them from American influence — and not a single one had acquired any familiarity with a gun.

Although William Auld at York Factory was most co-operative, there was no room at the fort. The parties would have to winter on the north side of the Nelson River above the factories. Provisions were of course in short supply, since Auld had not anticipated feeding a hundred extra men over the winter. In early November Miles Macdonell complained to Auld's subordinate, Edward Cook, that he had only a month's worth of provisions at hand and had been unable to find game to kill for fresh meat. "I was aware of considerable difficulties in prosecuting this Scheme, which a desire to forward your Lordship's views led me to undertake," Macdonell reported to his employer, but "the troubles attendant on it have already exceeded my expectations." In another letter to Selkirk, Macdonell reported serious flooding on the Pembina River in the spring of 1811. Selkirk's response was to suggest another location for the centre of the colony, perhaps at the mouth of one of the rivers emptying into Lake Manitoba. This reaction suggests that at this point, at least, Selkirk was not wedded to a settlement at the Forks.

From William Auld at York Factory both Alexander Wedderburn and Selkirk received some unsolicited negative comments written in the autumn of 1811. Auld was an old hand in the Bay. He was also not very adventurous. His lack of enthusiasm for the projects which Miles

Macdonell and William Hillier were to lead was transparent, but his comments probably deserved a better hearing than they received. From the outset, Auld warned about mixing Scotsmen and Irishmen, a melange preferred by Selkirk for political reasons. Auld was equally concerned about the lack of experience with local conditions on the parts of both Miles and Hillier. He illustrated the problem in two ways. First, he flayed Miles' plans for using flat-bottomed boats to traverse the rocky rivers to the south. Secondly, he pointed out that the new governor made promises that could not possibly be honoured in the rough conditions of the wilderness. Not surprisingly, moreover, Auld saw the colony as a competitor for the limited amount of experienced manpower at his disposal.

In a letter to Selkirk dated 31 May 1812, Miles Macdonell described at length the events of the winter of 1811-12. All his party were in log and clay houses before the first of November, and had physically survived the winter very well. There was no shortage of food, little frostbite (although the temperature was often fifty degrees below zero), and the onset of scurvy was easily correctable by the use of spruce juice. Despite these facts, Macdonell complained of lack of co-operation from the local HBC men. The non-physical side had not gone so well. Cabals had formed among the men, and on New Year's night the Irishmen in the party had attacked the Orkneymen.

Subsequently one of the Orcadians had refused to drink spruce juice, and was confined in a separate hut which his companions burnt to the ground the first night he was placed there. A little group of dissidents — nine from Glasgow and four from the Orkneys — refused to submit to authority. They spent the remainder of the winter in isolation. In the spring they refused to enter HBC service, insisting that they were not being treated in accordance with their recruitment promises. They could only be sent home, "there being no controlling power in this country to manage them." Macdonell emphasized strongly the need for a proper judicature in the colony, suggesting a military establishment based on martial law. A strong power would be necessary to keep order, he insisted, lest "we may be all overturned by the tumultuous onset of our own people." Macdonell concluded his report by observing that William Auld insisted that according to George III c. 138, all legal matters in the country were cognizable only in the Canadian courts.

The problem of jurisdiction was a serious one, and both Selkirk and the HBC began attempting to grapple with it. But Miles Macdonell was already displaying certain tendencies which would only become more pronounced over time. One was a moralistic censoriousness against the established employees of the HBC, accompanied by serious difficulties in co-operating with anybody. Another was a tendency to paint himself into corners over minor problems to which he responded with harsh and repressive disciplinary measures. In the isolated wilderness of western Canada, men needed to be inspirationally led, not heavily disciplined. The new governor's stiffness and pugnacious inflexibility were not encouraging signs in a man who was to be the leader of a frontier settlement.

Given the difficulties he had experienced over the winter, one might have expected that Macdonell would hurry to the Forks as soon as possible in the spring, striving to get his men on the site of the colony in time to do some planting. Instead, he hung around York Factory feuding with William Auld over experienced boatmen for the journey to the Red River and dealing with the disciplinary loose ends of the winter. The problem of the disposition of what William Auld labelled the "Glasgow Insurgents" and the "Irish Criminals" was a difficult one. Auld insisted that sending them back to Britain for action was not very useful, since their offences were cognizable only in Canadian courts. Negotiations with the troublemakers dragged on until late June, when most finally agreed to be co-operative; the remainder would be sent back home. This delay was probably unavoidable, although Miles then proceeded to wait still longer for boatmen and the total breakup of the ice on the rivers.

While it was true that the breakup of ice on northern rivers was always very late, Macdonell would have been well advised to get on with his journey to the south on foot, as several of his successors would do. Instead, the beginning of July found him still at York Factory. Having decided to send some of the recalcitrant home and having allowed William Hillier his complement of men, Macdonell had only a relative handful — twenty-two — left. He wrote, "a man of one nation is prejudiced against going with one another — I shall go on with any number — take possession of the tract & hoist the Standard." He finally started up the Hayes River on 6 July. The journey south, once undertaken, was relatively uneventful. Miles Macdonell and his tiny party, ultimately reduced to nineteen, would not reach the site of the settlement until 30 August 1812. Another year had been lost. No seed would be planted in 1812.

The contrast with the planting of crops at Fort Astoria was instructive. Despite the need to travel around the southern tip of South America to arrive on the Pacific Slope, the beginnings of settlement could be swifter there. The *Tonquin* had departed New York in September of 1810, arrived at the mouth of the Columbia in April 1812, and within days the party had begun building and planting. The HBC ships had left Stornoway in July of 1811, but the advance party intended for Red River would not get seed into the ground until May of 1813. To some extent the difference was in climate and accessibility. It took two months to sail to Hudson Bay and from Hudson Bay Miles Macdonell required another two months to reach his destination — four months travel as opposed to seven sailing from Atlantic to Pacific. But because of the climate, the timing in the Bay had to be perfect. When it was not, as had been the case with the first Red River party, years could be lost.

During the period he was at York Factory, Miles had written a letter to his cousin John Macdonell, who was in the service of the NWC. John replied on 27 June 1812. It was not a hostile letter. The soil was good at Red River, but the winter weather was severe, John reported. The area was thinly populated by First Nations and some Canadian freemen and halfbreeds, "not to be trusted & in general outcasts from our employ." The Nor'Wester observed that Selkirk's settlement schemes in the past had gone astray, adding: "The great are often ungrateful, I sincerely wish you may find his Lordship an exception."

The 1812 party for Red River fared little better than the first. That party was shipped from Sligo, Ireland, with Lord Selkirk himself in charge of the departure. The group was again a mixture of Highlanders and Irishmen, mostly single young men but including a few families with small children. Forty adult Highlanders, some with families, came from the island of Tyree in Argyleshire. Most were young, although a few were in their forties and fifties. The final return showed fifty adults (over fifteen years of age) bound for the settlement, plus four children between 8 and 15, and six children under 8. Another thirty-nine were destined for HBC service. The Irish were recruited by B. H. Everard in the Sligo area. The leading settler was to be Alexander Maclean, a Highlander, who had a family and was given a number of prize Merino sheep by the earl. William Auld would later complain that fourteen men, plus six more for the sheep, were required just to unload the McLean party at York Factory.

As leader of the party, Selkirk chose Owen Keveny, an Irishman who exuded competence but had no North American experience. He added Dr. Thomas McKeevor from Dublin as doctor/surgeon, and an Anglo-Irishman named Andrew Langston in place of Archibald McDonald, who had originally been intended to assist in leading the new settlers. McDonald had become a protege of Selkirk, who decided that the young man was not yet ready for full leadership. The party departed on 24 June aboard the *Robert Taylor*, sailing in company with the *King George* and the *Eddystone*.

The 1812 voyage to the Bay aboard the *Robert Taylor* became another debacle of the first magnitude. The Irish and Scots once again did not get on together. The Irish, encouraged by Langston, insisted that the Scots were receiving better treatment. As early as 5 July "Vox

Populi" had written to Keveny that the passengers would not stand watch until "your treatment towards us is greatly changed." This document was written a line apiece by the conspirators. According to later testimony, the chief problem was more to do with insufficiency of promised rum than of food. Owen Keveny had responded with brutal discipline, either clapping the troublemakers in irons or forcing them to run the gauntlet between men equipped with clubs. Memories of the gauntlet still dominated Donald Gunn's account of this voyage when it was first published in 1869.

Langston complained that the passengers were being treated like transported felons. He subsequently plotted to seize the ship and was himself placed in irons. Four passengers, including Langston, were eventually shipped back to Britain from York Factory because of their mutinous behaviour. Keveny reported from York Factory that he was ready to take the new settlers inland, but there was a shortage of both boats and experienced hands. He warned Selkirk not to expect more than half of the previously promised fifty boats for 1813. Believing that to have another party winter at York Factory would hamper further recruiting, Keveny determined to press south to join Macdonell, who had only just arrived in Red River himself and had enjoyed no opportunity to prepare for fresh arrivals.

Owen Keveny managed to get the remainder of his contingent, including the women and children, to Red River by early October 1812. At Point Douglas this party met the one led by Miles Macdonell, which had only itself arrived at the Forks two months earlier. There was little enough food or shelter for the first arrivals. The second group was thus forced to push on to Pembina, in modern day North Dakota, where Métis and freemen might be able to supply them with buffalo meat. Keveny's boats arrived at Pembina on 27 October, flags flying and pipes playing. Whether such enthusiasm would greet the following spring was another matter. How Macdonell would deal with the party of two to three hundred settlers which Selkirk had promised for 1813 was another matter entirely.

The winter of 1812-13 was a difficult one for the colonists. No crops had been planted, and so the newcomers had to rely on meat supplied them by mixed-blood and freeman hunters. The newcomers had to collect the meat from the hunters' lodges. Lacking sufficient horses and dogs, the men themselves were harnessed to huge sleds loaded with frozen meat. For days they tugged, without snowshoes. According to Donald Gunn, they had to consume so much meat to keep up their energy that "all they brought to the fort was very little more than would be required to feed themselves until they should return to the hunting tents again." The settlers would probably have starved, added Gunn, if the North West Company had not supplied them with provisions, consisting of wheat, barley, potatoes, and some farmyard animals.

6. The War of 1812:

The United States declared war on Great Britain on 18 June 1812. Whatever the results of the War of 1812 in the eastern part of the continent, in the western country, especially on the Pacific, it proved a godsend for the NWC. John Jacob Astor would later acknowledge that "as soon as war was declared I considered Columbia in danger if not lost." Around the Great Lakes the NWC would ally with the British in successful military action.

Ironically enough, on the very day war was declared, Lord Selkirk wrote from Sligo in Ireland to William Hillier, the man in charge of the HBC forces in North America. Hillier was described by Selkirk as "a magistrate, & his people . . . police officers or posse comitatus called out to protect a market from rioters." Selkirk issued his own declaration of war to his private police force. "You know how anxious we are that in repelling the violent aggressions of the Canadians," Selkirk emphasized to Hillier, "you should never exceed the bounds of moderation, or allow any provocation to lead you into an imitation of their lawless proceedings." Hillier was to use due process to apply his force. He was to invoke the Law of England, giving the NWC "solemn warning" about trespassing on HBC land. "We are so fully advised of the unimpeachable validity of these rights of property, that there can be no scruple in enforcing them whenever you have physical means. If they make a forcible resistance, they are acting illegally, and are responsible for the consequences of what they do, while you are safe so long as you take only the reasonable and necessary means of enforcing that which is your right."

Selkirk's advice not only assumed that the HBC charter would be fully recognized by the British authorities in London, but by the Canadian authorities closer to the scene. In actual fact, the British government had not yet given its view and would avoid taking a stand on the validity of the charter throughout the fur trade conflict. As William Coltman would later point out, how lawyers judged the charter depended on what information they were given about its history. Coltman himself suspected that the lawyers had not been informed of the extent to which the HBC had failed to enforce its monopoly over many years. Moreover, Selkirk could not anticipate the ways in which the war might change the dynamics of the fur trade competition.

Selkirk also wrote to Miles Macdonell about a possible war with the United States, not knowing it had already been declared. He expected that men from the two fur companies could work together to defend the Northwest against the Americans. He promised, "if . . . you can hold out for a while, & let me know where you are to be found, reinforcements shall come to you through one route or another, & it will go hard with me, but I will have a share in your adventures." He would indeed.

~4~

The War of 1812 and the Fur Trade

*T*he West, particularly what is now the American Midwest south of the Great Lakes, had been for many years one of the major sources of contention between the United States and Great Britain. The British decision to close the region to settlement in 1763 had become a long-standing grievance for the American colonists. In a fit of impetuousness, British negotiators eager to end the War of the American Revolution had agreed to give up to the Yankees the trans-Appalachian region south of the Great Lakes. It seemed small matter that Britain's aboriginal allies claimed most of this territory. Like the Loyalists, the First Nations could be sacrificed to hasten an end to a war the British government felt it could no longer afford.

Having taken the step of abandonment, the British subsequently had second thoughts. These were aided by pressure from Britain's native allies, who did not want to become wards of the expansionistic Americans, and from Britain's Canadian colonists, who did not wish to surrender their access to the fur trade in the region. And so Britain found reasons for not abandoning its forts in the Old Northwest and beyond. One attempt was made to settle the dispute (and other outstanding Anglo-American issues) in Jay's Treaty, negotiated in 1794. This led to the British withdrawal from most of the disputed points, including Detroit.

Britain continued to maintain a military and naval presence in the region south of the lakes. Fur traders continued to compete in the West as well. In 1806, the Montreal merchants organized the Michilimackinac Company, which complemented rather than competed with the NWC in the Michigan-Wisconsin-Minnesota area. John Jacob Astor's American Fur Company, established in 1808, contended actively with the NWC in many areas south of Lake Superior. This competition eventually produced the South West Fur Company in 1811, a joint venture of the NWC and Astor. Despite the uneasy agreement between Astor and the Nor'Westers, relations between the British and the Americans in the region continued to be tense. By 1812, the Americans were hoping to establish a trading post at Prairie du Chien, deep in the interior, to compete with the British there.

On the eve of the opening of the war, the Americans were actively attempting to persuade the Indians in the Louisiana Territory to remain neutral should hostilities erupt. Many tribes were invited to Washington for this purpose in the summer of 1812. The British trader Robert Dickson succeeded in convincing the aboriginals of the upper Mississippi River, especially the Sioux over whom he had great influence, not to become involved in the various peace negotiations. Born in Dumfries, Scotland, Dickson was closely related with a number of other Scots resident in Upper Canada — especially William and Thomas Dickson, the Clark brothers, and Robert Hamilton. Like many Scots Lowlanders, he had little but contempt for the Highlanders of the NWC. Dickson had spent many years in the upper Mississippi region, taking a Sioux wife in 1797 and trading with his own company in what is now Minnesota and Wisconsin before joining the Michilimackinac Company in 1807. Instead of co-operating with the Americans, Dickson began recruiting among "His Majesty's Indian Allies" in the late spring of 1812. The western interior and Pacific Slope were distinctly sideshows during the War of 1812. But from the standpoint of the fur trade, the military machinations of the war were a matter of considerable importance.

1. Fort Michilimackinac and the Western Interior:

In the days immediately following the American declaration of war, while the Americans massed invading armies on the borders of Upper Canada, the British achieved an outstanding if unexpected victory in the West. A small contingent of American troops, occupying Fort Michilimackinac on Lake Huron in early July 1812, had not received word that war had been declared. Captain Charles Roberts, the British commander at Fort St. Joseph on the St. Mary's River, however, had already received a letter from General Isaac Brock ordering him to attack Fort Michilimackinac. Roberts had been offered the assistance of the North West Company in the region, which had quickly provided him with nearly 200 voyageurs and several parties of Indians (Sioux, Menominee, and Winnebago led by Robert Dickson) totalling about 400 effectives.

This force set off for Michilimackinac on 16 July in an NWC schooner and a number of canoes. The subsequent attack was a complete surprise to the defenders. The American commandant, Lieutenant Porter Hanks, readily agreed to surrender, concerned that his troops might be massacred. Roberts was able to report of his Indians that, "as soon as they heard the Capitulation was signed they all returned to their Canoes, and not one drop either of Man's or Animal's blood was Spilt." Roberts decided to use the fort as his western base. Robert Dickson led his warriors on to Detroit, where news of their coming helped General Brock capture the town in August.

Michilimackinac was virtually the only good news for the British in the early summer of 1812. But it was an important victory, not merely on the morale front. In the short run it secured the West for Great Britain and exposed the Americans to aboriginal depredations on their western flanks. Equally important from the standpoint of the fur trade, it sealed a longstanding alliance between the Canadian authorities and the North West Company. Even before the triumph, Captain Roberts had been instructed to "afford every assistance and Protection Possible to Promote the Interest and Security of the North West Company." The Nor'Westers had obviously responded in kind. In September of 1812 a corps of voyageurs was formally embodied in the West, which provided many Nor'Westers with military uniforms, including those red coats which so impressed the native peoples. It would prove very difficult for the Hudson's Bay Company to break up this cosy arrangement between the NWC and the Canadian governments, especially in Lower Canada, in years to come. As for the uniforms, they would be eventually employed against the Red River settlement, worn proudly by NWC partners harassing the settlers.

Early in 1813, Robert Dickson was appointed as Indian agent and superintendant for the First Nations west of Lake Huron, his salary to be paid out of the secret-service fund. He was instructed to restrain his warriors from acts of cruelty, and to encourage his aboriginals to push the Americans out of the West in such a way that "the Indians only are to appear as the movers in such proceedings." Thus the British continued a long-standing policy of using the aboriginals as stalking horses for their own interests, a tactic that Lord Bathurst would soon see extended into the fur trade wars.

Dickson spent the remainder of the campaign raising aboriginal warriors for the British. His forces helped fend off the Americans at several posts in 1813. Dickson then headed off for Prairie du Chien to raise a substantial force which the Americans erroneously suspected of preparing to attack the Missouri settlements as far south as St.

Louis. As a result of Dickson's influence, the Americans spent the entire war on the defensive in the western interior. A number of American military posts were abandoned. The British might have done even better in the West had they controlled the Great Lakes in the latter days of the war; a western supply line based on the fur trade routes was hardly very satisfactory.

Certainly the Nor'Westers had a direct interest in the outcome of the military activities in the West, since they might well influence the final boundary settlement between British North America and the United States. In the end, the British abandoned the fur traders (and First Nations) in favour of peace, restoring the status quo of 1811. One British officer wrote that the Crown's negotiators as usual "have shown themselves profoundly ignorant of the concerns of this part of the Empire." The British withdrawal from the region of the upper Mississippi would leave Drummond's Island on Lake Huron as the principal British military connection with the region. The British abandonment also had a considerable impact on Lord Selkirk, who now found much of his 1811 grant likely to end up south of the final American boundary.

2. Lord Selkirk's Highland Regiment

On the other side of the Atlantic, the coming of war led Lord Selkirk to undertake his own military initiatives. He was somewhat delayed, however, by various affairs on the home front. Through the latter half of 1812 he was involved in various political matters, including his own successful re-election to the House of Lords as a representative peer for Scotland. He also found time-consuming his duties as Lord Lieutenant of Kirkcudbright, commanding home defence for the county. But depressing reports of the progress of the advance party he had sent to Hudson Bay, news of American raids on his Baldoon property in Upper Canada, and an erosion of support for his settlement plans within the HBC, all contributed to changing his thinking. Reports from North America made clear that Canada was having trouble protecting itself from the Americans. There were obvious advantages to defending British interests in North America with Highland soldiers, especially if they could ultimately be settled at Red River.

On 23 January 1813 Selkirk wrote to his Highland associate Alexander MacDonald of Dalilia that all previous plans for Red River were in abeyance. Instead, he intended to propose to government that he raise and lead a corps modelled on the Canadian Fencible Regiment for "service in America, during the present hostilities there." A stipulation would be added that the men should settle in Red River at the close of their service, their families transported to the colony at government expense. Only married men were to be recruited, and allowances would be paid to maintain families left at home. Selkirk hoped government would pay the allowances, as well as outfit and provision the troops. Apparently he was unfamiliar with the sorry details of the Canadian Regiment, which had been summarily disbanded in Glasgow in 1803 after a mutiny against its officers. The Regiment never actually got into service. Its complex history had made government, and especially the British Commander-in-Chief, the Duke of York, highly suspicious of Highland recruiting for North American service. Nonetheless, a week later, Selkirk reported to MacDonald that the Secretary of War, Lord Bathurst, had approved his plan in general principle, and quick action would be essential to collect a respectable list of Highland-connected officers.

By 13 February 1813, Selkirk had, in a characteristic whirlwind of activity, assembled an impressive list of prospective officers, nearly all with Highland credentials and family connections. These, it was hoped, would facilitate local recruiting. Four days later he forwarded the outlines of his proposal to Lord Bathurst. What Selkirk offered was to raise, inside of six months, a Highland regiment of 1,000 men for North American service "on the principle that none but married men shall be admitted as recruits, & that upon the reduction of the regiment, the men shall be conveyed to the place of settlement [i.e., Red River] at the Expence of Government." Selkirk was to be a colonel with temporary rank, thus fulfilling a long-standing military ambition never fully satisfied by his duties as Lord Lieutenant. Moreover, military service was one of the few approved ways an important public figure like Selkirk could use to justify leaving Britain and his responsibilities during a wartime crisis.

Officers were to be recommended by Selkirk, and those from the regular army with rank of captain or below would get a permanent step-up in rank (the big selling point in collecting officers), while those with local influence appointed temporarily would receive an ensign's half-pay after reduction. A bounty of £5 per recruit was to be paid, and each soldier's family would get a £10 per annum allowance (partly based on pay deductions) until the family could be settled in America. In case of a protracted war, the colonel could discharge to the settlement one-tenth of any men who had served two years, providing they were replaced. The men were bound to full service until eighteen months after the peace, and would be discharged at Red River, thus assuring they would not disperse and find their own lands. Government would provide conveyance to Red River for soldiers and their families, as well as a year's provisions.

In return the men would serve as a local militia, training for three weeks per year at their own expense as a condition of their tenures. The scheme was a mixture of precedents established by previous North America regiments modified by Selkirk's own notions of how to defend and settle North America. Lord Bathurst immediately turned the proposal over to the Commander-in-Chief for final approval.

Any hope which Selkirk and his officers entertained of the ready acceptance of the new regiment was quickly dashed by the Duke of York, whose observations on the plan were returned to the earl at the beginning of March, 1813. The Duke's criticisms were directed to specific parts of the proposal rather than to its principles, although they were extensive and damning. Most related to "innovations" which Selkirk had included to speed recruitment. The commander-in-chief was particularly dismissive of payments of allowances to families and on discharging soldiers after two years of service. The government had been burnt earlier by North American Fencible regiments recruited in the Highlands, because of the special inducements required to raise them, and the commander-in-chief had no intention of becoming involved again. Characteristically, Selkirk took the criticisms not as rejection but as objections which could be met with counter-argument, revision, and further negotiation.

The earl thus responded with a lengthy memorandum to Bathurst which defended his proposals, given the unique situation in both the Highlands and in North America. The concentration on married men was an important part of the scheme, he emphasized, for it would provide North American reinforcements without affecting ordinary recruitment for other theatres of war; married men with families were not part of the militia conscription pool and seldom volunteered for overseas service. Married men and families were also essential to Selkirk's colony, of course. In conclusion, Selkirk insisted that the money was being invested in a permanent military force for the colonies, and "ought perhaps to be considered as an experiment." As was often the case, however, Selkirk was far fonder of experimentation than was the government.

At this point — with the Duke of York opposed to the scheme and Selkirk convinced he would ultimately win approval of at least a modified plan, for he seemed to have the support of the Secretary of War — Selkirk was presented with a marvellous opportunity. It arose out of the profound changes which were occurring in Sutherlandshire in the northern Highlands. William Young, the chief factor of the Marquis and the Marchioness of Stafford (later the Duke and Duchess of Sutherland), was reorganizing their Highland estates. He was converting the infertile mountain lands of Sutherlandshire to sheep farming, and removing the existing tenantry from the barren glens to the seacoast, where they would receive small plots of land and become crofters.

Most of the populace of the region accepted the changes, however sullenly, but the 2,000 residents of Kildonan parish were less amenable. They gathered to protest the moves in several large assemblages (which Stafford agents chose to view as "riots"), and appointed one of their number, a retired recruiting sergeant of the 93rd Regiment, to take their case to London. Kildonan parish was not abjectly pleading for mercy, but prepared to bid high for the land. Sergeant William Macdonald was authorized by the tenants of Kildonan to offer the Staffords more rent for their lands than the sheep farmer had agreed to pay. He was also to offer to the Duke of York leave to raise 700 effective men in the region — nearly a full regiment — to be "at the Commander in Cheif's disposel in aney part of his Majesty's Dominions at Home or North America, provided their aged Fathers and Mothers and Wives and Children cane with propriety keep their Native home." Neither the Marquis of Stafford nor the Duke of York would grant Macdonald an audience. Only the Earl of Selkirk was prepared to listen to the sergeant's proposals. With mounting excitement, his lordship recognized that here was the nucleus of his regiment.

Soon after his meeting with Macdonald, Selkirk visited the Marchioness of Stafford (the Kildonan lands were part of her inheritance and she supervised their management) to explain his project of a North American regiment. If he enlisted Kildonan men, could the Staffords accommodate their families until the war was over? The Marchioness found the proposal "impracticable," for "leaving the Families without the men to assist in settling them would only increase the difficulty." A later meeting with her ladyship and other efforts failed to turn up a satisfactory place for relocation of the families of the prospective soldiers.

Despite these difficulties, Selkirk continued to negotiate with Sergeant Macdonald, going so far as to prepare a jointly-initialled series of queries and answers which Macdonald took back to Kildonan. The earl's responses were based on the assumption of official approval of his plan for a Highland Regiment. He was now thinking of sending the families of the soldiers on ahead to Red River, provided they could obtain government allowances. While Macdonald returned to Kildonan under the distinct impression that he was to recruit for Selkirk's regiment, Selkirk believed that he had merely authorized the sergeant to collect a list from which recruits could later be selected. In the meantime, Selkirk submitted to government a modified version of his earlier proposals, based both on the objections of the Duke of York and the Kildonan windfall. Thanks to the Kildonan situation, he felt he had managed to meet all of the commander-in-chief's criticisms.

To Selkirk's chagrin, the commander-in-chief again rejected the Red River scheme on 14 April 1813, this time categorically and unconditionally. This rejection did not so much mark a conscious British retreat from an aggressive posture in the Mississippi country as it did a hostility to the recruitment of Highland regiments. One side-effect of the Duke of York's negative, however, was to ensure that the western interior of North America would not become a central feature of British strategy in the war. Not quite beaten, Selkirk immediately wrote to Bathurst offering to create a corps for Northwest frontier service composed of resident fur traders supplemented by a few disciplined soldiers. The soldiers would be conveyed to North America at government expense and would be settled in Hudson's Bay Company territories after the war. The earl offered his own services to lead this corps and to govern "those parts of North America which lie beyond the limits of Canada[,] a Territory not now included in any regular Government." Still attempting to get to North America and still hoping for some government assistance with Red River, Selkirk was also clearly trying to incorporate the Kildonan people. This final proposal was not taken very seriously by anyone. It is interesting mostly for its pointers to what Selkirk wanted most to salvage from the debacle.

This entire incident leads to one of the great "might have beens" of Canadian history. Had Selkirk succeeded in getting government approval for his regiment, the entire course of the development of western North America would have been likely altered. The settling at Red River of 1,000 armed and trained Highlanders and their families would have provided a major military presence in the heart of the continent. Not only would the Nor'Westers have been intimidated, but very possibly Selkirk could have defended the American portion of his grant and asserted British control over much of what is now the midwestern United States. Only one command decision stood in the way.

In the end, the only outcome of Selkirk's concerted efforts to combine the war in North America with Red River settlement was a personal commitment of sorts on his part to Sergeant William Macdonald and the people of Kildonan. This was based upon an assumption of government sponsorship which was not to be. For his part, Macdonald had returned to Kildonan in high spirits. He had quickly acquired a large list of over 1,300 recruits and families based upon his discussions with Selkirk. While Selkirk had stressed the provisional nature of his plans, Macdonald operated as though they were definitive.

To make the situation worse, many Kildonan residents refused relocation within the Stafford estates, instead selling their stock and effects in anticipation of their imminent departure to North America "with Lord Selkirk." Informed by the Staffords of this development, Selkirk was forced to a desperate series of last-minute improvisations to recover something from the shambles of the regiment idea. It would be at least partly his honour and credibility which were at stake. To do something for the Kildonan people, he would have to return to his pre-regiment plans for Red River and combine them with the Hudson's Bay Company requirements for young clerks and traders. He would also have to act quickly.

Late in April of 1813, Selkirk wrote to the Marquis of Stafford outlining his new plan. The people of Kildonan were the unfortunate victims of a great change for the general good, but would never be happy set upon small crofts. How much better such a "bold and hearty" peasantry would fare peopling British colonies overseas. The scheme Selkirk intended to propose involved sending able-bodied working men the first season to prepare the way, followed by their families over the next few years. Still looking for accommodation for those not immediately transported, Selkirk hoped the prospective emigrant families could be left temporarily on their own lands, or alternatively, relocated for the moment on lands which Selkirk would lease from the Staffords for the purpose. The Staffords were prepared to consider the latter option, although nothing ever came of it. As it became clear that Selkirk had not got his regiment and was recruiting on his own account, factor William Young wrote that the Earl "has brought himself in to an awfull scrape, and us to a world of trouble, for what can the people now do for themselves, without proper aid from the Government and certain pay to the people?" A few days later, Selkirk sent his own agent to Kildonan to inform the people of the altered arrangements and to select first recruits.

The Kildonan tenantry was informed that there would be no regiment. Selkirk was prepared to take to Red River 60 to 80 young men who "would proceed without their familys on the usual terms of paying their passage, who would on their Arrival either get a Few [a feu was a Scottish term for a small holding of land] on easy terms or a certain number of Acres to purchase from his Lordship." In addition, the Hudson's Bay Company wished for another 60 young men. Such a proposal was a far cry from the arrangements discussed with Sergeant Macdonald. It was little more than an ordinary emigration venture, restricted to the young and able.

As William Young queried, "how the others are in consequence of what Macdonald has heldout to replace their Corn and Cattle which they have sold off . . . is more than I can divine." Selkirk headed north at the end of May. He personally concluded arrangements with the prospective emigrants and gave many receipts for their passage money in his own hand. Selkirk always insisted that emigrants should pay at least part of their own expenses, lest they become mere objects of charity. But in this instance, his acceptance of much of the small capital possessed by the Kildonaners was probably a mistake, turning an affair of honour into a mere business proposition. John Strachan from Upper Canada would severely attack Selkirk in 1816 for these arrangements.

Many of those signed up were to be sent out in 1814. But the disparity between the final terms and Macdonald's earlier reports helps explain much of the subsequent Kildonan hostility to Selkirk, including the angry tone of Donald Gunn's account (in Gunn and Tuttle's *History of Manitoba*) of the recruiting conducted in Kildonan by the earl. In the end, Selkirk was forced to take 13 of the most importunate families in 1813. They sailed with 37 single emigrants (mainly young males) aboard the *Prince of Wales* from Stromness on 29 June. Selkirk realized that the Kildonaners were Presbyterians and his administration in Red River was headed by the Catholic Miles Macdonell, but he could only hope this was not a problem.

Along with the settlers, the *Prince of Wales* carried a large bundle of letters and instructions for Selkirk's agents in North America. Perhaps the most important item was a letter for Miles Macdonell about the thorny question of jurisdiction. Legal opinions had established that the charter was valid, wrote Selkirk, but "any violent overstretch of authority would be extremely pernicious to our cause," leading to parliamentary abrogation of the charter. Particular caution would be required with the North West Company, which would seize on any mistake, especially "any step that might give a handle for misrepresenting these proceedings as directed to any sinister object, & particularly to the invidious purposes of monopoly."

In a separate letter, Selkirk explained about the Kildonan settlers, noting that they had "a great deal of the old highland pride & warmth of feelings," and would prove loyal only if well treated. He worried about whether these Presbyterian sectarians would accept the leadership of a Roman Catholic, but hoped they would do so if their feelings were carefully considered. Selkirk added in another letter, "the distance at which we are placed, and the long period which must intervene between our communications, leaves a sort of melancholy impression of uncertainty in our correspondence." The earl had learned that he had no control over events on the other side of the Atlantic. He could only hope his agents were sensible.

As might have been expected from a venture conceived amidst such confusion, the Kildonan emigration of 1813 did not do well. Typhus was aboard the *Prince of Wales*, and five emigrants as well as the young surgeon hired by Selkirk to lead the expedition died on ship. Another thirty were weakened by the disease, some to die later. To make matters worse, the captain of the vessel refused to take the settlers to York Factory, where they were expected, and dumped them instead at Fort Churchill without proper provisions for a winter on the Bay. As the disappointments accumulated, it was no wonder that many of this earliest contingent of Kildonan settlers were not among Selkirk's most loyal supporters in the subsequent troubles with the North West Company. The fact that their fate was not entirely Selkirk's fault made little difference. Worst of all, the news of their arrival at Fort Churchill — and Selkirk's promise of more settlers in 1814 — helped push Miles Macdonell into his ill-fated Pemmican Proclamation.

When Macdonell had visited York Factory in September of 1813, awaiting the arrival of the Kildonan settlers who were not landed there, he discussed policy with William Auld and other employees of the HBC. His interpretation of the instructions from Lord Selkirk seemed to recommend bellicose behaviour. The traders at York Factory certainly favoured action. Of paramount importance was the fact that the colonists would not have enough food. Although the first contingent of colonists had been able to plant in 1813, it was almost impossible to farm, especially on Red River soil, using no agricultural implement but the hoe. William Auld complained to Lord Selkirk that the settlement had "neither ploughs, nor carts nor horses." Donald Gunn in his later *History of Manitoba* would complain that Selkirk shipped arms to the colony, but could not manage to send agricultural implements.

By this point Auld and Macdonell were barely speaking. An accumulation of incidents had soured their relationship, headed by Macdonell's unfortunate comments about Auld's mixed-blood family which had been passed on by a discontented Red River clerk. Macdonell believed he had the authority to regulate the trade in foodstuffs, especially pemmican. He was also certain that he had the superior military position, an assessment which was true in the short run. Macdonell was not given the letter from Selkirk while he was at York Factory, ordering a more cautious policy. Its suppression was probably part of Auld's mischief. The warning only caught up with him at Red River in December, too late to change his mind.

By the end of 1813 Selkirk could assess the effects of the first two years of colonization. He had virtually nothing to show for his investment. The labour of his subordinates appeared almost entirely wasted. Settling a colony would not be as easy as he had expected. Matters were not aided by his own errors of judgment. Selkirk's miscalculations, like his promotions, had a wide-reaching effect. All his undoubted assets of character — his enthusiasm, his altruism, his stubbornness, and his ingenuity — could become liabilities when they led him to overreach himself and when others had to pay the price for mistakes. The worst miscalculation of all, of course, was Selkirk's failure to appreciate the fierceness of the reaction of the partners of the North West Company to his schemes.

3. Astoria:

As in Red River, affairs on the West Coast led a life of their own. The communication links were so difficult that it was quite impossible to integrate strategy planned in the east or in Europe into any planning. Those on the spot were very much on their own.

The wintering partners of the North West Company had first learned of the American declaration of war against Britain at their annual meeting at Fort William on 18 July 1812. Unbeknownst to those gathered at Fort William, only two days earlier, the company's voyageurs on the Great Lakes had headed off for Michilimackinac. The news of the American action came by express canoe, which brought a copy of James Madison's proclamation of a state of war. The meeting was immediately galvanized into action, not over western forts but over Astoria. Here was a chance to beat the Americans. Donald McTavish and John McDonald of Garth were sent to London to arrange British naval support for the company's ship *Isaac Todd*, which would be sent armed to the Pacific Coast. The two men carried a letter explaining that the Nor'Westers expected "on this occasion that the government will come forward in a decided manner to let the World understand who are the proprietors of the country."

Other parties were ordered west overland to meet up with the *Isaac Todd* at the Columbia.

In England in the autumn of 1812, NWC agents lobbied for government naval protection for the *Isaac Todd*. The Colonial Office was told, "The territorial possession of the Countries bordering on the Columbia River, and finally the whole North-west Coast of the Continent of America, will depend on the present occasion." The government finally listened. In March 1813 Captain James Hillyar of the HMS *Phoebe* received secret orders to escort the *Isaac Todd* to the Columbia, where he was "to protect and render every assistance in your power to the British traders from Canada and to destroy and if possible totally annihilate any settlements which the Americans may have formed on the Columbia River."

Meanwhile, over the winter of 1812-1813, agents of John Jacob Astor were also in England, arranging for a fast armed ship, the *Forester*, to sail ostensibly to Canton, but with a stop at Astoria along the way. This vessel probably departed from England in the same convoy as the *Isaac Todd*. (The *Forester* got to Hawaii late in 1813, where its British crew mutinied and attempted to surrender the ship to an American privateer. The captain decided not to continue on to Astoria but to head for California).

Astor also simultaneously lobbied energetically in the United States for support for his trading post. He talked with American Secretary of State James Monroe, concerned to know whether the United States would "assert any claim" to the Pacific coast. He advocated an armed ship to patrol the waters off the Columbia River. Astor knew, of course, that such a ship was available and would be heading towards the region. Even so, he organized another vessel, the *Lark*, to sail to the Columbia under Russian documentation. (This vessel actually got away, and was struck by a gale off Hawaii in the summer of 1813. It drifted without masts and rigging for some days before eventually beaching at Maui.) In late March of 1813 a Boston merchant who gathered British intelligence reported on the voyage of the *Isaac Todd* and *Phoebe*. Astor actually went so far as to get American government approval for the dispatch of an armed naval vessel to the Pacific Coast, but at the last minute the crew was transferred to Lake Ontario.

In Astoria itself, news of the war between the United States and Great Britain finally arrived in January 1813. The overland party of the NWC arrived in Spokane late in December. Its leader, John George McTavish, had a copy of Mr. Madison's declaration of war. He displayed it openly, and told all and sundry that armed British ships would be in the Columbia in the spring. The American leader Donald McKenzie was at Spokane. He copied out the words of the declaration of war, and arrived with the copy at Astoria on 16 January, 1813. The Americans apparently determined to abandon the fort in the spring as indefensible. They knew of the Nor'Wester scheme of conquest, though not of Astor's desperate attempts to assist them.

By July of 1813, Astor learned that the *Phoebe* and the *Isaac Todd* had sailed, but would probably not reach the Pacific Slope until spring of 1814. He made a last desperate effort to force government action. In the end, he had to settle for an armed privateer escorting a merchant vessel. To elude the British naval blockade of New York, Astor again negotiated Russian sailing papers. But the British blockaders categorically refused to allow a vessel ostensibly chartered by the Russian-American Company to pass the blockade.

On the Columbia itself, the spring of 1813 was spent with Americans and Nor'Westers uneasily cohabiting. Both sides waited for the arrival of reinforcements, which were expected to be British. The Nor'Westers knew that the *Isaac Todd* was on its way, although they had no idea of its precise movements. The Americans had absolutely no notion of how hard John Jacob Astor had worked to provide them with United States military relief. In any case, the Americans saw no reason to change their earlier decision to abandon the post. At another meeting of the local partners, replete with what Alexander Ross labelled "mutual recrimination," Donald McKenzie spoke eloquently and at length about the inevitable decision. "In the present critical conjuncture," he argued, "there is no time to be lost: let us then, by a timely measure, save what we can, lest a British ship of war enter the river and seize all." He blamed "the absolute necessity of abandoning the enterprize as soon as possible" on Astor's failures "and a chain of misfortunes."

The partners signed a resolution of dissolution and eventual abandonment on 1 July 1813. It said:

> *We are now destitute of the necessary supplies to carry on the Trade, and we have no hopes of receiving more. We are yet entirely ignorant of the coast, on which we always had great dependence. The interior parts of the country turn out far short of our expectations. Its yearly produce in furs is very far from being equal to the expenses the trade incurs; much less will it be able to recover the losses already sustained, or stand against*

*a powerful opposition and support itself. In fine, circumstances
are against us on every hand; and nothing operates to lead us
into a conclusion, that we can succeed.*

The Astorians planned to depart in April 1814. In the meantime,
they proposed to the Nor'Westers that the interior fur trading be divided among the companies. The North West Company accepted the proposals of the Astoria partners for a division of the trade with alacrity.
Nobody had any idea where the *Isaac Todd* was, and it appeared quite
likely that something had gone wrong on the other side of the world.

On 20 August 1813, a ship suddenly appeared in the Columbia. It
was an American merchant vessel from Hawaii. Wilson Price Hunt
disembarked from the ship. He regaled the traders with his adventures with the *Beaver* among the Russians, who drank him under the
table. The chief Russian trader, Hunt reported, "is continually giving
entertainments by way of parade, and if you do not drink raw rum,
and boiling punch as strong as sulphur, he will insult you as soon as
he gets drunk, which is very shortly after sitting down to table." Hunt
was astounded to discover that Astoria was to be abandoned. He
argued against the decision, pointing out that there was no sign of
British relief. But he was easily outvoted.

At the annual meeting of the wintering partners of the NWC at
Fort William in July of 1813, a party of men was sent west with fresh
information about the *Isaac Todd* and with instructions. As a result,
the Company's West Coast leader, John George McTavish, determined
to act. He led a force of 75 Nor'Westers to Astoria, which arrived in
early October at the post by canoe. The Astorians were understandably skeptical of McTavish's news that the *Isaac Todd* could be expected momentarily. They refused to take any action, leaving McTavish
and his men to cool their heels in an open camp with winter just
around the corner. McTavish soon had a solution, however. On 8
October he offered to buy out the Pacific Fur Company, lock, stock,
and barrel.

The Astorians spent the period between 8 October and 12
October deliberating on the NWC offer. On the one hand, the company agreement made no mention of liquidation by sale. On the other
hand, a British warship might arrive any day. The threat of the warship won out. Gabriel Franchère wrote, "expecting every day to see a
warship arrive to deprive us of what little we had, we listened to
those proposals and after several consultations set a price upon our
furs and our remaining merchandise." Several more days were spent

dickering over the price. The final agreement was made on 16 October. All assets would be turned over to the Nor'Westers. The staff at Astoria could either join the NWC or leave. The assets were valued in detail. The valuations were probably reasonable (or even a bit high) under the circumstances, which was a forced sale under threat of military conquest.

Mr. Astor, of course, did not agree. For the remainder of his life he groused about his heavy losses, and particularly about the undervaluation of the furs at Astoria. Such complaints might have had more legitimacy had any of his relief vessels ultimately reached Astoria. But they did not. Instead, at the end of November the HMS *Raccoon* appeared in the Columbia. At first the vessel's identity was not clear, and more than one Astorian probably spent an uncomfortable few hours wondering if the arrival was American. It was not, of course. The *Raccoon* had been detailed to convoy the *Isaac Todd* at Rio de Janeiro. It had arrived ahead of the remainder of the ships in its convoy. On 12 December 1813, Captain William Black of the *Raccoon* took formal possession of Fort Astoria. According to Gabriel Franchère:

> We entertained our guests as lavishly as we possibly could.
> After dinner the captain had guns distributed to the employees
> of the company and we all gathered, thus armed, on a platform
> on which a flagstaff had been erected. There the captain took
> a British flag he had brought for the purpose and had it run
> up on the staff. Then, taking a bottle of Madeira wine, he broke
> it across the staff, declaring in a loud voice that he was taking
> possession of the establishment in the name of His Royal
> Majesty. And he changed the name of the Fort from Astoria to
> Fort George. Indian chiefs had been assembled to serve as wit-
> nesses to the ceremony, and I explained to them, in their lan-
> guage, what had taken place. Three rounds of artillery and mus-
> ketry were fired, and the health of the King was drunk, accord-
> ing to the usual custom on such occasions.

Thus ended the fur trade wars on the Pacific Coast, which was now effectively British from Spanish California to Russian Alaska. Unfortunately, this little ceremony so many thousands of miles from the centres of power, would ultimately come back to haunt the British. Fort Astoria may have been purchased by the NWC, but it had been subsequently included in a military conquest during the War of 1812. As such, it should have been returned to the Americans by article one of the Treaty of Ghent.

Unlike John Jacob Astor, the partners of the North West Company did not complain overmuch about the deal made at Astoria. At their 1814 meeting at Fort William, they agreed that "the Advantages derived from the Arrangement" were "considerable." What the resolution of the Pacific Coast conflict meant, of course, was that the NWC could turn its truculent attention to the HBC and to Red River, which was now a more essential provisioning post than ever for the transcontinental canoe brigades.

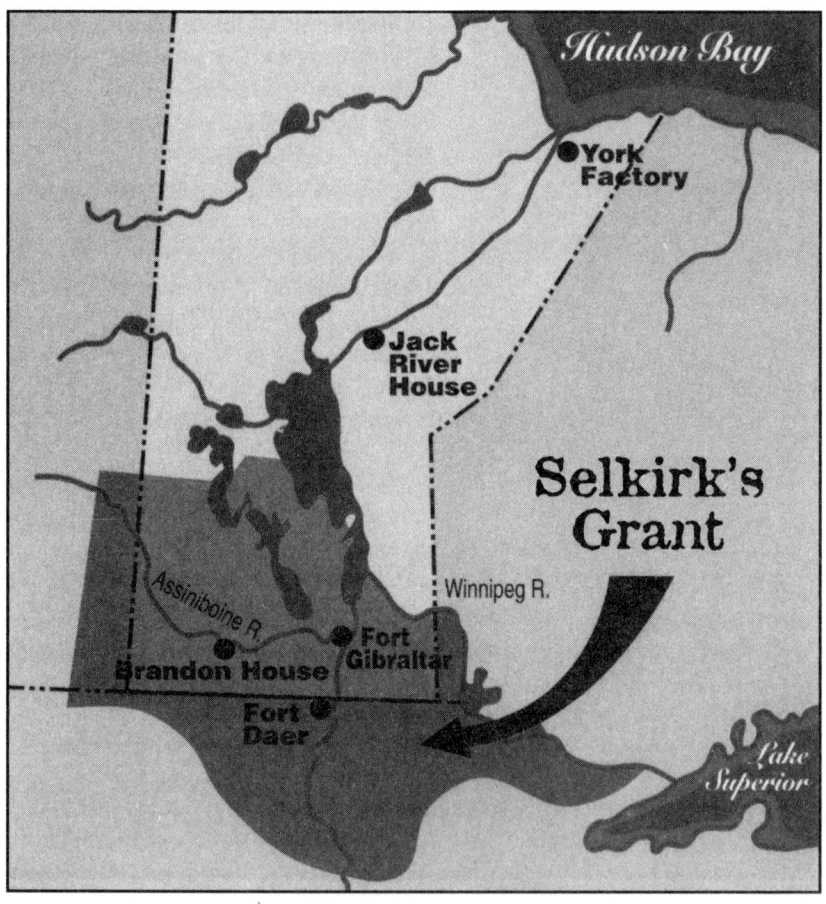

~5~

The Pemmican Proclamation
and Its Consequences

*O*ver the winter of 1813-14, the little settlement of cold and unhappy Europeans at Red River continued to rely heavily on the resident hunters for a food supply. The produce of a few patches of ground cultivated with the hoe was quickly consumed. The adult male settlers persevered in their roles as human beasts of burden, dragging sledges through deep snow drifts from the camp of the hunters to their compatriots. Meanwhile, their leaders began to prepare for the first showdown at the Forks between the Hudson's Bay Company and the North West Company. On the West Coast, the Astorians readied themselves to depart Fort George (as it was now named) for eastern Canada.

1. The Pemmican Proclamation:

*M*iles Macdonell issued his ill-fated "Pemmican" Proclamation on 8 January 1814. In the yet "uncultivated state of the Country," it said, food was scarce for the population of the settlement. Therefore, no persons trading furs or provisions within Selkirk's territory employed by either the Hudson's Bay Company or the North West Company could remove any provisions from the territory for the next twelve months "except what may be judged necessary for the trading parties at the present time within the Territory to carry them to their respective destinations." Application to Macdonell for permission to remove provisions would be required. All provisions would be paid for at customary rates in British currency. Disregard of the regulation would result in prosecution, with goods and conveyances seized and forfeited. William Hillier met Macdonell at

Pembina shortly after the proclamation had been issued, advising that it contradicted Selkirk's instructions. Macdonell replied, "No damn them, I'll settle them my own way."

The Nor'Westers always argued that this proclamation was the "*casus belli*" for the ensuing fur trade wars. In their version of events, an uneasy peace had been maintained between the NWC and the colony until Macdonell had assumed "powers greater than those usually delegated to governors appointed by the crown." Macdonell insisted that the colony was a jurisdiction with its own laws, and acted upon this insistence. William Coltman - who later investigated the fur trade wars for the British government — was unsympathetic to this perspective. He pointed out in 1818 that the appointment of Miles Macdonell as governor had not been submitted to the Crown as was required by Parliament. Moreover, Macdonell had never taken any oaths of office. Macdonell not only proclaimed his authority, of course. He also sought to enforce it. The defenders of Selkirk and the HBC could do little better than to justify Macdonell's action as necessary given the conditions that he faced in 1814.

The attempt to distinguish the settlement from the HBC by forbidding both fur trading companies to remove provisions was never very convincing. All the traders knew that it was the North West Company which would be most affected by the prohibition, because it was most dependent on the foodstuffs from the Red River region. Observing the forms specified in the law book which Selkirk had sent Macdonell, the governor made an effort to "publish" the proclamation by posting it at the gates of several North West Company posts, including Brandon House.

From Fort Gibraltar, former XY fur trader John Wills officially responded that he refused to acknowledge "an authority in that district capable of executing such a Proclamation." He added his own threat "to bring down the Brigades from Fort Dauphin and Swan River." According to HBC fur trader Peter Fidler, Wills also said "that he would assemble the Indians to assist his people to forcibly resist the said Proclamation being carried into effect." Privately, in a letter to Macdonell, Wills observed that provisions would be scarce in the spring, and "I should be very sorry to part with any . . . if there is a possibility of avoiding it." The Nor'Wester described the regulations as a "piece of inhumanity unheard of, admitting you had a right to do so." He could not acknowledge Macdonell's authority until he had consulted with other partners in the district.

In early 1814, Miles Macdonell was not particularly worried about North West Company threats. From a military perspective, he was quite sanguine. In a letter to William Auld dated 4 February, he commented, "I have sufficient force to crush all the N Westers in this river should they be so hard as to resist openly my authority." Although he expected some opposition in the spring, he added, "We are so well armed & I have a parcel of fine active stout fellows that will execute any order they receive." So long as the opposition did not send in reinforcements, his assessment was correct. The young men of the settlement had received some cursory training with weapons and Macdonell had several light cannon at his disposal.

Meanwhile, Macdonell's employer in London was deluging the Liverpool ministry with position papers on many subjects, ranging from the abolition of the slave trade to the reconstruction of Europe. In one paper, Lord Selkirk called for a confederation of African nations brought about by the British, who were "a civilised people, actuated by disinterested views." The superior knowledge of the British should enable them to dominate the confederacy, he argued.

His most interesting suggestions were contained in another paper discussing a prospective American treaty and its effect on the aboriginal people. He did not want to abandon native allies of the British in the lands between Detroit and the Mississippi. He advocated instead another confederacy to inhabit Indian territory, free from both British and American sovereignty. Once again, the superior British would dominate the natives.

His lordship was clearly concerned to provide a buffer zone along the western boundary between the United States and British North America. Selkirk was especially adamant that the United States should be left no opening to claim the Northwest as an extension of the Louisiana Purchase. The country north of the height of land dividing the Mississippi from the waters of the Hudson Bay, he insisted, was as British as Canada or Nova Scotia. It should not be a topic for treaty discussion with the Americans.

Such blatantly imperialistic views, in which Britain would dominate native peoples through its obviously superior "civilization," were all part of the assumptions with which Selkirk attempted to colonize western Canada. Such imperialism is no longer fashionable, but we cannot understand Selkirk without taking such attitudes into account. He had no doubt that British civilization was superior to American, not to mention aboriginals and mixed-bloods.

Selkirk's concern with higher affairs of state came at a time when Red River's prospects seemed, from his perspective, to be unsettled but not particularly threatened. Neither he nor most of his North American agents understood the potential virulence of the North West Company response to Red River. Certainly Miles Macdonell expected that the Nor'Westers would accede to his superior force and accept his proclaimed authority.

To nobody's surprise, the Hudson's Bay Company in the person of William Auld acknowledged the governor's jurisdiction and supported the principle that provisions could not be removed from the territory without license. In a letter to Macdonell, Auld reported that the Kildonan people were ill chiefly because of their "abominable filthy habits," adding that he had introduced naval discipline to prevent them being "smothered in their own excrement." He noted that Macdonell would get no support for his pemmican proclamation from William Hillier, who had not been consulted in the affair. Auld was wrong about the absence of consultation with Hillier, but not about his lack of support. In a separate letter to Hillier, Auld articulated his misgivings. He confessed, "We are but poor matches for the Canadians either in cunning or unjustifiable aggressions."

Although Auld did not yet know it, he was being replaced. The instructions from the HBC's committee of management to his successor Thomas Thomas emphasized two points which were to be changed. First, there must be an end to "the blind adherence to antiquated customs" which meant that "the quantity of work done by our people both labourers & tradesmen bears no proportion to the days work of a man in any part of Britain." Three-fourths of the staff were to be cut. Second, "as you are opposed to a set of people who proceed upon a systematic plan of violence to prevent the Indians from trading with us, and to deter our people from protecting them when attempting, it is evident that no success can be expected until you are enabled to repel force by force."

One apparent inconsistency is evident in these instructions, and perhaps more were implied. How could the work force be cut by three-quarters at the same time that a more concerted opposition to the North West Company was expected? The answer to this question lies in the theory of the committee of management that most of their older employees at the Bay were indulged Orkneymen totally lacking in backbone. The new recruits which Selkirk had sent and was continuing to send were supposed to be harder working, particularly when put under tighter discipline. Moreover, the group would be protected by a small mobile contingent of trained Highlanders and Irish headed by William Hillier, which had been especially organized for the purpose.

Lord Selkirk certainly had no reason to be unhappy with Macdonell's proclamation, since in a series of letters in April of 1814 he suggested something not dissimilar. In one letter he complained that Macdonell had co-operated too closely with the North West Company, which would allow his enemies to misrepresent his intentions. In a later letter, Selkirk added: "I have omitted mentioning that

Notice should be given to the Partners or Servants of the NWCo at the Forks to Quit Possession — in the manner pointed out in Burn's Justice — Article 'Distress — Tenant holding over' — considering them as Tenants at Will — This should be done in writing, & verbally also, before enough of witnesses to prevent any question as to the Notice being received — the same should be done at all the other Posts of the NWCo. within the Territory of Ossiniboia."

Selkirk wanted the Nor'Westers warned by the same legal procedures followed by many an improving landlord in the Scottish Highlands. Such action presumed that his title to the land was unchallenged, which was hardly the case. As William Coltman later commented, to seize by force a trading post occupied by others, without any formalities required by law, was an excessive act. It presumed the absolute validity of both the HBC charter and Selkirk's grant, neither of which had ever been tested in any court.

Food for the colony was in short supply. The proclamation could be defended on those grounds, especially as it was directed against all fur traders. Selkirk might have commented that merely warning the Nor'Westers was less provocative than actually seizing pemmican. But the governor might have responded that there would have to be some further symbolic action of authority beyond a mere warning. Seizing the valued pemmican would be such an action.

Certainly the early signs were encouraging for Macdonell. In April of 1814, William Auld's report on NWC reaction indicated that he had won the first round. John (le Borgne) MacDonald had wanted to meet the governor with force, but other NWC partners in the region apparently had accepted the proclamation.

Meanwhile, John Wills was quite ill. He would soon be replaced as the NWC's head of the Red River District and would die at Fort Gibraltar before the year was out. William Auld had asked Wills, "what the opinion in England would be if you permitted Strangers (not to call his association by a worse term) to carry out provisions from your own lands when you must purchase English provisions either in England or here from the HBC's stores to subsist?" Auld claimed Wills had no response. Auld further opined to Macdonell, "I don't think either we or the Canadians will lose a drop of Blood; the Bourgeoisie will bluster & Strut a bit & that will be all." Moreover, he added, "you have but to beckon with your finger & every Canadian servant who is free this year will repair to your Standard." The Nor'Westers were bullies, concluded Auld, and he did not expect serious trouble. Despite their disagreements, Auld seemed obviously prepared to support Macdonell on this issue.

William Auld's encouragement was a bit premature. The Red River governor and the Nor'Wester Wills continued to exchange tense letters. Macdonell insisted it was his "indisputable duty to endeavour to secure to the British Empire this part of the Country," while Wills maintained that he could do nothing until the wintering partners had met at Fort William. In the meantime, Macdonell would keep the pemmican. In late May the two men met for a person-to-person conference, walking together along the river bank in the lush spring growth. Wills continued to deny Macdonell's authority. It would take a commission from the Privy Council to issue such a proclamation, argued Wills, who added, "You are too weak altogether to attempt the establishing of regular law in this country."

2. Gabriel Franchère Journeys East:

On the Pacific Coast, 4 April 1814 saw the embarkation up the Columbia of those employees of John Jacob Astor's Pacific Fur Company who chose to take advantage of the Nor'Wester offer of transportation east. They became passengers on what Alexander Ross described as "the first grand movement of the North West Company on the Columbia." This expedition was not the first attempt at an eastern journey from Fort George. James Keith and Alexander Stuart had earlier left for Fort William to carry the news of the takeover of Astoria, but their party had been attacked by Indians. Stuart was saved only when a stone pipe he was carrying prevented the barb of an arrow from entering his body at his waistcoat pocket. This second attempt contained a large body of voyageurs, as well as the Astorians. Donald McKenzie carried the papers of the Pacific Fur Company for John Jacob Astor.

The diary of Gabriel Franchère tells the story of this early effort of crossing the continent, in the process demonstrating that the overland route was no easy journey. Franchère had been born in Montreal in 1786. He was one of those Canadians who had signed on with John Jacob Astor in the spring of 1810. He had travelled aboard the *Tonquin* to the Columbia in 1810. During his entire service with Astor he had kept a diary of his experiences, devoting a substantial portion of it to detailing his return to Lower Canada in 1814. Franchère's account provides an excellent description of the state of western communication in the early days of the fur trade wars.

According to Franchère, the Astorians left what was now named Fort George in ten canoes, each carrying seven crewmen and two passengers. Five of the canoes were of bark and five were of cedar. The party was well armed, since hostile natives were still a great concern. The expedition left Fort George under a salute with flags flying. Only a week out, one of the canoes overturned and sank in shallow water. The crew managed to save all the baggage, which had to be dried and redistributed in the remaining canoes. By 16 April the river began narrowing and mountains were visible to the southeast.

The party bought some horses from some Snake Indians, and Franchère rode one at the side of the river. A day's riding so fatigued him that he returned to his canoe. To the rear, canoes could be seen trying to catch up. To Franchère's surprise, a child's voice called out, "Arretez donc, arretez donc." When the canoes landed, he recognized the wife and family of a mixed-blood hunter who had been ordered to obtain provisions from the Snake people. The wife's story was one of disaster. Her husband and his companions had been killed by natives and she and her two children had spent the winter hiding in the mountains. Franchère saw the deaths as a vengeance for the previous hanging by the traders of one of the Indians for theft. "This event," he wrote, "the massacre of the *Tonquin's* crew, the disastrous end of Captain Cook, and many other similar instances demonstrate how those Europeans who have relations with barbaric people must refrain from treating them on the basis of a too marked inequality, or to punish them for their misdeeds, according to the customs and codes where often there is an enormous disproportion between the crimes and the punishments." By this point the party was heading more north than east. It would continue to move north by northeast until it reached Lesser Slave Lake.

On 21 April, the party lightened the load of three canoes, and those who were crossing the continent carried on in them. Two days later, the small flotilla arrived at the NWC post at the mouth of the Okanogan River. One of the traders gave Franchère a letter to carry to his brother in Canada. The canoes continued eastward, meeting with John Stuart and John Clarke — who had ridden by horseback from Fort Spokane — on the 30 April. On 4 May the enlarged group reached the mouth of the Flathead River. Six days later, the travellers saw ahead of them a chain of high mountains totally covered with snow. On 11 May the canoes left the Columbia for a small stream earlier named the Canoe River by David Thompson. Franchère calculated the distance at nearly 1,200 miles, and calculated that the party had travelled at the rate of about 30 miles a day. The Canoe River quickly became unnavigable. The party stopped, stowed the canoes, and divided the baggage. Each man got about fifty pounds, including provisions from a sack of pemmican found at the spot. Thus prepared, the party of 24 began hiking overland toward the mountains.

In the course of fording a very swift river, one of the party lost a sack of salt pork. The group became very concerned about shortness of provisions. On 14 May they began to climb a mountain, pausing frequently to catch their breath. Progress was slow, since each hiker had to follow exactly in the deep tracks in the snow of the person ahead, plunging up to their knees. "It was as though we had put on and taken off, at each step, a large pair of boots," reported Franchère. A day later they descended. Soon they reached the banks of the Athabasca River. Supper consisted of a few handfuls of dried corn grilled in a pan. On 17 May the party came across an old North West Company trading post, "surrounded by smiling and lush prairies and superb groves." Several free traders, along with pemmican and fresh meat, were found there. Franchère had earlier struck his knee on the branch of a tree, and it was very painful. He managed to get a place in a canoe brought down the Athabasca by other traders. Most of the party continued on horseback or on foot.

The party abandoned its canoe on 19 May, knowing that Rocky Mountain House was nearby. This post, said Franchère, was maintained by the North West Company chiefly to facilitate the mountain crossings of its employees. Four fresh canoes were prepared, and on 24 May the group glided away from the mountains. A canoe mishap on the 25th drowned two voyageurs and resulted in a substantial loss of supplies. A few days later, the travellers met a bark canoe heading toward Rocky Mountain House. From a letter carried in this canoe, Franchère and his companions learned of the Battle of Lake Erie fought on 10 September 1813.

They then obtained more canoes and set out on the complex river system to the south of the Athabasca, heading eastward. On 2 June, the group passed the mouth of the Little Slave Lake River. A day later they were forced to walk along the narrow and boulder-filled river which Franchère called the La Biche. On 5 June they crossed Lake La Biche. Here they met a former voyageur who lived at the lake with his family. Franchère read to this man several letters he had held for two years. This man provided the party with dried meat and tallow. The worst of the journey was now over. Franchère's group had reached the Beaver River, which led into the more commonly travelled canoe route east.

The Franchère party descended the Beaver River and carried their baggage overland to the North Saskatchewan River. On 10 June they arrived at Fort Vermilion, where both the NWC and the HBC had posts together on the North Saskatchewan. According to Franchère, the forts of the competitors were "usually built close to one another, surrounded by a common palisade so that from the outside they

Miles Macdonell

Chief Peguis

Gabriel Franchère

Colin Robertson

appear to form a single square. The houses are separated by a light palisade so that they can go to one another's aid in case of attack." His description provides a graphic example of how employees of the two companies often co-operated in a hostile wilderness. However, this sort of arrangement would prove a built-in recipe for trouble when hostilities between the companies heated up.

At this point, the men of the two companies were still getting along. The NWC clerk in charge took two quarters of buffalo from his ice-house and provided supper for the visitors. The newcomers were surprised to find in one of the large rooms of the post a full-sized carriole. It had been built in the room by men who had not measured the doors in advance. They were thus unable to get it out.

After a well-needed rest, the party continued on its way. Travel along the Saskatchewan was swift, the canoes carried along by a heavy current. The travellers were even able to hoist their sails. On 20 June the party reached Cumberland House on English Lake. Two days later their hosts held a ball in their honour. By 25 June they arrived at the Great Rapid of Lake Winnipeg and five days later at Fort du Bas de la Rivière on the Winnipeg River. The men from the West Coast had passed Red River within just a few days of the first confrontation over the pemmican proclamation.

3. The Pemmican Proclamation Enforced:

On 25 May 1814, Sheriff John Spencer of Red River went to the White Horse Plain. With the assistance of several freemen, including Jean-Baptiste Lagimodière (grandfather of Louis Riel), he seized 96 bags of "artfully concealed pemmican." There followed a series of "arrests" by the respective parties, as well as the capture of more pemmican by Sheriff Spencer. On 10 June he took 479 bags of pemmican, 94 kegs of fat, and 865 pounds of dried meat in bundles. The Nor'Westers complained of the confiscation of two canoes and the arrest of their crews at the foot of Lake Winnipeg, which they demanded be released "unless you mean to declare War against us."

Macdonell responded by freeing the men but keeping their arms. He added, "you cannot suppose yourselves possessed of any civil or military authority here." The Nor'Westers answered that they would send Deputy-sheriff Joseph Howse, whom they had arrested, to Montreal for trial on charges of burglary. They insisted, "The Laws of our Country will determine which of the two parties, that took up arms first." Macdonell stood firm, insisting that there was "no Tribunal at Montreal competent to try" Howse. As it turned out, a court eventually did try Howse, finding him innocent of criminal intent. His arrest was a distinct escalation of events, the first time the Nor'Westers had claimed an alternate authority to that of the colony. They employed an appointment as justice-of-the-peace issued by Lower Canada. Henceforth, both sides would claim to be enforcing "the law" in Red River.

In mid-June, John McDonald of Garth, Duncan Cameron, John (leBorgne) McDonald, John Wills, and J. D. Cameron — the North West partners currently resident in the Red River region — wrote to Miles Macdonell as "British Loyal Subjects." The question of Macdonell's authority must be settled by a higher tribunal, they maintained, but in the meantime they were willing to meet him "on the most liberal plan." They admitted that the American War had put them in a difficult position. The Americans were disrupting commerce on the Great Lakes, and the British government had granted them permission to send their trade goods through the Bay this year to avoid possible trouble with the United States. They concluded, it was "necessary for the existence of your infant Colony that a perfect understanding & an intercourse of mutual good offices should exist between' us & you."

Macdonell replied with the same note of conciliation. He was pleased to be able to make an amicable settlement. "We must make mutual sacrifices for the exigencies of the times." He released substantial amounts of fat and pemmican, and promised to release more in return for Nor'Wester commitments to help feed his people over the ensuing winter. The North West partners agreed to his terms the same day.

According to Gabriel Franchère, who visited Red River within days of the settlement, the agreement was that half the pemmican would be left for the colony and the other half returned to the Nor'Westers, each side reserving the right of appeal to the courts in Lower Canada. And so Macdonell had seemingly won his point. The lesson seemed to be that if the Nor'Westers were met with sufficient firmness, the "bullies" would back down. In a subsequent memorandum on the pemmican affair, Lord Selkirk himself noted that "Capt. MacDonnell so far from suffering himself to be bullied by the Canadians, compelled them to submit to his authority, and to respect the Company's jurisdiction." That the American war presented special circumstances did not seem any more important than the fact that the partners lacked clear military superiority. In any event, the North West Company had conceded to Macdonell's authority only for the moment.

In his own report to Selkirk, Macdonell emphasized the enormous advantages in manpower which the Nor'Westers enjoyed, despite their capitulation. That he had enjoyed a military advantage in the winter and lost it by the following summer perhaps suggests that he ought not to have been so ambitious in the first place. According to his reckoning, the NWC had 120 voyageurs, 12 bourgeois, plus 200 to 300 freemen and mixed-bloods at their disposal. This figure did not include aboriginals. For his part, Macdonell had 28 armed men, and he was never reinforced by Mr. Hillier.

Macdonell also waxed lyrical about the crops in 1814. For the first time, he drew Selkirk's attention to the Canadian freemen and their families, although he made no proposals about enlisting their support or settling with them on favourable terms. As for the NWC, he wrote, "it will require more force than we yet have to dispossess them forcibly."

The annual meeting of the partners of the NWC at Fort William in 1814 was an unusually spirited affair. The subject of the pemmican business was on everyone's minds. Officially, the compromise with Miles Macdonell was endorsed. Those who had permitted pemmican to be seized were censured at a special meeting, however. "A full determination was taken to defend the Property at all Hazards." By this time, the Nor'Westers were aware that the war with the Americans was over.

Gabriel Franchère had left Red River on 2 July and soon entered the "White River," the Winnipeg River. His party made 34 short portages and was at Lake of the Woods on 4 July. His canoes were soon in the Rainy Lake River. Like the Wolseley Expedition a half century later, what impressed Franchère most about this part of the journey was the mosquitoes: "...we were tormented by them the whole way and they followed us even into our canoes." They crossed Rainy Lake and passed Kakabeka Falls. Franchère mentions 36 portages at the lower end of the Kaministiquia River, but found nothing otherwise untoward about this leg of his journey. He arrived at Fort William in the midst of the summer meeting. He described the fort, built on drained marsh at the mouth of the Kaministiquia River, as looking "more like an attractive village."

Franchère wrote that his knowledge of Chinook led the Nor'Westers to hope they could get him to return to the Pacific Slope, but he was anxious to get to Montreal. While he was at Fort William, James Keith arrived from Astoria with news of the arrival of the *Isaac Todd* in late April 1814, thirteen months after she had sailed from England. The vessel, a slow sailor, had become separated from her escort at Cape Horn and had ended up alone on the coast of

California. Here it discovered the English naval sloop the *Raccoon* aground in San Francisco Bay. The *Raccoon* was careened and repaired, while the *Isaac Todd* continued on to the Columbia.

The censures made at Fort William against those who had compromised with Macdonell stung deeply. Alexander Greenfield Macdonell, no relation, made a partner despite his part in the pemmican business, reported to John McDonald of Garth: "You see myself and our mutual friend Mr. Cameron so far on our way to commence open hostilities against the Enemy in Red River. . . . Something serious will undoubtedly take place — nothing but the complete downfall of the Colony will satisfy some, by fair or foul means — a most desirable object if it can be accomplished — so here is at them with all my heart and energy."

Although the partners always maintained that Macdonell and Cameron carried on their subsequent campaign against the settlement without instructions from the Company — Macdonell's letter does not contradict the assertion — the letter does indicate how Macdonell responded to the censures and ridicule he had received for failing to stand up to Miles Macdonell. It is difficult to believe — whatever official action was or was not taken — that Macdonell and Cameron were returning to Red River without a clear idea of what was expected of them. What was obviously required was the destruction of the colony by any means necessary.

On his annual visit to York Factory in late summer of 1814, Miles Macdonell showed the strain he had been operating under for some time. He suffered what amounted to a nervous breakdown. The immediate problem was not the threat from the Nor'Westers but a combination of his continuing deteriorating relationship with William Auld and his own inability to keep the financial accounts of the settlement in a satisfactory manner. Macdonell was a soldier, not an accountant. To his colleagues Macdonell exclaimed, "I am a villain — the Colony will be ruined all by my fault." His letter to Selkirk explaining his difficulties was rambling and incoherent. He admitted great disappointment that Selkirk had not come himself with the year's shipment of settlers as he had promised. The new crop of people was not a prepossessing one, he thought. They were likely to cause trouble. Fortunately there were not many of them.

In a separate letter to Selkirk, Northern District superintendent Thomas Thomas wrote that Macdonell appeared incapable of carrying on his position. Thomas was not certain of the extent to which the confrontation with the Nor'Westers had led to his problems, but Macdonell had clearly been emotionally disturbed for some time. The arrival of James White as second-in-command apparently allowed

Macdonell to recover quickly from his illness. At least, the governor returned to Red River, arriving back at the settlement on 19 October. Here he found the situation far more menacing than he could have anticipated, given the earlier agreement to resume a friendly intercourse. Sheriff John Spencer had been arrested on 6 September under a Canadian warrant, and shipped east in a canoe for Fort William. Those in charge of the settlement had declined to rescue him. Duncan Cameron refused to replenish any of the provisions which Macdonell had allowed the NWC to have over the summer. He went further, and positively forbade the free Canadians to supply the settlement with any meat.

Macdonell had earlier sought to prevent the freemen and mixed-bloods from hunting buffalo without restriction, at least during the food emergency. Cameron took down from NWC gates the order forbidding the practice, telling the freemen that they should not be limited in this way. He bought up all the meat that the hunters could kill. Moreover, Cameron was now dressed in full military uniform, describing himself as a captain in his Majesty's service. Rumour had it that every Nor'Wester in the district had come back from Fort William with military appointments, swords, and uniforms. Macdonell served notices to quit upon the North West Company post in October of 1814, probably an unnecessary provocation given the circumstances, but one which fulfilled his employer's orders.

Duncan Cameron found many settlers at Red River discontented with their lot. Conditions were much more difficult than they had expected — or been promised — and improvement was slow. Towards the close of 1814 Cameron received a letter from one disgruntled settler, asking him to relieve a "poor distressed people" by transporting them to Montreal in the spring. The correspondence makes clear that Cameron had encouraged such a request, but he plainly had much raw material to work with in stirring up trouble.

4. Gabriel Franchère Heads to Montreal:

Franchère left Fort William on 20 July in an express canoe bound for Montreal. Fellow Astorians John Clarke and Donald McKenzie were among the six passengers aboard this canoe, which was manned by 14 voyageurs. Travel across Lake Superior was hampered by heavy mists, but the canoe arrived at Michipicoten Bay, on the north shore of the Lake, on 26 July. Here the party met another canoe containing the captain and crew of one of the NWC's schooners. The vessel had been abandoned and burned by the captain when an American detachment had attacked Sault Ste Marie.

It was decided to return the express canoe to Fort William with this news. Franchère transferred into the smaller canoe on the water. In the hurried exchange of canoes, his party failed to take any eating utensils. They were forced to moisten flour into little cakes which were cooked on flat stones. Franchère obviously regarded this bannock as part of the "wretched life" he led until the next post was reached. On 31 July several NWC canoes went to Sault Ste Marie to examine the damage wrought by the Americans. "The sawmills, warehouses, houses and so forth had all been destroyed and were still smoking," Franchère reported. The Americans had apparently hoped to capture the annual fur shipment from the West, but had been too early.

The actual Sault Ste Marie was a rapid into which Lake Superior emptied, about 1,500 feet wide and three-quarters of a mile long. At its lower end, one bank belonged to the Americans and the other to the British. On the American side, the chief resident was a Mr. Nolin and his mixed blood family. On the north side, NWC agent Charles Ermatinger had built a substantial establishment. Franchère's party tarried for some weeks at the Lake Huron end of the Sault, partly because of the American threat, partly to wait for the fur canoes from the west. The fur brigades arrived on 25 August. There were 44 fur-laden canoes and three express canoes, containing a total of 325 armed men. Franchère estimated the value of the furs at 200,000 louis, or over £100,000 in 1814 money. Truly these furs were a prize worthy of contention.

The brigades crossed Lake Huron and entered Lake Nipissing. A number of portages took them to the Ottawa River. More portages around the rapids and waterfalls of the Ottawa brought Franchère to Hull on 31 August. Two days later he was in Montreal, after an absence which he calculated at "four years, one month and six days." His "perilous journey" was over. From Astoria it had taken five months and involved literally hundreds of portages. Franchère's diary recorded the loss of the lives of several voyageurs, almost constant danger — mainly from the nature of the terrain transversed — and frequent deprivation in the form of loss of sleep and short rations.

5. The Robertson Mission and New Threats to Red River:

Colin Robertson was once described by George Simpson — who did not like him — as a "frothy trifling conceited man . . . who read novels, became sentimental and fancied himself the hero of every tale of Romance that passed through his hands." Six feet tall, with flaming red hair, Robertson was also known as a bon vivant and a risk-taker. He was in many ways the antithesis of the dour, careful Macdonell. Born to a family of weavers, Robertson had spent some years with the NWC, and had retired in 1809 with a decent testimonial. He immediately applied to the HBC for employment, pointing out the value of the fur trade in the Athabasca region and advocating that the venerable Company enter seriously into that trade. The HBC was in no position to undertake an initiative into the Athabasca in 1810. Robertson went off to Liverpool as a merchant. He was summoned back to HBC headquarters on Fenchurch Street early in 1814. On 15 March he again submitted a plan for trading in the Athabasca, and a month later he was on his way to Montreal to carry his proposal into execution. He was instructed to recruit a fur trader in Canada and to find a Montreal business firm to act as the HBC's local agent.

Unfortunately, Robertson's voyage to Quebec was delayed in Ireland waiting for a convoy to cross the Atlantic. As a result, he did not arrive in Lower Canada until 27 September, far too late to get anything organized for 1814. Moreover, he was convinced that there had been an information leak. Simon McGillivray had arrived only two days after Robertson in Quebec, and seemed to know all about the Athabasca venture which Robertson was to set afoot. Even if there had not been "whispers" in London, Robertson's loud talk and recruiting among former NWC servants quickly had given the game away. Or at least his actions gave away some of the game. The Nor'Westers had always suspected that Red River was only a cloak for an HBC foray into Athabasca. Robertson confirmed the suspicion. In some apparent attempt at disguising his mission, he appeared in Canada as a Red River land agent, conducting all business in the name of the colony. His "easy affability and lavish notions" soon brought numbers of retired and discontented fur traders to his door. One of those Robertson wooed was John Clarke, late of the Pacific Fur Company, who had recently arrived in Lower Canada with Gabriel Franchère.

On the very day of his arrival in Lower Canada, Robertson heard rumours of Métis threats against Red River. The fur trade community was a small tightly-knit one, and everybody seemed to know everybody else's business. Robertson recruited John Pritchard, who had also recently left the NWC service, to return to Red River. Pritchard had been one of those Nor'Westers who had abjectly surrendered pemmican to Macdonell early in 1814. He had subsequently been accused of cowardice by his colleagues. At his own request, Pritchard was sent west over the winter to warn the settlement about the threats against it.

Robertson reported the rumours he had heard to Lord Selkirk. The earl replied in December of 1814 that he found the threats of the Indians worrisome, but that he did not think the Nor'Westers would risk infamy by actually inciting them.

Colin Robertson was not the only person who heard rumours of trouble for Red River. Miles Macdonell's cousin John, retired from his partnership in the NWC to a farm near Glengarry, picked up similar reports of inciting the aboriginals to violence against the settlement. "The strongest argument I have heard used to raise a jealousy in the natives is by inculcating upon their minds a belief that they are Robbed on their Lands with no indemnification," he wrote to a correspondent. Macdonell could see no particular justification for this fear, but added, "Self preservation may justify acts that in other situations would become criminal."

Lord Selkirk was shown copies of this correspondence early in 1815, and took immediate alarm. But terminology and a lack of complete understanding of the social structure of Red River misled him. It is not clear from his letter exactly who John Macdonell meant by "natives," but it is likely that he intended to refer to the mixed-blood children of the freemen who often worked for the North West Company. Had Macdonell meant "Indians," he probably would have used that term. Selkirk, of course, immediately assumed that the danger was from the aboriginals.

In early February of 1815, Joseph Berens, the governor of the HBC, wrote officially to Lord Bathurst at the Colonial Office. He forwarded a letter from Lord Selkirk alleging that the settlement at Red River "is in immediate danger of being destroyed, through the machinations of certain persons who are endeavouring, by malicious misrepresentations, to inflame the minds of the Indians against the Colonists." The evidence was not conclusive, wrote Berens, but sufficient to call for precautions to prevent the "horrible consequences" of an attack.

A few days later Selkirk penned another letter to the HBC. This one responded to the letter from Miles Macdonell's cousin, offering it as evidence that the threats against the colony were serious. Selkirk spent much of the letter denying that the Indians had been mistreated by Macdonell. His examples made plain that he thought solely in terms of the aboriginals. While he had earlier thought of the

Nor'Wester threats as an "idle menace," he now realized that some of the partners "have lived from early youth at a distance from the restraints of civilized society" and "believed that the remoteness of the country would shelter them from the law."

Selkirk himself wrote to Bathurst in early March of 1815, seeking to correct any misapprehensions which might have arisen from a conversation the two had conducted a few days earlier about Red River. The earl insisted that there was no question in his concern for his settlement of serving the pecuniary interests of one party in a commercial rivalry. Rather the issue was one of protecting innocent subjects from massacre. The intention was not to incriminate the NWC, he insisted, but merely to demonstrate the danger. In preventing an impending breach of the peace, "the persons who may be suspected," ought to be "the very last who are consulted." This reference was to discussions Bathurst had recently held with representatives of the NWC. Denying that the conduct of the two companies was similar, he insisted the HBC was responsible for its employees and its board was "composed of gentlemen, who have too much regard for their character, to give any instruction, that is even of a doubtful nature."

Unlike the partners of the NWC, the leadership of the HBC could not escape justice by disappearing into the interior of the country. The NWC could evade responsibility for the acts of any partner by disavowing them, he emphasized. Nevertheless, the settlers still needed protection and had not caused trouble. As usual, Selkirk took a high moral ground he would have difficulty sustaining.

Lord Bathurst responded to the HBC representations by writing Lieutenant-General Sir Gordon Drummond of Lower Canada to enquire into "the grounds of the fears expressed by them," without interfering in any way in the dispute between the two companies. On this occasion, Bathurst did demonstrate a concern "to secure the lives and properties of His Majesty's subjects established on the Red River." For a variety of reasons, neither he nor anyone else proved able to do so.

~6~

The Settlement Dispersed

*U*ntil 1815, a good deal of posturing and threatening had been carried on by all parties involved in the escalation of the fur trade wars. But precious little real violence had taken place. So far nobody had actually gotten killed and very little property had been seriously damaged. That situation would change dramatically in 1815. The year's big event would be the destruction of the Lord Selkirk's Red River settlement by the Nor'Westers. In the background, however, many other significant developments had occurred — developments that would have an equally profound effect on what would become Western Canada.

1. The Dispersal of the Settlement:

As early as January 1815, if not before, virtually everyone in the western territory knew that the North West Company would attempt to drive the Red River settlers out of their homes in the spring. HBC fur trader George Holdsworth wrote to Miles Macdonell that the presence of adequate provisions for the settlers was a blessing, since the Nor'Westers hoped to use scarcity to induce the settlers to leave. As Holdsworth well knew, the NWC had fertile ground for the sowing of discontent. For the settlers, the first couple of years at Red River had been miserable. First, they experienced an extremely long and difficult journey to Red River. They suffered many further privations once arrived. Whatever promises they thought had been made to them had rarely been fulfilled. To top everything off, Miles Macdonell was hardly a charismatic leader.

Although Selkirk had feared trouble between the Catholic Macdonell and the Presbyterian Kildonaners, little evidence of sectarian hostility actually surfaced. Apart from the hardships of adjusting to frontier life, which would have made anybody unhappy, much of the problem was with Miles himself.

Macdonell was really a number of problems, rolled into one conflicted package. For example, he was not actually a Highlander, but a North American of Highland background. The difference was crucial. He never really understood the people under his command, and had little but contempt for them most of the time. They were — he thought — ignorant, dirty, stubborn, and full of nothing but complaints. Miles never appreciated that the dazed response of his Highlander charges was not simply to hardship, but also to totally unfamiliar conditions and circumstances.

The second problem was that Macdonell was essentially a military man with a military man's perspective on life. He handed out muskets and expected the settlers to fight. He lacked compassion and flexibility. Once he had an idea in his head, he could not be talked out of it. His response to business matters was to avoid them as long as possible, and then to pass them along to his underlings. His successor Robert Semple reported to Selkirk in September of 1815 that there was much evidence to suggest that "the dispersion of the Colony to have been occasioned, not so much by the efforts of the Canadians as by the errors of those who had the direction of it. . . . Captain MacDonell was careless and profuse in great matters, whilst on little points he frequently displayed a niggardly parsimony. That he was liberal in his promises but wanting in the performance of them, in so much that at length even his own men and the Colonists lost all confidence in him, and knew not what to trust to."

For most settlers, Miles Macdonell was not so much a presence but an absence, often away from Red River. Certainly Macdonell gradually lost the respect of most of the other leading men of the settlement and the HBC. As Semple pointed out, his attitude seemed to be that he "was surrounded by envious men whose chief wish was to throw obstacles in his way, and whose greatest pleasure it would be to see him fail in all his plans." It did not help matters that he became very much enamoured of Christina McLean, the wife of Alexander McLean, and usually deferred to her opinions in preference to those of others. Mrs. McLean was obviously attractive, since she would subsequently become involved with Colin Robertson in a similar sort of way.

The story of the spring of 1815 is one of the rapid deterioration of any support for Miles. At the end, he was left alone to face the combined opposition of the Nor'Westers and his own settlers. Not surprisingly, he lost his nerve and gave up entirely.

Once again, the settlement needed food over the winter of 1814/15. The efforts of the NWC to interfere with the food supply proved fairly effective. The freemen drove the buffalo away, and the Nor'Westers prohibited any freemen from hunting for Red River despite their contracts to do so. Macdonell attempted in February to make peace with the freemen camped near Turtle River led by Peter Bostonois. His emissaries were surrounded by a group of NWC servants, freemen and mixed-bloods who were well-armed. This gathering held the settlers captive for six days while attempting to lure Miles himself into the camp. According to John McLeod, one of their prisoners, the freeman party painted their faces daily, sang Indian songs, and beat Indian drums.

As it turned out, Macdonell spent most of the winter of that year on the plains, avoiding the settlers while attempting to find meat for them. He never properly explained why he had abandoned Fort Douglas at such a crucial time. It seems likely that he was trying to recover his mental equilibrium by not interacting with other people. When he came to Fort Daer in early March, he had Peter Bostonois arrested on the complaint of John McLeod. In retaliation, a large party led by Cuthbert Grant captured a number of settlers. Miles freed Bostonois and was subsequently visited by Grant and his men. Macdonell thought he had smoothed matters over, for the visitors repeated "Faisons la paix, faisons la paix" as they departed.

As for Duncan Cameron, he spent the winter offering to free discontented settlers from their 'bondage'. He insisted that the surest way to obtain what was due them "is to get whatever you can out of their store & I will take any article that can be of use here off your hands & pay you in Canada for them." Cameron told any settler who would listen that the NWC would transport the people of Red River to Canada free of charge, providing them with land, livestock, and provisions at the end of their journey. According to John Pritchard, the Nor'Westers had practiced "every insinuating art . . . to gain the good will of the Settlers; they were extremely lavish of their Wines, frequently gave Balls and other diversions." The settlers were told that the HBC charter was worthless, that Selkirk could not to be trusted, and that, in the end, the Indians would scalp them all.

The governor eventually responded to reports from Fort Douglas of continued turbulence at the Forks. He arrived at Fort Douglas in early April to discover that in his absence the Nor'Westers had finally won over the colonists. Most of the settlers had taken their families and their baggage to the NWC's Fort Gibraltar. Only the McLeans and a few other families remained at Fort Douglas, forced from their houses by threats of violence. Most of the loyalists were older men. They were joined by Peter Fidler, who had been surveying lots along the river.

Led by the renegade George Campbell, the rebellious settlers then entered the store at Fort Douglas and — under orders from Cameron — removed the settlement's artillery pieces. The rebels carried the cannon to Fort Gibraltar as well. On the occasion of one of these forays, one of the loyal settlers opened the window and told George Campbell to speak with reason and he would be heard. Cuthbert Grant was heard to reply, "no reason here."

Macdonell was not entirely abandoned, for the settlement's employees had not yet deserted him. Bound by contracts, many of which would expire on 1 June, the servants knew perfectly well they would not receive what was due them if they left their employer early. The governor spent the next several months in the curious position of being besieged in fortified quarters by his own settlers. At one point he arrested a NWC clerk, William Shaw, for leading the party that had attempted to break down the doors of "Government House" on 5 April. The disaffected settlers attempted to rescue Shaw, but were beaten off by the governor and his servants. The NWC sent an emissary to attempt to bail Shaw. On the negotiator's second visit to Macdonell, someone touched the governor on the shoulder and showed him a warrant for his arrest. It had been issued by Norman McLeod and called for Miles to appear before a justice of the peace at Fort William. Macdonell ignored it on the grounds "that a governor could not be legally taken from his government in such a manner." The arrival of John Pritchard on 16 April raised spirits momentarily, but Macdonell's tiny body of men was being depleted by desertions.

Affairs turned desperate in early June. The contracts of many of the HBC and colony servants expired. Macdonell attempted to retain the servants, at least until it was time to meet the ships at York Factory. He offered advances on wages and the remission of fines which had been levied for previous misbehaviour. The servants took the money and then promptly departed for Fort Gibraltar on 5 June. Macdonell was now left with only a handful of supporters, most of them officers of the settlement.

He still had cannons, however, which he ordered fired against the marshalling "enemy" on 10 June. Those riding around outside the fort, according to Archibald McDonald's daily journal, "was of all nations, viz. natives, half-bloods, Scotch, Irish, English & Canadians." Unfortunately, one of the cannon had been improperly loaded and exploded. It seriously wounded Messrs. McLean and Warren. The accident with the cannon took the heart out of the little party still supporting Miles. They met and advised him to surrender to the NWC but Macdonell continued to vacillate. On 15 June the wedding of John McIntyre to Catherine Sutherland was disrupted when some of the guests were taken prisoner by the Nor'Westers. Archy McDonald got away only by brandishing his sword and his pistol. A shot was fired at him but missed. Miles himself was obviously disheartened, and again disappeared for a few days.

Nor'Wester Duncan Cameron as "Captain, Commanding Officer in Red River" stepped into the vacuum and ordered both colony and Company to depart immediately. On 16 June, Henry McKenzie, a senior member of the NWC, arrived at the Forks. Macdonell's supporters tried to obtain a "fair peace," but were told that only the surrender of the governor would end hostilities. The remaining band of loyalists — led by Surgeon James White, Peter Fidler, Alexander McLean, and John Pritchard — wrote a public letter to Macdonell, asking him to surrender for the good of the colony. They entered into a verbal agreement with the NWC, based upon the unconditional surrender of the governor. Macdonell warned that once he was in custody, such agreements would not be honoured. But under severe pressure, he gave in and allowed himself to be taken prisoner. Wasting no time, on 18 June the Nor'Westers then sent off their prisoners in canoes with 134 erstwhile settlers, bound for Upper Canada. A broken and embittered Macdonell, under close arrest, would follow soon afterwards.

As John Pritchard confessed ruefully to Lord Selkirk in a letter dated 20 July 1815, "Foolishly relying upn the N.W. Company's assertion [that they only wanted their prisoner] We flattered ourselves that they would then suffer us to enjoy our fields in peace; but they were no sooner in possession of his person than the delusion vanished."

The delusion vanished in startling fashion. When the remaining leadership of the shattered Red River colony met with the Nor'Westers at Fort Douglas after Macdonell's arrest, Duncan Cameron introduced them to four men who called themselves "the North West free halfbreeds." All four were the mixed-blood sons of retired NWC partners; two were clerks apprenticed to Cameron and the other two were longstanding employees of the NWC. These men told the shaken settlers that they, the halfbreeds, owned the land around Red River. They added that both the HBC servants and the settlers had two days to leave the settlement.

The evidence is simply not available to ascertain the extent to which the mixed-bloods had developed these demands on their own. Two points are clear. One was that some in the NWC were closely related to the developing mixed-blood leadership. The other was that this group — soon to be known as the Métis — had their own grievances against the settlers. Selkirk had not sufficiently taken their feelings into account, and his local agents had failed to deal with them appropriately.

This error was perhaps most clearly underlined when Macdonell had imperiously issued regulations about the running of buffalo — the lifeblood of the Metis. To further display a disdain for the friendship of the Métis was beyond folly. The mixed-bloods later complained to Colin Robertson of the Miles Macdonell regime, "No one would ask us in to take a Glass of Rum, or even to warm themselves."

The loyalists drafted an anguished letter to Selkirk, dated 20 June, noting that "if we quit the Country it will be with the greatest sorrow; but we cannot remain without protection; for want of power to redress our wrongs and a security for our property, our best efforts towards the maintenance of our families must ever be paralized." The document was signed by 28 men, including some settlers, a few Irish and Scottish HBC employees, and four Norwegians who had been brought out in an ill-fated attempt to maintain a herd of reindeer.

Having introduced the remaining Red River settlers to the mixed-blood leaders, the majority of the Nor'Westers left the region in their canoes, carrying Miles Macdonell with them. The rump party of settlers and servants still had to face the wrath of the mixed-bloods, who continued to insist that the country belonged to them and not to Lord Selkirk. Armed parties of Métis burnt houses during the daytime and fired on the terrified settlers at night.

Fortunately for the settlers, some of the aboriginal residents of the region came to their assistance, offering to help them retreat by boat from the area. The Saulteaux chief, Peguis, even attempted to negotiate with the mixed-bloods at Fort Gibraltar, but reported ruefully that they were too determined and too strong. A party of 40 loyalists, including a handful of women and children, were then loaded onto a collection of small boats. The colony's remaining cattle and sheep were carried in other vessels. Archy McDonald sadly entered in his journal on the evening of their departure, "We have been driven from a country whose fertile soil, wholesome climate, natural productions & beautiful scenery promised to us and our children ages of happiness." The colonists, led by Peter Fidler, proceeded to Jack River on Lake Winnipeg, where they would be met in August by Miles Macdonell's alter-ego — Colin Robertson.

2. The Mission of Colin Robertson:

Colin Robertson had spent the winter of 1814-15 in Montreal organizing the HBC thrust into the Athabasca. He had found a Canadian business firm with which he could work. Maitland, Garden and Auldjo was a wholesaling operation in Montreal with little experience in the fur trade. Its closest connection to the NWC was through the marriage of junior partner George Auldjo to the daughter of a Nor'Wester. But Auldjo was not active in business with Red River. The firm wholesaled in Upper Canada and exported mainly potash, timber, and wheat. George Garden would become a trusted friend and associate of the Selkirk family. His firm was able to supply Robertson, who worked in the name of Lord Selkirk, with trade goods. In the process, Robertson so inextricably tied the finances of Selkirk to those of the HBC that it was almost impossible to separate them. He later insisted that he had no orders from Selkirk to operate in the manner he had done.

Another initiative of Robertson while he was in Montreal involved John Jacob Astor, who had only just wound up his Pacific Fur Company and had no love for the Nor'Westers. Robertson went to New York to discuss an alliance of Astor and the HBC. The American was not ready for such a definitive move, but he was certainly willing to help harass the Nor'Westers. During the War of 1812, Astor had obtained a virtual monopoly of a Brazilian tobacco much favoured by the aboriginals in the Northwest. He was quite prepared to share the "NW Twist" with Robertson, who wrote to the HBC, "I have got an excellent lot of Tobacco for the Indian trade which belonged to Mr. Astor." Robertson added, "The North West Co. Have been obliged to purchase an inferior quality for the trading department, as that gentleman [Astor] held every ounce of North West Twist in the Country."

Robertson also was able to collect a party of fur traders and voyageurs for western service. He offered high wages and was able to recruit among recently retired Nor'Westers, many of them discontented with the Montreal partnership. Few of those signed up were possible leaders of an expedition, however. Robertson had tried desperately to hire Donald McKenzie, formerly of the Pacific Fur Company and Astoria. But he was unable to win McKenzie over. John Clarke, another former Pacific Fur Company man and ex-Nor'Wester, was the closest Robertson had come to hiring a potential leader. Clarke turned down an appointment with the Indian Department, which Robertson had to outbid for his services. But the more Robertson dealt with Clarke, the more dubious he became of Clarke's soundness. A vain man himself, Robertson could recognize overweening vanity when he saw it in others. Moreover, Clarke was fond of excessive display and expenditure, another Robertson failing. Other Robertson recruits included Robert Logan, Pierre Decoigne, and Aulay McAulay. By April, Robertson had pretty much faced the fact that, to increase his chances of success, he would have to winter himself at least one season in the interior.

On 17 May 1815, Robertson left Lower Canada for the interior with 16 canoes, 20 officers, and 157 men. He reported to Andrew Colvile that the senior men were experienced but apprehensive of the NWC, which had already tried to sow dissension among the new recruits. Whether word had yet reached Montreal of a confrontation in February 1815 between the NWC and the HBC at Ile-à-la Crosse (at the southern edge of the Athabasca country, now in Saskatchewan) is not clear. But several men had been killed at this time. The ultimate destination of Robertson's expedition, of course, was the Athabasca country itself, although Robertson did not intend to accompany it that far. Whatever his intentions, they were quickly altered by events. As Robertson's brigades headed west, they began to pick up intelligence of the dispersal of the Red River settlement. In early July Robertson reached the NWC post at Lake la Pluie. There Nor'Wester John McLoughlin (later of Oregon fame) confirmed that the settlement had broken up. McLoughlin claimed that the settlers had been driven away by a new nation calling themselves "the free Halfbreeds of Red River."

Two days later, in the river of Lake la Pluie, Robertson met a flotilla of ten NWC canoes going eastward. On board these canoes, he later reported, were at least a dozen of the wintering partners of the NWC on their way to the annual meeting at Fort William. The partners were heavily armed, and Duncan Cameron was still in his regimental uniform. Also aboard one of these canoes was Miles Macdonell — under arrest and carefully guarded — on his way to Montreal to stand trial. Warily, the brigades passed each other without incident.

In another two days, Robertson's party met yet another brigade of Nor'Westers, this one carrying the disaffected settlers of Red River. Although he could not know it, the colonists were already grousing continually. They complained about having to live on food that was not fit for animals. When they got to the lakes they moaned about having to paddle canoes like slaves. It is not recorded what the hardy voyageurs had to say in response.

3. Reorganization by the Hudson's Bay Company:

A restlessness had developed by early 1815 on the London committee of the HBC. Major confrontations were brewing in British North America over which they had little control. William Auld was now in London, doing his utmost to undermine Lord Selkirk, whom he blamed for his dismissal. "The Earl of Selkirk's influence," he wrote one correspondent, "is as you know quite paramount — he attends regularly at the board every Comm'ee day and nothing is too minute for his inspection or to trifling for his employment." Selkirk and Colvile were "utterly destitute of honour & honesty," and not as well off as people imagined. Selkirk, for example, "borrowed the money which he paid for the stock he holds of the Company's funds." Auld would have been pleased to have access to the reports of Selkirk's estate manager in Scotland. These would soon indicate a serious decline in the earl's financial position due to the agricultural depression which accompanied the end of the Anglo-French wars.

Certainly an increased interest in the West was evident among the HBC directors. A committee vote in early April 1815 ordered large-scale copies of Arrowsmith's manuscript map of those parts of the Company's territories where it was desirable to gain further information for "completing the Topography of the Country." The directors still had never seen the territory, but they could at least now visualize it on a map.

At the same committee meeting, a new governor of the HBC's territories in North America was nominated. No evidence survives to suggest why Robert Semple was selected. Born in Boston in 1777, Semple had joined his parents in Loyalist exile after the American Revolution. He became a merchant who travelled extensively around the world, and the author of several travel books. While there is more than a hint that Semple had served as a spy for the British government in Europe, using his American identity as an entry to places a Briton could not go, he was nevertheless far more English than American. He had never visited North America in the course of his travels. Moreover, Semple had no administrative experience, much less familiarity with colonial government or the fur trade.

The appointment did provide a Company-sanctioned government for Red River, thus responding to the NWC's insistence that Miles Macdonell was only Selkirk's agent and held no proper post. Macdonell was not replaced, for he was a Selkirk appointment. The nature of Semple's relationship to the settlement or the soon-to-be-deposed Macdonell was not at all clear.

A few weeks after announcing the choice of Semple, the General Court of the HBC met on 19 May 1815 to provide "a more regular Form of Government . . . in the Company's Territories in Hudson's Bay." It voted resolutions appointing a governor-in-chief and a council competent "to form a Council for the Administration of Justice." It also extended judicial powers to the governors of Assiniboia (Red River) and Moose Factory. Sheriffs were appointed, one for Assiniboia, one for Moose, and one for the remainder of the territories "for the execution of all such process as shall be directed to them according to law." The resolutions were separately voted on by the proprietors, and then individuals were nominated to fill the various posts and councils. Robert Semple became governor-in-chief and Miles Macdonell was named governor of Assiniboia.

The Company immediately forwarded Lord Bathurst a copy of the proposed ordinances to be executed by this new system of justice. It added its anxiety that "such Ordinances should receive the sanction of His Majesty's Att'y and Sol. General, before they are acted upon." A subsequent letter to Bathurst, drafted by Selkirk, re-iterated the Company's claims and rights under the charter. It emphasized that the Company had always exercised jurisdiction "as far as circumstances required." With the increasing population of the country, "new rights & varied interests have arisen, which call for a more regular & effectual administration of Justice." The company had its own legal opinions, but since the royal prerogative was involved, it sought confirmation from the Crown's legal officers. Nevertheless, since immediate action was required, the Company had instructed its newly appointed governor and council to administer justice in the territory.

The reasons for the new system of justice were obvious. The Pemmican Proclamation and the subsequent problems which Macdonell had in enforcing it had underlined jurisdictional uncertainties that had never been satisfactory resolved. To some extent, the HBC may have been seeking post facto confirmation of Macdonell's performance. More importantly, the Company was trying to avoid any fresh difficulties of a similar nature. The easiest way to escape the tortured procedures of the Canada Jurisdictions Act of 1803 (43 George III, c. 138) was to put in place a system which would have at least tacit government support. While it was no doubt necessary to build Assiniboia into the Company system of the administration of justice, this action merely underlined the close relationship of the HBC and the Selkirk settlement. Most of this ostentatious administrative reform came too late. The time to resolve the jurisdictional issues by unilateral action of the HBC was past. But as a consequence of the reorganization, Robert Semple did set sail on a Company vessel in 1815 to take up his post in the HBC territories.

4. Dissension in the North West Company:

The HBC was not the only player in the escalating fur trade wars that sought to rethink its position in 1815. So too did the North West Company at its annual meeting at Fort William. This meeting was attended by London merchant and agent Simon McGillivray, who administered McTavish, Fraser & Company. McGillivray had for years acted as a principal spokesmen for Nor'Wester interests in Great Britain, especially with the Colonial Office. From the outset of the grant to Lord Selkirk, McGillivray had opposed it, insisting that Selkirk's "success would strike at the very existence of our trade." By 1815, it was clear that the crisis in the fur trade and in the North West Company was getting worse. McGillivray thus sailed from Liverpool to New York in April, and had gotten from Montreal to Fort William in the remarkably good time of 18 days.

The problems within the North West Company went far deeper than the controversies with Lord Selkirk and the HBC, which only exacerbated existing conditions. In the first place, furs were a non-renewable natural resource and the territory for their harvest becoming increasingly limited and less accessible. The fur trade had for several centuries followed the cycle of exhausting one region of furs and then moving on to the next. The North West Company had always been in the vanguard of the opening of new regions, acting as though it had no limitations and no serious competition. In 1815, it found neither of these assumptions were any longer true.

A final settlement with the Americans, following the War of 1812, was in the works which would run the 49th parallel as the international boundary across the Prairies to the Rocky Mountains. The North West Company had lobbied hard with the British government for a boundary further south in the region west of the Great Lakes, but had failed to make any headway with the Foreign Office. Despite years of exploration and activity in what is now the Dakotas, Montana, Washington and Oregon — not to mention the southern part of Selkirk's land grant — it was now apparent that the Americans would supplant the British and Canadian influence in those regions.

It also appeared that John Jacob Astor would dominate the fur trade in the United States. Astor had no particular love for the North

West Company, although he had occasionally tried to work with them. Soon to be pushed north of the 49th, the Nor'Westers knew that there was still one great underexploited fur trade territory — the Athabasca region. As the NWC had always feared, however, the HBC was now prepared to compete actively for the Athabasca. Indeed, Colin Robertson's brigades were in the summer of 1815 poised to enter the region. Although most of Robertson's trade goods and supplies had come initially from Montreal, over the long haul the HBC could supply the Athabasca from the Bay at considerably less expense than that provided by the NWC's fur trade route.

To make matters worse for the Nor'Westers, they had won the battle for the Pacific Coast trade. Ironically, the net effect of the victory was to extend their supply lines still further and to increase costs considerably. Alexander Ross would later additionally blame the NWC's Pacific Coast problems on arrogance and inability to adjust to new conditions. "The maxims of trade followed by the company of the east of the mountains, their mode of voyaging and their way of dealing with Indians," wrote Ross in his *The Fur Hunters of the Far West*, were "founded on false principles, and when they are reduced to practice in the Western districts, they are found to fail."

As with all fur trade operations, returns on investment on the Pacific Slope were slow to be realized. The NWC's vessel *Isaac Todd* carried a cargo of furs to Canton in 1814. That cargo brought $101, 155.40 in revenue from fur sales in the Chinese emporium. Most of that total — $81,404.30 — was in beaver. The NWC could not know in 1815 of this windfall. Because of trade restrictions in Canton, after 1815 it would ship most of its furs to Asia from the east coast in American vessels, thereby reducing its profits and further lengthening the timelines.

If the NWC could not substantially reduce its costs and speed up its turnover, it would sooner or later go under. The high costs were associated with the extended transportation network, which had all sorts of hidden ramifications. For example, not only were hundreds of voyageurs required to handle the canoes, but their native families and those of the traders had to be accommodated at most of the posts.

The problem of costs had been disguised for many years by the absence of competition faced by the Nor'Westers. At the same time, even under monopoly conditions the junior winterers increasingly felt hard done by and restive. They felt that the company's success was being achieved at their expense, and they were quite critical of both the merchants of London and Montreal as well as the senior partners. Alexander Ross wrote of "two classes of expectants in the North West Company's service, who have invariably had the same promises held out to them." According to Ross, one class was generally fortunate, the other generally unfortunate. The fortunate ones were "the aristocratic twigs of the day, or those connected with the men in power." The unfortunate were those who lacked patrons and who had nothing in their favour but hard work and energy. The latter class eventually discovered that their "zeal and faithfulness have all been in vain," retiring in "all the bitterness of disappointed hope." Whether the company could ever take full advantage of talent was another matter.

A journal kept by Simon McGillivray, recording his visit to Fort William, has survived. It was not a full account of the meeting, but rather concentrated on matters of real concern to McGillivray. It demonstrates that from the beginning of the 1815 meeting, the external threat from Lord Selkirk and the HBC was only a small part of the agenda. The most pressing business of all for McGillivray involved heading off an internal revolution led by the wintering partners.

The impending confrontation with the winterers was momentarily deferred while the Nor'Westers celebrated their recent triumph over the Selkirk settlement. Simon McGillivray personally accompanied the prisoners Miles Macdonell and John Spencer up to Fort William. He interviewed each prisoner in turn inside the fort. Macdonell was informed that McGillivray had it on the "highest authority that the power he [Miles] had assumed was entirely unauthorized & unwarrantable", but he was unrepentant.

Miles was met at Fort William by one of his sons, who had come west to warn his father of impending trouble. The two Macdonells were incarcerated together. Sheriff Spencer in his turn apologized profusely, blaming Macdonell for all the problems. In a later conference with Spencer, Simon McGillivray told him that "it was now our object to make a public example of the fallacy of the grounds upon which he had acted." The NWC sought to convict the governor. If Spencer's "evidence should in the opinion of our Lawyers be sufficient for that purpose, we should probably decline prosecuting himself." The sheriff responded with alacrity to this suggestion of a deal, offering to provide evidence that he was only acting only orders of Miles Macdonell.

The larger question of discontented partners and employees still lurked during the early days of Simon McGillivray's visit. He was told by Norman McLeod that John McGillivray was unfit to head the Athabasca department and would have been replaced "were his name not McGillivray." A few days later Simon accidentally stumbled into a meeting of the winter partners, vehemently discussing the plug tobacco issue. McGillivray was conciliatory, but the winterers protested that solutions were being offered "before they were ready." Simon Fraser spoke of retirement, to which McGillivray responded that the Columbia business had been so expensive that it would be difficult to settle the explorer's account. On 17 July, McGillivray entered the council chamber early in the morning. He hoped to get on with the business of the meeting, beginning with the staffing of departments. He was told by the wintering partners that they needed more time "to consider matters & compare Ideas."

The winterers called McGillivray and McLeod to the council room around noontime. John Haldane spoke for the disaffected. They had appointed a committee and had come to some unanimous resolutions. The winterers wanted answers from the agents before they proceeded with other business. The resolutions dealt with the rate at which currency would be exchanged, the Columbia trade, and the commission charged on the equipping of that trade. McGillivray argued that the wintering partners were only part of the whole concern, and should not take so extreme a line on issues that mattered to all. He succeeded in opening a discussion on the topics mentioned, defending the agency with vigour on these matters. He warned that such criticism was tantamount to cooperation with the "Common enemy", always a favourite strategy of beleaguered management.

The parties met again later in the day and the following one to "arrange the Departments," that is, to fix the postings for the coming year. This business was absolutely critical to the traders. Unpopular figures — especially those who were vocal in their criticisms — could be isolated to remote postings for years on end. Many partners were unhappy with their assignments in 1815, and several threatened to resign, rather than accept them. Simon McGillivray noted "there seems a general wish to retire from the Country, some from getting old & tired of it, others from a dread of opposition." In the end, the dissidence was smoothed over. The parties agreed to expunge the minutes of the last two days of discussions. McGillivray conceded that the resignations would be overlooked, saying "it was only to meet the wish of the Wintering Partners and a sense of the value of these Gentlemens services in such critical times that we could sanction the thing at all or permit any partner who had over thrown up his share to return into the Country."

Although Simon McGillivray did not record such matters in his journal, the 1815 meeting at Fort William also initiated a number of other important decisions respecting the fur trade, chiefly in the Columbia district. The district was divided into two parts, to take effect in 1816. James Keith was put in charge of the Columbia section, and in 1816 Donald McKenzie (of the Pacific Fur Company) returned to the coast to manage the interior or inland section. McKenzie's appointment was not popular with senior partners.

The interior district, called New Caledonia because of the similarity of its terrain to that of Scotland, was to be supplied henceforth via the canoe routes from Fort William. It would expand its trade into the country of the Snake and Nez Percé tribes, at considerable loss of life. The new Columbia district would continue to be supplied via the Columbia River, which was listed in the British Custom House books as a Foreign Continental Colony until 1824. The exportation of goods to it ranged from 26,000 pounds in 1817 to 12,500 pounds in 1821 in one or two vessels. The costly business of employing special express canoes for communicating news was given up. Only one annual general express would henceforth be sent.

On 20 July, towards the close of the meetings, a ball was given in honour of the Red River colonists, who had arrived at Fort William from the west. McGillivray recorded, ". . . all is fun & good humour. Our officers appear in uniform for the first time and dancing kept up till daylight." But such gaiety could not disguise the fact that the NWC was a badly divided operation in 1815. Not surprisingly, and despite their victory at Red River, the Nor'Westers would seek again to negotiate with their HBC rivals late in that year.

5. The Red River Settlement Re-established:

After Colin Robertson had passed the Red River settlers heading east in NWC canoes, he did not hesitate for an instant. Leaving most of his brigade to continue to the loyalists camped at Jack River on Lake Winnipeg, he headed straight for Red River to investigate the disaster for himself. At the site of the settlement, Robertson spoke to a number of mixed-bloods, who told him that the NWC had employed them to drive away the settlers.

They had been furnished with arms and ammunition by the fur traders, he reported later to Lord Selkirk, and they expected rewards for their services when the Nor'Westers returned in the autumn. Other freemen, including Jean-Baptiste Lagimodière, informed Robertson that they had been offered rewards by Duncan Cameron to drive out the settlers, but had refused. Robertson also found that the crops, while badly damaged, had not been completely destroyed.

Having learned all he could at the Forks, Robertson went to the rendezvous point at Jack River. Here on 22 July he found his own brigade, a number of the settlers from Red River, and another HBC brigade which had come south from York Factory. The HBC men, who included Thomas Thomas, the governor of the Northern Department, and James Bird, were most impressed with John Clarke. They selected Clarke to head the Athabasca party. Robertson did not protest the loss of his appointment overmuch, partly because he was in the process of agreeing with the party of settlers to lead them back to Red River. He intended to supply some much needed energy and direction to the beleaguered settlers. Robertson did insist on a formal instruction from Governor Thomas before he did so, however. Along with the settlers, Robertson took two clerks, two interpreters, and a handful of Canadian voyageurs and Norwegians to help get in the crop.

On 19 August 1815, Robertson, 40 settlers and 17 HBC employees arrived back at the Forks. They were greeted with enthusiasm by the aboriginal residents, chiefly the Saulteaux, who mistrusted the mixed-bloods in the area. Although the various parties of marauders had done considerable damage to the crops, there was something to salvage. The harvest would have been a very good one had it been left intact to maturity. As it was, the settlers managed to preserve about 400 bushels of wheat, 200 bushels of barley, and 500 bushels of potatoes. Robertson also put them to work catching catfish in the river, which were dried and salted. As well, a number of small dwellings were hastily erected to provide shelter for the winter. Robertson made arrangements with sympathetic local mixed-bloods to supply the little community with meat for the winter.

When Nor'Westers Duncan Cameron and Alexander Greenfield Macdonell arrived back at Fort Gibraltar on 13 September from their sojourn at Fort William, they discovered to their surprise that the Red River colony was not destroyed after all. Instead, a rump of settlers had re-established themselves. Their new leader — Colin Robertson — was popular and decisive, rather than detested and ineffectual like his predecessor. The charismatic Robertson's declared motto was, "When among wolves, Howl."

Robertson's early meetings with the Nor'Westers seemed concilliatory. Before Alexander Macdonell headed off for his post at Qu'Appelle, he told Robertson that he hoped there would be no reoccurrence of the violent behaviour of the previous spring. So did Robertson, since he had too few people to make a successful defence if actually attacked.

While Colin Robertson was putting the settlement back into business, Robert Semple and a party of new settlers arrived at York Factory on 27 August. Semple was greeted by news of the earlier disaster at Red River. Within a few days, however, he had information of

Robertson's successful intervention, and ordered Robertson to be placed in charge of the settlement until Lord Selkirk could make alternate arrangements.

Semple had originally intended to go to the Forks in the following spring, but instead he decided to accompany the 84 new settlers departing for Red River. He was impressed with the newcomers, finding them "the mildest people, in their manners, I ever met with." The "indolence" of the recruits was balanced by their being sober, honest, patient, obedient, obliging and good-natured, he observed.

Meanwhile, at the Forks of the Red and Assiniboine Rivers, Colin Robertson remained in a state of "fancied security" until 14 October, when he received a desperate letter forwarded from Brandon House. It was written by John Richards McKay, the HBC post-master at Qu'Appelle, requesting assistance. The 'halfbreeds' threatened his post, wrote McKay. "They have got two of the Captain's Cannon in their War house pointed to us to prevent us from working, they are determined on Killing us all. . . . perhaps this will be the last letter you will have from us." McKay had received a 24-hour ultimatum from Alexander Fraser, a mixed-blood NWC clerk, to abandon the country or be killed. He was ultimately saved by the local aboriginals, who came to his assistance.

Characteristically, Robertson responded swiftly to what he took to be a resumption of hostilities. He immediately marched a small squad of men to nearby Fort Gibraltar, capturing Duncan Cameron and two clerks, Seraphim LaMar and Charles Hesse. Robertson also demanded — and received — some of the arms that had been seized in the spring from the colony. The prisoners were freed a few days later only upon Cameron's solemn assurance that neither he nor any of his associates would disturb the settlement and that he would endeavor to promote friendship with it. Two days after Cameron's liberation, Robertson received the letter of temporary appointment from Semple.

On 17 October, Robertson sent Jean-Baptiste Lagimodière east with urgent dispatches intended to update Lord Selkirk. Lagimodière was a former Canadian voyageur who had settled near Red River. Unlike most freemen, however, he lived with a European wife (Marie-Anne Gaboury) and welcomed the establishment of the settlement.

On 3 November Semple himself arrived at Red River. His initial report to Lord Selkirk from the settlement was quite encouraging. "The Colours were hoisted, the guns were fired, at night we laughed, and drank and danced and now the serious Calculations of the Colony Commence."

Grain was in the bins. Buffalo and partridges were plentiful. The "miserable system of treachery and ingratitude" exhibited by the

Highlanders in 1815, so contrary to their character, Semple wrote, could only have been caused by mismanagement at the top. This conclusion seemed even more evident when "Half Breeds and Old Worn Out Canadians" began to be "kicked about" by Colin Robertson. The two men would soon be at loggerheads, but at the beginning seemed able to work well together. Semple left Red River in mid-December for a three-month tour of the neighbouring HBC posts, leaving Robertson in charge of the settlement. At the time of the governor's departure, everything appeared sufficiently tranquil for him to risk a lengthy absence from Red River. Semple's total misreading of the potential threat to the settlement augured ill for the future.

6. Government Gets Involved:

As he had promised, Lord Bathurst wrote in the spring of 1815 to Governor-General Sir Gordon Drummond in Quebec. He ordered Drummond to enquire about the Indian menace to Red River, and to protect the settlement as far "as can be afforded without detriment to His Majesty's service." Drummond was not to act in such a way as to affect the dispute between the two great fur trading companies. The governor-general doubtless found this a difficult assignment. He was well over a thousand miles from Red River, and had no real authority in the Indian Territories. Under the circumstances, he did what any good bureaucrat would do. Drummond ordered his *aide-de-camp* to write William McGillivray of the NWC that "some of the Servants of the North West Company are suspected of being concerned in the diabolical Plot against Red River." Drummond sought to ascertain from McGillivray if "there exists in your opinion any reasonable ground" for suspicions for the safety of the settlement from Indian atrocities. He added that if anything did happen, the NWC would be "considered responsible in the eyes of the world."

Lord Selkirk and the HBC would later complain bitterly about this appeal for information from a man they regarded as one of the chief villains. But Drummond was probably quite right in thinking that this appeal was about all that he could manage. The HBC's local agents themselves approved of Drummond's approach to the problem, admitting that a military relief force was unworkable.

William McGillivray responded to John Harvey on 24 June, 1815, ironically enough at about the same time the Red River settlers were being removed by canoe from the settlement. He began by noting that a copy of Bathurst's orders had already been transmitted by Henry Goulburn to the NWC in London. It had been fully answered there. Lord Selkirk had been enticing people to Red River with "golden but delusive promises," said McGillivray. The NWC could not be held responsible for any hostile actions of Indians against Selkirk's people or the HBC. (One of the many ironies of this dispute was the fact that the "Indians" under Chief Peguis were Selkirk's greatest allies.) Citing the Canada Jurisdictions Act, McGillivray held that "individuals in the Indian country are personally responsible for their own criminal acts." Moreover, Selkirk was the aggressor, for "Under the guise and cloak of Colonization, he is aiming at maturing an exterminating blow" against NWC trade. Miles Macdonell had acted in the capacity of a "Bashaw" in his proclamation. McGillivray concluded, "in all such attempts hereafter, the North West Company would assuredly be justified in repelling force by force."

As a result of the McGillivray-Harvey correspondence, the Canadian agents of the HBC were informed that all unfavourable impressions of North West Company conduct had been removed from the mind of Sir Gordon Drummond. Instead, Drummond was now convinced that any trouble "will arise principally from the conduct of Mr. Miles MacDonell," who had asserted "Powers which cannot possibly in His Exc'y's Opinion have rested in him or in any Agent Private or Public of any individual or of any Chartered Body." Although the legality of Macdonell's proclamation was still to be settled in a British court, Drummond had already declared which side he would back. He so reported to Lord Bathurst.

7. Lord Selkirk Intervenes:

With the Anglo-French wars finally over, it was now possible for Lord Selkirk to take a personal hand in the affairs of his settlement. Previously he had been forced to issue orders from afar, only able to shrug his shoulders and carry on when things went wrong. The obstacle was partly "indifferent health," but also his responsibilities during wartime, both as lord-lieutenant of Kirkcudbright and as a member of the House of Lords. Now, his great genius for improvisation could actually be employed productively. While packers prepared Lady Selkirk's grand pianoforte and harp for shipment to Quebec, the HBC instructed Selkirk on the guidelines for any negotiations with the North West Company.

The major point in any agreement, the HBC committee stressed, was "the preservation of the Chartered rights of the HBC, avoiding any concession which can fairly be constructed into a Imbition [sic] of our priviledges." The committee hoped an offer of long-term access into those rights would appeal to the NWC, since "It seems possible that they will prefer their immediate advantage to any remote interest which they might have to contest our rights at the expiration of the agreement. Only if the Montrealers would acknowledge the charter and property rights of the HBC could there be negotiations on pulling out of Athabasca and Canada. Selkirk could concede the right of transit through Port Nelson, although if it were so valuable there should be concessions elsewhere. The HBC would willingly agree to make no arrangements with any other fur trading company except the NWC. Even if what he would find in Lower Canada upon his arrival had not disposed Selkirk to oppose any deal with the NWC, his instructions made it quite impossible for the two companies to reach an agreement.

Selkirk sailed with his family for New York from Liverpool in September, 1815. In his last letter before departing, he proclaimed, "it is necessary that I should obtain justice for those who have thrown themselves on my protection." Whatever had motivated him earlier, he would now be driven by a patriarchal sense of honour to his settlers. While Selkirk was sailing west, Archy McDonald was heading to England from Hudson Bay with first-hand information of events in Red River and a manuscript description of events which would be published in 1816. In New York Selkirk learned of the destruction of the settlement not from McDonald but from a young Irishman who had apparently come east from Red River with the settlers. From the very beginning, Selkirk was convinced that there had been collusion between the NWC and the mixed-bloods. He was equally certain that the government would have to take action. He was in Lower Canada by early November, eager to get an investigation moving.

Lord Selkirk immediately penned a letter to Sir Gordon Drummond, attempting to resurrect the notion of military protection for Red River. A decision not to send troops, he maintained, could hardly be taken "upon the mere ex parte statement of those from whom the danger was apprehended." Enclosing narratives of recent events, he insisted "it would surely be most disgraceful to the British government, if these lawless ruffians should be suffered to make open war upon their fellow subjects." The culprits were "Canadians, mixed with the bastard sons of others, who have thrown off the restraints of regular society, & cohabiting with Indian squaws have formed a combination of the vices of civilized & savage life." Selkirk now had some better appreciation of who the dangerous "natives" were. But he had absolutely no understanding of their background or their point-of-view. He never acquired one.

The report received from his military advisors hardly disposed Sir Gordon Drummond to action. The country was too isolated, wrote Major W. H. Robinson. What "would the Officers become, exiled in a Country where they can have no society, employment, or amusement?" Robinson had more cogent objections as well. Introducing the soldiers into the midst of a private war would be a nightmare. The boundary claims of the United States would add further complications. "The lives of men are too precious," he concluded, "to be sported with in such Experiments."

While Drummond consulted with the military, Selkirk wrote to Joseph Berens of the HBC in London, outlining his thinking from his new North American vantage point. The news of the dispersal of the settlement dampened his expectations for negotiations, he began. The NWC's natural arrogance had been enhanced. He doubted they would be accommodating unless the Crown backed HBC jurisdiction, which was unlikely. Athabasca had to be pursued, for it must have been fears for its commercial interests which had induced the NWC to attack the settlement. He did not expect a fair investigation of the dispersal. The NWC had a "strange ascendancy" over Bathurst through undersecretary Henry Goulburn, and the governor of Lower Canada shared the prejudice in favour of the Nor'Westers. Surely someone at the HBC, he wrote, must have enough weight at the Colonial Office "to prevent an undersecretary from throwing aside our representations as waste paper."

Here, as elsewhere, Selkirk resolutely refused to admit that government might legitimately prefer the NWC position. As he had written Sir Gordon Drummond, there were 150 colonists at his remote and dangerous settlement who required military protection. Not so far removed from the days of feudal fealty, Lord Selkirk was ready and willing to take matters into his own hands.

After an incredible winter journey by foot across Canada
J.B. Lagimodière arrives in Montreal with word for
Lord Selkirk of disaster at Red River.

~7~

The Battle of Seven Oaks

*T*he seeming ease with which Colin Robertson re-established the Red River colony in the autumn of 1815 would prove to be more than a bit deceptive. Within a few months, the violence of the fur trade wars would reach a new peak, both in the Red River region and in the Athabasca. The key figures in the escalation of hostilities would be the local residents of the western country — not the First Nations but the mixed-bloods, a group to which Lord Selkirk and his Red River people had paid virtually no attention in establishing their settlement.

1. Negotiations between the Rival Companies:

To Lord Selkirk's surprise, he found himself in early December of 1815 meeting with John Richardson of the NWC to discuss an arrangement between the rival fur trading concerns. Both parties agreed such an understanding was desirable. Richardson was Scottish-born and educated at King's College, Aberdeen. After many years in the fur trade he became a partner in Forsyth, Richardson and Company in 1790, one of the business firms which had organized the XY Company in 1798-9. The rivalry between the NWC and the XY Company threatened to allow violence free rein in the interior and to ruin both trading organizations financially. In 1804 the two companies merged, with the XY Company receiving one-quarter of the shares in a newly reorganized NWC. Richardson thus had considerable experience in fur trade amalgamations.

From the outset, Richardson wanted to know whether the arrangements to be discussed extended only to partitions of the trading area, or whether union could be considered as well. Selkirk responded that union had never previously been seriously discussed by the HBC managing committee. He could only present a proposal to them. Selkirk was empowered to negotiate partitioning arrangements, however. Richardson replied that a complete union was the best solution to the rivalry, although he admitted many obstacles to achieving it. With union not on the agenda and Selkirk insisting — as he had been instructed — upon recognition of the HBC charter prior to any serious discussion, there was little chance of any real understanding being reached.

The NWC subsequently proposed a partition of trading areas "to prevent collision" and to enable the trade to be carried on with "order and economy." It refused to concede anything in the Athabasca. It wanted the region around Red River "held co-operatively." Red River was essential to both parties since it produced "the Provisions to furnish the Depots necessary for carrying on the General Trade." As an alternative, the NWC offered a joint-trade arrangement for the years 1816 to 1822, with management under the direction of NWC agents at Montreal. Profits would be shared one-third by the HBC and two-thirds by the NWC. Neither party was to regard this arrangement as affecting the charter issue. Selkirk riposted that he could allow the NWC to manage the western trade only were the HBC allowed to control the trade in its chartered region and the question of the charter was submitted to binding arbitration by "eminent legal characters at London." The question of the settlement was not raised in terms of the joint-trade agreement, although presumably the NWC would have wanted co-operation between the companies at the Forks.

Selkirk wrote to Andrew Colvile in mid-December that he was surprised to be negotiating with the NWC so quickly. He obviously did not appreciate how stretched the NWC was already, how desperate the situation had become. Had he been more willing to bargain, he might have won further concessions. As it was, he told his brother-in-law "you will be much less surpriz'd to hear that it has ended in nothing." There was no surprise because the HBC did not really want to negotiate at the end of 1815. In principle Selkirk thought the proposed division "preferable, even to the exclusive possession of our own Territories." But he was apprehensive of the legal effects of a joint venture with a company of such limited liability. Nevertheless, the key was the Athabasca country. Were the HBC thrust of 1815 pursued aggressively, "I have no doubt that in another year, they will hold a different language." Selkirk added that he was preparing actively for the spring, hoping to head west himself to re-establish his settlement "in respectable force."

The discussions between Selkirk and the Nor'Westers concluded on 27 December 1815, with the Canadians rejecting any agreement based on charter recognition. They had hoped, they wrote Selkirk, to found an understanding on "the practical pecuniary Interest of both Parties," leaving "abstract pretensions and theories, to remain either wholly dormant" or inoperative. Selkirk's insistence on form over substance would mean great losses, they argued, for the two parties would have to return to a "pecuniary Contest." The NWC had, in its own way, been quite open about its financial concerns. But it misunderstood Selkirk here as always. The earl was not motivated chiefly by a balance sheet. He was certainly not prepared to sacrifice his settlement to economic advantage. For his part, Selkirk seemed unable to appreciate just how eager the Nor'Westers were for an agreement.

To Andrew Colvile, Selkirk reported early in the New Year on the further negotiations with the Nor'Westers. He was not impressed with the legal opinions obtained by the NWC regarding the charter, he wrote. He thought the NWC refusals to accept binding arbitration "in plain English . . . amount to this, that it is not for their interest, to have the rights of the HBC brought to a decision, & that they will therefore stave off the question as long as they can." Selkirk then moved to what for him was the crux of the matter: "Thus our legal rights will remain an empty name, till we can obtain such a decision, as we can expect to see supported by the public forces; unless we can in the mean time obtain a superiority of force in our own hands, so as to give effectual support to the jurisdiction & drive those who question it to become the appellants."

2. Selkirk Prepares for Spring:

At the beginning of 1816, Lord Selkirk had moved no further thinking about the use of force than to suggest to Andrew Colvile that the HBC might consider organizing company servants into a small para-military group if government was not forthcoming with support. He was still thinking in terms of a small team of well-armed and well-disciplined men who could be moved to any quarter "to face down all their bullies." This was the old Hillier plan revived, of course. But the use of military force was increasingly on Selkirk's mind. All arguments against force had been removed by the opposition in 1815, he wrote Colvile. Earlier, the NWC could have aroused public opinion "against the employment of a private military force, instituted, (as they would have said) for the purpose of enforcing an odious & illegal monopoly." But the occurrences of the previous summer had demonstrated that "for our own security we are under the necessity of organising what force we have, in such a manner as to be effective." While Selkirk was thinking in terms of defence against aggression, military force could also be put on the offensive as well.

In the concluding paragraphs of his letter to his brother-in-law of 6 January 1816, Selkirk demonstrated his ability to seize the opportunity at hand. While contemplating the need for force, he wrote, he had learned of a large body of soldiers who would be discharged from Canadian duty in early spring. These men, mainly Swiss veterans of European campaigns, would make first-rate settlers and an ideal private army. Selkirk suggested that he would defray half the expenses of recruiting the soldiers from the regiments of DeMeuron and De Watteville "for our mutual defence."

In later January, 1816, Selkirk visited York in Upper Canada for the first time. Here he interviewed some of the disaffected settlers who had been brought east from Red River the previous year, taking detailed notes of their testimony and opinions. His findings were in most respects predictable, but in some ways a bit surprising. A substantial number of the settlers interviewed thought the pemmican proclamation had been key, but not in the ways that Selkirk might have expected. The critical event, the settlers argued, was the arrest of John Spencer. The officers of the settlement had refused to rescue Spencer because he had been taken under a legal warrant issued under 43 George III c. 138. This scrupulous regard for Parliament suggested to the settlers that, contrary to what they had previously been led to believe, the law was against them. Selkirk already knew that the confusion over law in Red River was a serious problem. But such responses probably opened Selkirk's eyes to some legal realities that had not previously occurred to him. In the remote areas of legal jurisdiction in the West, it was best always to act as if the law were on your side.

Most settlers seemed to have few particular grievances with Miles Macdonell, who was regarded as a distant figure usually away from the settlement. Much of their hostility was directed at his underlings. Miles was disliked mainly for handing out muskets and expecting the settlers to fight. Clearly Selkirk could not expect to defend Red River from aggression with these sorts of people. Another class of settler, more experienced at soldiering, would be required. The interviews confirmed the desirability of negotiations with officers from the disbanded regiments. Selkirk left his attorneys to pursue the ringleaders among the disloyal settlers of 1815.

Selkirk returned to Lower Canada and, in a typically feverish whirlwind of activity, began to organize his westward expedition. His efforts were redoubled after the arrival on 10 March of Jean-Baptiste Lagimodière with dispatches from Red River. Lagimodière, with one companion, had travelled overland, mainly on foot and snowshoes, to the south of Lake Superior and through Sault Ste Marie and York. It was an incredible journey of some 1,800 miles — in the middle of a Canadian winter. Legend has it that Lagimodière burst into the middle of a ball at the Selkirk house in Montreal, bringing news of the re-establishment of the settlement by Colin Robertson. On 11 March Selkirk wrote to Sir Gordon Drummond, seeking to complete arrangements for an officer and a few soldiers to escort him into the interior. He was prepared to pay a young DeMeurons officer and a subaltern's guard himself, he wrote, to provide personal protection from the NWC's violence. This matter was quite separate from that of the defence of the settlement, he argued. Drummond reluctantly agreed to the request, offering to detach a subaltern, two sergeants, and 12 men to be provisioned, conveyed to Red River, and returned — all at Selkirk's expense. These men, Drummond emphasized, were to be used only to protect the earl against assassins or robbers.

Selkirk wrote to Colin Robertson in March that he hoped to arrive at the settlement sufficiently supported to prevent trouble. Three or four "fully manned" canoes would be dispatched under the command of Miles Macdonell. Robertson was to arrest the ringleaders of the destruction of the settlement in 1815, using warrants which Selkirk was forwarding. He realized that it would be necessary to evict the North West Company by force, he added, but wanted this done regularly under a legal warrant from the governor. This dispatch and its enclosures were sent westward with Jean-Baptiste Lagimodière. Unfortunately, Lagimodière, while an experienced bushman, was not a very discreet messenger. As he travelled west, he told whoever would listen to him in the taverns of Upper Canada of his mission. Word soon got to the Nor'Westers, who sent out orders for his capture and the seizure of his dispatches. Lord Selkirk's messenger was in fact captured near Fond du Lac (now Superior, Wisconsin) on 16 June 1816. No pretence of legal warrants was offered for this action, which amounted to a kidnapping. Lagimodière's dispatches were eagerly read by the Nor'Westers at Fort William, who reached new heights of anger at the thought of being summarily "evicted" from the Forks. Excerpts from the captured dispatches were later used in NWC polemics as evidence of Selkirk's intentions.

Selkirk's relations with Sir Gordon Drummond were never very good. Drummond bridled at this British "Milord" arriving in Lower Canada as an important player in the fur trade. The relationship deteriorated badly in mid-April of 1816. The key issue was the armed escort which Drummond had agreed to provide at Selkirk's expense. Drummond was now having second thoughts. He accused Selkirk of intending to employ the escort to protect his servants and followers, adding that the NWC partners were now also requesting military escorts, to which they were as entitled as Lord Selkirk. Nothing he had written, Selkirk insisted, suggested that he was planning to extend the escort to his followers. At the same time, if the escort did not defend his dependents, those dependents would have to be independently armed. He would not trust his life or those of others to the good faith of the NWC. If Drummond wanted to provide escorts for the Nor'Westers, that was his business. Drummond accepted these arguments, but only for the moment.

After having made clear without effect his displeasure about the armed escort, Sir Gordon Drummond, in one of the final acts of his administration, rescinded the order. The De Meuron Regiment was about to be disbanded, and he had no other troops available. If he had hoped by this action to keep the earl out of the Indian Territories, he was sadly mistaken. Selkirk's response was simply to enter openly into negotiations with officers of the disbanded Swiss regiments to recruit soldiers as settlers for Red River. To common soldiers he offered lands ready for cultivation in the settlement. Making clear his intentions, Selkirk wrote Captain Steiger of the De Watteville Regiment that he did not expect long service from his "settlers," but merely a year's employment. The numbers were to be substantial, as many as 80 men from each of the De Meuron and De Watteville units. Drummond's action only cleared the way for the employment of a large contingent of mercenaries without any confusion of roles. Whatever the moral and legal implications of the subsequent use of the mercenaries, in terms of practical strategy they were a brilliant stroke.

Lord Selkirk was not the only antagonist in the fur trade war who was recruiting among the disbanded regiments. The NWC signed up as clerks several De Meuron non-commissioned officers, including Frederick Heurter and Charles de Reinhard in April of 1816. Heurter would later testify that he was told by Norman McLeod "that I must by all means take my Regimentals along with me to the Indian Country, saying we shall shew a little Military practice to the Hudson's Bay Company." While the Nor'Westers hired only a handful of mercenaries to supplement its existing forces in the interior, Lord Selkirk was preparing to buy a small army to defend his settlement.

By early May, two separate expeditions were heading westward to relieve Red River. One was led from York in Upper Canada by Miles Macdonell, still on bail from charges filed against him in Lower Canada. Feeling embarrassed and guilty about having surrendered so abjectly in 1815, Macdonell had volunteered to lead a return party to the settlement. His offer had been accepted, mainly because he still held the formal commission of appointment as governor of Assiniboia. The Macdonell party consisted both of men and of live-stock. Because of the animals, its westward progress was slow and tedious. The other expedition came from Lower Canada, commanded by Captain Frederick Matthey of the De Meuron regiment. It consist-ed of 60 former De Meuron soldiers, most of them still in their regi-mental uniforms and well-armed.

While his expeditions headed westward, Selkirk remained in Canada dealing with last-minute details. He was becoming increasingly aware that he was very much on his own. There would be little if any support from the Imperial government, either for defending Red River or bringing to justice those responsible for the dispersal of 1815.

3. The Athabasca:

L ord Selkirk was convinced that victory over the NWC was inti-mately connected with the expedition to the Athabasca country which Colin Robertson had left at Jack River at the end of July 1815. While Selkirk may have been correct, competing successfully with the NWC in the Athabasca would require more than merely send-ing an HBC expedition into the region. Overcoming the stranglehold which the Nor'Westers had over the aboriginals would be a real prob-lem. The NWC had operated alone in the Athabasca for a quarter of a century. Selkirk was aware of the extent of NWC influence, for he wrote of it in his book on the fur trade, and John Clarke certainly should have taken it into account.

As Colin Robertson's successor, John Clarke finally left Jack River on 4 August 1815 with his voyageurs, arriving at Cumberland House on the Saskatchewan River on the 14th of that month. Clarke subse-quently complained about the absence of trade goods available at the time of his departure from Lake Winnipeg.

But trade goods were not his biggest problem. From the very beginning, the NWC attempted to induce his people to desert and intimidated the aboriginals not to trade. Such strategy ought to have been exactly what Clarke was expecting, but in his various accounts of his treatment he always seemed surprised by the vehemence of the Nor'Wester opposition. One voyageur deserted to NWC protection, and Clarke responded by seizing several of the enemy. Clarke did not lack a willingness to meet force with force. These tussles and the need to repair much worn canoes delayed his departure for English River until 20 August. By Clarke's own account, the expedition left Cumberland with only six bags of pemmican per canoe, and was shadowed by two NWC canoes until its arrival at Athabasca. Clarke would later claim that the pemmican supply at Cumberland House was totally inadequate, although critics would insist that he had cavalierly refused to "drag grease" into the interior, expecting instead to be able to trade for provisions on the spot. Clarke had perhaps spent too much time on the relatively friendly West Coast.

To Clarke's surprise, no Indians were to be found anywhere as he entered the Athabasca region. The natives were intimidated by the NWC from trading with the newcomers. As a result, he was unable to acquire any more provisions, and was forced to press on ahead of his party down the Athabasca River. Fortunately, the advance group managed to kill six buffalo, which provided food until its arrival at Athabasca Lake. While his men coming up behind were short of food, the Nor'Westers continually tempted them with provisions, even leaving pemmican by their encampments at night.

At this point Clarke's people still remained loyal. Robert Logan headed off for Ile-à-la-Crosse, arriving on 13 September. Clarke and his main party reached Lake Athabasca on 4 October. Here Clarke met a small group of traders he had dispatched from Jack River in early August. They were supposed to announce to the aboriginals that the HBC was coming, but the Nor'Westers had worked hard to prevent any contact with the natives. Finally, Clarke spied an Indian family in two canoes. He sent a party to pursue the unsuspecting aboriginals, and managed to open a trade with them.

Food remained a constant problem. Clarke was eventually forced to divide his party. He kept 16 men at Lake Athabasca, sent 15 to Great Slave Lake, and dispatched 13 to Calimunt. Meanwhile Clarke and the bulk of his officers proceeded with 48 men up the Peace River. This "squadron of invasion" — as the Nor'Westers labelled it, had no provisions and was totally dependent on a single Cree Indian who was hired to hunt for it. Unfortunately, the hunter killed only three animals during the trip. Nor'Wester John McGillivray commented on the emaciated appearance of Clarke and his men, while simultaneously giving orders that the NWC people not supply their rivals with food.

Clarke again pushed on ahead of the main body, reaching Fort Vermilion on the Peace River on 27 October. He waited for the remainder of his people, but they did not catch him up. He was forced to walk for four days without food searching for aboriginals from whom he might obtain provisions. He found a band, but they were unable to help him very much. Nevertheless, he returned to his party with what provisions he could carry, only to find that in his absence his head clerk George McDougall had made a deal with the Nor'Westers by which goods and men along with their engagements had been surrendered in return for some food. With his men dying of malnutrition, Clarke was eventually forced to make another similar arrangement to save his own life. The Nor'Westers agreed to furnish his party with provisions and to conduct it to Fort Wedderburn.

Others in his expedition were not so fortunate. Sixteen died of starvation, 13 of them trying to return to Fort Wedderburn. These men were part of the relatively unheralded casualties of the fur trade wars, their deaths receiving far less publicity than those killed at Red River a few months later. Clarke reached Fort Wedderburn on 8 February 1816 and wintered there. Some of the Nor'Westers were impressed by his "perseverance." When he finally reached Cumberland on 15 June 1816 with what was left of his original brigade, he found almost no useful trading goods for a return to the Athabasca and none to supply him. He offered to rush to the assistance of Red River, but was ordered not to do so.

4. The Renewal of Trouble in Red River:

According to Peter Fidler, postmaster of Brandon House, rumours that the mixed-bloods were planning to drive away the re-established settlers were rampant after Christmas of 1815. The reports were initially little heeded since Duncan Cameron had pledged peace. At Fort Douglas, Colin Robertson heard similar stories in January and February of 1816. Robertson later testified that at the beginning of February he had visited Cameron at Fort Gibraltar and complained about the "impropriety of exciting alarms in the minds of the Settlers." Cameron insisted that the reports did not come from him. He said he was heading for Qu'Appelle, where he would do his best to advocate friendship.

Robertson then went to Fort Daer at Pembina, where he heard more stories of a massed attack. At the end of February, Robertson wrote to Governor Semple at Brandon House that some danger was to be apprehended. He advised Semple that in the spring the settlers should not be placed upon their lands or allowed to farm them. Instead, they should remain within Fort Douglas until the period of expected danger had passed. When Duncan Cameron returned from Qu'Appelle in March 1816, he again appeared in British regimentals. Settlers reported to Colin Robertson that Cameron told them that he had driven them away once and could do it again. John Pritchard, who was hunting on the prairies, later claimed that "the language of every free Canadian we saw was 'mefiez vous bien, pour l'Amour de Dieu mefiez vous bien.'"

At the NWC post of Fort Qu'Appelle on the Saskatchewan River, the Canadian northern express arrived around 12 March. The arrival of the express was always an occasion for celebration, and this was no exception. A day later, the HBC men observed that a new flag had joined the NWC one on the flagpoles of the fort. According to Peter Fidler, this "flag of the Half-breeds" was "about 4 1/2 feet square, red & in the middle a large figure of Eight horizontally of a different colour." It had first been seen by the HBC traders in the previous autumn. The display of the flag was accompanied by renewed rumours of a great attack on the Red River settlement in the spring. At about the same time that the "Half-breed" flag appeared at Fort Qu'Appelle, mixed-bloods from all over the western plains began to assemble at Fort Gibraltar.

In the advance planning for the settlement of Red River, absolutely no attention had been paid to the mixed-bloods and their "freemen" associates as important players in the region. Selkirk had recognized the presence of the First Nations, whose friendship would have to be cultivated and whose aboriginal land title would have to be respected. But his early writing on Red River, the fur trade and the First Nations — including his *A Sketch of the British Fur Trade* published in early 1816 — offered no suggestion of the existence of the mixed-bloods and freemen. Nor did any of his instructions to Miles Macdonell suggest a policy for dealing with them. Macdonell's journal certainly recognized the existence of these local residents, but the governor, while he employed them as hunters, did not treat them as a distinct people with their own aspirations and interests, worthy of a concerted effort of cultivation. He would come increasingly to appreciate that the mixed-bloods were the main warriors of the NWC. Accepting the mixed-bloods as a force was hardly the same as understanding them, however.

Colin Robertson decided to seize Fort Gibraltar again, claiming that if he delayed he would not have sufficient strength to do so later. He wrote Semple of his intentions, but acted before he received any reply. Duncan Cameron was again placed in custody, and Robertson later testified he found in Cameron's room an open letter in the Nor'Wester's handwriting inviting Indians to the Forks to pillage in the spring. This letter led Robertson to seize the remaining papers at Fort Gibraltar and ship them to Fort Douglas for careful scrutiny. Among these papers were a number of earlier letters written to HBC people, which had been opened and obviously read. Robertson also found a

Cuthbert Grant

Robert Semple

This somewhat fanciful depiction of the Battle of Seven Oaks
was produced many years later.

circular letter from Cameron and Alexander Macdonell written from Qu'Appelle in February 1816 which said, "the spirit of our people particularly the Halfbreeds will require to be roused, and we think that the appearance of a few of their color from the nearest posts would again have the desired effect." A number of other letters related to the events of 1815. Here, Robertson insisted, was clear evidence of NWC duplicity and instigation.

On 18 March, John Siveright, a clerk of the NWC at Gibraltar, asked Robertson whether he intended to stop the winter express as it passed the Forks. Robertson replied that he had three men ready to seize the express, but if it was not concealed, he would be satisfied with examining the letters from Qu'Appelle, Swan River, and Fort des Prairies. If these contained no evidence of plans against the settlement the express could proceed. Otherwise, he would detain it until Semple's arrival.

The express arrived the following day, and when Robertson opened a letter from Alexander Greenfield Macdonell at Qu'Appelle, he read: "A storm is gathering to the Northward ready to burst on the heads of the rascals who deserve it; little do they know their situation; last year was but a joke. The new nation under their leaders are coming forward to clear their native soil of intruders and assassins." This letter did not suggest that the "new nation" was being instigated or encouraged by the Nor'Westers, but in another letter Macdonell wrote, "Sir William Shaw is collecting all the Halfbreeds in the surrounding departments, and has ordered his friends in this quarter to prepare to take the field; he has actually taken every Halfbreed in the country to the Forks from Fort des Prairie, it is supposed they will when collected together form more than one hundred, God knows the result." Other correspondence from the three posts which Robertson opened was in the same vein. Robertson carefully bundled the entire express up and put it away without opening any more of the letters. Or so he would claim.

On 19 March, Sheriff Alexander Macdonell at Pembina received a letter from Robertson informing him of the seizure of Fort Gibraltar. Macdonell, accompanied by Messrs White, McLeod, Pritchard, and several constables, immediately proceeded to the NWC post at Pembina, where he arrested its occupants and seized their arms and ammunition. Among the guns was one which George Sutherland insisted had been forcibly seized from him the previous spring by the Nor'Wester Alexander Greenfield Macdonell. The Nor'Westers arrested were sent to Fort Douglas in the custody of P.C. Pambrun and John McLeod. In the meantime, Robertson had heard that two of the cannon taken from the settlement the previous spring were hidden at Bas de la Rivière. He sent John McLeod and a party of five men to search for the artillery, but they were unable to find it.

Governor Semple arrived back at the Forks from his western tour at the end of March. His immediate instinct was to allow the detained express to proceed, but when he had read some of the opened correspondence he decided to retain it as evidence of the NWC intentions. Semple formally sent a letter to Robertson on 12 April approving of his actions in seizing Fort Gibraltar, arresting Cameron, and opening the letters in the express. The measure was demanded by the conduct of the Nor'Westers, the governor wrote, and the seizure of the express "was a step arising out of the former and which has happily furnished its own justification to the fullest extent."

Robertson advocated sending Cameron and the intercepted letters to Hudson Bay and thence to England, but Semple insisted "that he did not see any harm the said Cameron could do as a Prisoner." This disagreement appears to have marked the opening of the quarrel over policy between Robertson and Cameron that would end with the former departing the settlement in early June. From Robertson's perspective, Semple (whom Robertson persistently referred to in his writing as "Mr. Simple") placed too much trust in both friends and enemies in a place that was "a hotbed of Hypocrisy, desertion, and party spirit." Robertson did not approve of the release of all of the traders arrested except Cameron, for example, despite their solemn promises not to disturb the tranquility of the settlement. Robertson continued to advocate the dispatch of Duncan Cameron and the captured express to England. He also recommended that Forts Douglas and Gibraltar be consolidated in order to make defence easier. Perhaps most important of all, Robertson insisted that all the settlers should reside at or near one of the forts and should not be placed upon their farms until after the menace was over.

In early May, the HBC trader James Sutherland set out with his furs from Qu'Appelle for the Bay, having been assured by Alexander Greenfield Macdonell that he could proceed unmolested down river. Sutherland and his party were subsequently stopped in a crooked and rapid part of the river by a large party of Canadians and mixed-bloods led by Cuthbert Grant. According to Peter Fidler the attackers had "their faces all painted in the most horrid & terrific forms & dressed like Indians and all armed with Guns, Pistols, Swords & Spears, & several had Bows & Arrows; and made the War-whoop or yell like the Natives in immediately attacking their Enemies." The cargo of furs and provisions was seized. Sutherland and his party were forced to sign an agreement not to bear arms against the NWC before they were freed, having been kept prisoners for a week. Upon learning of this incident, Governor Semple decided to send Duncan Cameron and the captured evidence to the Bay, which was done on 18 May. John McLeod took the Nor'Westers and part of the letters found in Cameron's possession to York Factory.

The settlers returned from their winter haven at Pembina at the end of April and Semple had sought immediately to locate them on their land. They were assigned separate lots, given seed, and encouraged to plant extensively, while rumours of potential destruction swirled all around them. At the end of May, a number of settlers placed on their lands came to Colin Robertson, still in charge of Fort Gibraltar, and asked him to shelter them until the danger had passed. Robertson answered that they must apply to Governor Semple, who told them to remain on their lands. The "differences of opinion" between Robertson and Semple had now reached an open break, and Robertson debated about leaving "if he could not concur in the expediency which he doubted, of the measures to be taken for their [the settlers] common protection."

While Robertson and Semple were disagreeing over what should be done, Brandon House was attacked on 1 June by a party of mixed-bloods, Canadians, and aboriginals. Peter Fidler later described the scene: "A little after noon about 48 Canadians, half-Breeds, & Indians, but mostly half-Breeds appeared in the plain all in horse back with the Half-Breeds flag flying, this little army marched in regular order in an oblong square; one was near the middle beating an Indian drum & accompanying it with an Indian Song, the greater part of the rest bearing Chorus." The party galloped to a point opposite the NWC fort on the other side of the river, then turned their horses and charged suddenly into the HBC fort, which was manned by only a few under-armed HBC servants. They ransacked the post and celebrated for days, while the residents of the post — most of whom were fur trade families living in buildings surrounding the fort itself — moved out on to the plains to take shelter with the Cree and Stone Indians. The attackers eventually moved down the river toward the Forks. No-one had been seriously injured in the incident, although Brandon House had been stripped of its rum, tobacco, and ammunition. Up to this point in 1816, the "new nation" of mixed-bloods had intimidated fur traders and settlers alike. It had destroyed property, but had not actually killed anyone.

Word was brought to Fort Douglas of the destruction of Brandon House on 9 June. The aboriginal who reported this news also claimed that Alexander Greenfield Macdonell — with Canadians, mixed-bloods, and Indians — was heading down the Assiniboine River publicly proclaiming an intention to destroy the settlement. Governor

Semple finally decided that Colin Robertson's long-expressed fears were justified. Two forts could not be defended. He marched to Fort Gibraltar, still occupied by Robertson, to order its destruction and the movement of its palisades to help protect Fort Douglas. Although Robertson had now seen most of his recommendations accepted by Semple, the major one of keeping the settlers within the fort remained unresolved. Robertson later argued that he did not want to have to stay in Fort Douglas with Semple while the two men were still at logger-heads. He requested permission to depart Red River to go to the aid of the HBC traders he had sent to the Athabasca. The request was grant-ed. Robertson left with the parting words, "the Colony is nearly ruined, — time will show who has been the cause of it."

At Lake Winnipeg, Robertson had second thoughts, and he returned to within 15 miles of the Forks. He wrote Semple again offer-ing his services. The governor declined them, writing that Sheriff Alexander Macdonell had been put in charge of the colony in his absence. Robertson then resumed his journey. On 16 June an aborig-inal named Moustache arrived at Fort Douglas, claiming to have escaped from the mixed-bloods who were encamped at Portage la Prairie. He said that the heavily armed party would arrive at the Forks in a day or two. The chiefs of the local Saulteaux generously offered to assist the settlement, but Semple — in the first of several fateful miscalculations — said it was not necessary.

5. Battle at Seven Oaks:

On 19 June at about 7 p.m., a party of armed men on horseback was spotted moving slowly on the prairie by a man using a spyglass in the watch house of Fort Douglas. "The half-breeds are coming, the half-breeds are coming," he yelled. The party consist-ed of about 60 mixed-bloods, free Canadians, and aboriginals — accounts of the numbers vary from 50 to 70 — with the mixed-bloods in the majority. The horsemen would subsequently maintain that they were attempting to go around Fort Douglas and the settlement, but there was nothing but open prairie behind them. They could have made a much wider sweep to the northwest had they sought to avoid a confrontation.

The armed party had just about reached the lots of the settlers, who were weeding potatoes in the fields, when Governor Semple asked for 20 volunteers from the fort to accompany him to meet the intruders to "determine their intentions." Six officers from the fort joined the makeshift platoon.

Semple was particularly concerned for the safety of the settlers in the fields, which was understandable given his refusal to keep them within the fort. William Coltman, the commissioner who later investigated the Seven Oaks incident for the British government, was convinced that the governor's disagreement with Colin Robertson — in which Semple was now being proved demonstrably wrong — aggravated Semple's lack of sense and caution on this day.

The governor refused to wait for his small artillery force, assuring his people that he intended no battle. Several witnesses said that the governor had a paper which he intended to read to the intruders. On his way to meet the mixed-blood party, Semple was met by settlers running to the fort, and was informed that some had been made prisoner. Alexander Murray and his wife, Alexander Sutherland, and William and Alexander Bannerman were detained. These actions were probably made independent of any orders from NWC associates Cuthbert Grant or Alexander Fraser, who were leading the mixed-bloods that day. They "of course would irritate" Semple, Sheriff Alexander Macdonell later testified, adding "I have reason to think that it would enrage the Governor against the North West servants to see these settlers taken prisoner so inoffensively attending their own lawful labours." One of the retreating settlers warned Semple to be careful, to which he replied, "I am only going to speak to them."

Semple and his party marched single file along the left bank of the Red River past a number of settlers' houses until they reached a bend in the river at what was called "Seven Oaks." John Pritchard, one of the few survivors of the attack, insisted that Semple's group was not aware how numerous the other party was. Pritchard and others from the settlement also claimed that the NWC party was dressed as Indian warriors in full war paint.

At the bend in the river, dotted with tall oak trees, the well-armed horsemen surrounded the governor's party in a rough half-moon. Most testimony agrees that at this point a Canadian named Bouché or Boucher rode up to Semple and said something like "What do you want?" John Pritchard insisted that the question was asked in an "insolent tone," which may have further aggravated the governor, who after a brief verbal exchange attempted to grab either Boucher's gun or the reins of his horse. At this point it is not clear whether or not Semple gave an order to fire, or who actually fired the first shot. The preponderance of testimony is that the first shot was fired by a settler, although most of the surviving eyewitnesses were from the mixed-blood party.

In any event, a round of firing, most of it from Grant's men, followed the initial shot. In the ensuing battle, the mixed-bloods had all the advantages. Most of the settlers were not soldiers and were unfamiliar with guns, while their opponents — hunters and plainsmen — used them almost daily.

Semple was quickly wounded and several settlers killed. Semple's wound was in his thigh. He told Cuthbert Grant, to whom he pleaded for mercy, "I am not mortally wounded, and if you could get me conveyed to the fort, I think I should live." Grant promised to do so, but in the confusion of the fighting, he did not remain with the governor.

Grant soon lost control over his forces, who not only continued wildly firing their weapons but ignored various attempts on the part of the settlers to surrender. Semple himself was mortally shot in the chest by an aboriginal named Machicabaou. Before the shooting finally ended, 21 settlers were dead, including a number of the settlement's officers and leaders. Only one member of the NWC party was killed. In a frenzy of blood-lust, some of the settlers' bodies were mutilated and stripped of possessions following the actual confrontation. It was this part of the incident at Seven Oaks that Lord Selkirk and his friends always regarded as the "massacre." One of the few settlers to escape was John Pritchard, who was physically protected by a Canadian named Lavigne whom he had known when employed by the NWC.

Seven Oaks was clearly a spontaneous eruption of violence between two armed forces emotionally prepared for trouble, rather than a deliberately planned incident of mass murder. The mixed-bloods were probably as shocked by the bloody result as the settlers. Up to this point, the "war" in Red River had been conducted with little loss of life. From a legal standpoint, however, the absence of premeditation might lessen the nature of the offence — turning it from "murder" into "manslaughter" — but cannot fully exculpate those involved. Neither can the likelihood that Semple's people fired the first shot. Cuthbert Grant's party was armed and in the process of criminal activity — kidnapping and the display of armed threats, at the very least — when the incident occurred.

Only a handful of the party, and those chiefly not mixed-bloods, was involved in the post-battle slaughter and mutilation. Nonetheless this brutal behaviour horrified the world beyond Red River, confirming in the minds of many the notion that the mixed-bloods were little short of savages. Lord Selkirk would become a man possessed in his legal pursuit of those at Seven Oaks, although he never achieved a single conviction in the courts for their acts. The brûlés might have had an even worse press if most people were not convinced that they had been put up to their actions by the NWC. At the same time, laying the responsibility on the Nor'Westers for the savage behaviour tended to downplay any separate grievances that the mixed-bloods were attempting to address, such as their share in aboriginal rights.

6. The Settlement Dispersed Again:

At daybreak on the morning after Seven Oaks, acting governor Sheriff Alexander Macdonell attempted to rally his forces. Initially the remaining settlers agreed to defend Fort Douglas, and their defensive position was strong. With the assistance of the Saulteaux, Macdonell buried the dead. Later reports that the mutilated bodies were left for weeks on the battlefield to be scavenged by dogs and coyotes were gross exaggerations.

John Pritchard arrived with a message from Cuthbert Grant and Alexander Fraser, the two leaders of the mixed-bloods, demanding that the fort be surrendered, the settlers removed, and all property abandoned. If not, the Métis would murder all the settlers. These threats were probably part of the older rhetoric of intimidation rather than ones to be taken literally, but after the events of the previous day who could be certain? John Pritchard drafted and circulated a petition, supported by others, calling for capitulation. Most of the settlement signed. Macdonell understandably felt abandoned and suspicious of Pritchard, who had mysteriously escaped death at Seven Oaks. On 20 June he negotiated an agreement with the "chiefs of the Halfbreeds," allowing the settlers safe passage out of the Red River Valley. This hasty surrender was perhaps giving in too easily, considering the settlers' fortified position and the fact that the foe had no artillery, but the settlement was clearly very demoralized.

Two days later, after making out a full inventory of all the public property at Fort Douglas, Macdonell turned everything over to Cuthbert Grant, who signed a nine-page document receiving the goods. He wrote, "Received on Account of the North West Company, by me Cuthbert Grant Clerk to the North West Company, Acting for the North West Company." By signing the receipt as a clerk of the NWC, rather than as a chief of the new nation, Grant suggested that he did not himself believe that he was acting principally as an autonomous leader of his people.

Grant now refused to allow the settlers to depart, since he had received new orders to detain them until the arrival of Alexander

Greenfield Macdonell from Qu'Appelle. Sheriff Macdonell, no relation, observed that this would deprive Grant of the honours of the victory. Grant finally agreed to keep his word, and ordered the settlers to leave immediately. Sheriff Macdonell loaded his people and as much baggage as could be carried into eight boats, and the little flotilla started down the river towards its ultimate destination at the Bay. One of the acting governor's concerns was for the remaining documents which Colin Robertson had intercepted at Fort Gibraltar. These were now in his custody. Fearing that his party would be searched for this incriminating evidence, before embarkation Macdonell instructed one of the women of the settlement to tie the letters around her middle under her skirt.

On 23 June, the fleet of settlers heading north met a large brigade of Nor'Westers heading south under the command of Archibald Norman McLeod. The brigade of eight canoes had left Bas de la Rivière on 19 June, having been previously armed and instructed in "the manual and Platoon exercises" by De Meurons Charles de Reinhard and Frederick Heurter. Accompanying the canoes was a batteaux carrying two brass cannon mounted on field carriages. Heurter later testified that when he remarked on the relative weakness of this force, he was informed that this was only one of a number of parties that were converging on the Forks to attack the settlement. John McDonald was bringing 40 men from Swan River, and Alexander Greenfield Macdonell was coming from Qu'Appelle with 80 mixedbloods who were to make the first assault.

McLeod ordered the boats from Red River to stop, and commanded a general search of their effects. His orders were to search everywhere, stated Heurter, especially in trunks and boxes, looking for "all account Books letters & papers of whatever nature." There were no keys for Governor Semple's trunks, which were broken open with an axe. Meanwhile, the girl with the letters hidden around her waist stood unobtrusively on the shore. The acting governor and the settlers were eventually allowed to proceed, although several, including John Pritchard, were detained as prisoners.

Macdonell was persuaded that the detention of Pritchard was really a ruse by the Nor'Westers to disguise the fact that he was a turncoat who had been spared at Seven Oaks to sow dissension. Pritchard did not know of the presence of the documents. The settlers apparently escaped without actually taking an oath never to return to Red River, although Sheriff Alexander Macdonell had to find bail for an appearance at Montreal before he was released. Peter Fidler, who with his family was heading from Brandon House to the Bay, was also halted and threatened with death should he return to Red River.

After releasing the settlers, the NWC brigade continued to the Forks. There Messrs. McLeod and McKenzie assembled all the mixed-bloods and congratulated them on their efforts. They distributed presents. Each of 40 mixed-bloods got a capot, a pair of green trousers, a cotton shirt, a silk handkerchief, a leather jockey cap, and a feather.

The two Nor'Westers also harangued the Saulteaux for not being supportive. They then ordered a lake schooner labouriously constructed by boatbuilder Donald Livingstone to be destroyed. According to Frederick Heurter, the entire assemblage then moved to Seven Oaks to view the site of the battle, with more praise given to individuals who had distinguished themselves in the action, including the brutal bits. Most of the NWC partners then departed for the West, leaving Alexander Greenfield Macdonell and Archibald McLellan in charge of what remained of Red River. In late June of 1816, after years of contention and strife, the North West Company appeared completely victorious and in control of the region. Its triumph, however, would be short-lived.

~8~

Lord Selkirk to the Rescue

*U*p to the summer of 1816, the fur trade wars had been generally waged to the advantage of the North West Company. The Nor'Westers had thoroughly beaten the American traders on the Pacific Slope, and were well ahead on points of the HBC in the interior of North America, both in Red River and in the Athabasca.

Their antagonists, led by Lord Selkirk and the directors of the Hudson's Bay Company, had typically thought in terms of a commercial conflict rather than of open war. The HBC entrance into the Athabasca in 1815, for example, assumed that the arrival of a large corps of fur traders in the region would result in a bidding competition for furs, not in the violent treatment meted out to John Clarke and his associates.

Perhaps only former Nor'Wester Colin Robertson on the HBC side fully understood the reality of the situation, but he had not actually led the Company's forces into the Athabasca in 1815 and he had neutralized himself in Red River at the time of Seven Oaks. Occasionally somebody on the HBC side, such as Miles Macdonell in early 1814, would enjoy a momentary advantage of force. But it would soon trickle away in the assumption that one victory was all that was required to face the "bullies" down.

At the outset, the NWC traders had several great advantages in this conflict. In the first place, they recognized very early on in the struggle that it would be a life-and-death encounter. They were under no illusions of what would be required to emerge triumphant. In the second place, the Nor'Westers had, in the mixed-bloods, a resident cavalry. Once the *bois-brûlés* were mobilized and motivated, they made extremely good shock troops. Finally, the NWC was accustomed to violence in the fur trade. Indeed, as a number of observers pointed out, the company had made intimidation and violence an integral part of their western operations for many years.

Then, in 1816, a morally outraged Lord Selkirk went on the offensive. Within months, he completely altered the course of the conflict. He did so, of course, by following the maxims of Colin Robertson rather than those of the British drawing room or counting house. The liberal lord, the high-minded philanthropist, met the Nor'Westers on their own violent terms, without scruples, which surprised them considerably.

1. Selkirk Heads West:

Lord Selkirk finally departed from Montreal for Red River on 18 June 1816. In order to avoid being ambushed by the NWC around Fort William, he planned to travel to his settlement via the old voyageur route along the proposed international boundary through Fond du Lac. Selkirk hardly travelled alone, although he would not pick up his military escort of a sergeant and six men from the 37th Regiment until Drummond's Island near Sault Ste Marie. The earl was accompanied from Montreal by his manservant William — we never learn his surname — and by Dr. John Allan, a Royal Navy surgeon who was his personal physician; both had been with him since the departure from Liverpool in 1815. Selkirk had earlier travelled in North America in 1803 and 1804 with a personal manservant, whom he never once mentioned in his detailed journal of the tour. But he had not had a personal doctor in tow as well in 1803-4. The presence of such a figure indicates that Selkirk was still in ill health. Another person in Selkirk's canoes was Archibald McDonald, returning to the West.

Also among those in the Selkirk party departing Lower Canada was Captain Jean-Baptiste Chevalier de Lorimier who had been seconded to Selkirk by the Indian Department as a guide. A mixed-blood (his mother was an Iroquois from Caughnawaga), Lorimier had commanded a force of Indian warriors in the War of 1812 and spent much time in American prisons, severely damaging his health. Another member of the group was William Laidlaw, a young Scottish gentleman farmer who had been recruited by Selkirk to run his farm at the settlement on shares. At the Bay of Quinte, the group was joined by Lieutenant A.B. Becher of the Royal Navy, who had been ordered by Captain William Fitz William Owen (presently surveying the Great Lakes for the British government) to travel west with Lord Selkirk to "take such observations & sketches as circumstances might admit of" for the benefit of His Majesty's service.

Allan, Lorimier, and Becher formed a triumvirate of "gentlemen" later joined at Fort William by Captains Frederick Matthey and Proteus D'Orsonnens of the De Meuron Regiment. These men became quite close to one another and to Selkirk during the course of their adventures together over the next few months. They all passed well beyond being neutral observers to becoming active partisans on behalf of Selkirk, his colony, and the HBC.

Selkirk left his wife Jean, Lady Selkirk, in charge of his business in Canada. Like many female members of the Scottish upper classes, Jean Wedderburn Douglas had been well-educated and prepared for a life of business. She was not only astute and fully conversant with her husband's affairs, but she was a skilled hostess (blessed with great beauty) who charmed most of the males who came into contact with her. More than one of Selkirk's associates was secretly in love with her. From her base in Montreal, Lady Selkirk directed her husband's Canadian enterprises. She dealt with the merchants supplying the fur trade and the settlement as well as the lawyers defending Selkirk's interests. As the sister of Andrew Wedderburn-Colvile, she was able to inform her brother of what was happening in Canada in the course of what were ostensibly family letters. When Selkirk put himself at risk at Fort William through ill-judged actions, his wife travelled to Quebec to plead his case with Sir John Coape Sherbrooke, the governor of Lower Canada. She became immediate friends with the Sherbrookes, and remained close to Lady Sherbrooke for many years. Jean did not alter Sherbrooke's course, though she may have softened it a bit.

At Drummond's Island, the British military outpost to the south of Sault Ste. Marie in Lake Huron (now on the American side of the border), the Selkirk party on 22 July attended a public council with the aboriginals and the Indian department. Here Catawabety, a Chippewa chief from Sandy Lake, told the gathering that the NWC people at Fond du Lac had offered him rum and other presents if he and his people would make war on the Red River settlement. He had refused, said the chief, because the Nor'Westers admitted that they had no military orders for such action. Catawabety further testified that James Grant (the NWC partner at Fond du Lac) had offered him a reward if he would send his young men after some HBC messengers who were heading west earlier in the spring. This was Selkirk's first intimation that Jean-Baptiste Lagimodière might not have gotten through with his dispatches to the settlement. When asked by the earl about the Indians at the Forks, the Chippewa chief assured Selkirk that they were quite pleased that the settlement had been established.

Two days later, the Selkirk party was preparing to depart from Drummond's Island when Miles Macdonell arrived to report that he had been within a day of Red River when he learned of the incident at Seven Oaks. He had immediately turned around to warn Selkirk of impending danger. According to John Allan, Selkirk was exhausted and asleep in his tent and so was not told about this news until the following morning. There is a suggestion here that Selkirk was not very well at this point. The earl's immediate response to the news was that Semple was too sensible to have provoked such violence. MacDonell also reported that a number of Red River officials and settlers, notably P.C. Pambrun, John Pritchard, John Bourke, Louis Nolin, John Spencer, and Donald McPherson, were being held at Fort William. These people were all eyewitnesses to the events at the Forks.

Selkirk determined to head west via Fort William to interview the witnesses who were being detained. He would then carry on to the settlement via the American route, which ran along the modern-day international boundary to Lake of the Woods. Before departing he wrote to John Askin, an Indian Department official and magistrate at Drummond's Island, requesting that he accompany the party to Fort William. As an interested party the earl was in an awkward position of attempting to act as a magistrate investigating the NWC. Askin begged off the request, saying he could not spare the time. He did provide Selkirk with a set of provincial statutes, a copy of Burns' *Justice of the Peace* (a standard manual of the day), and a French Bible for taking oaths. Selkirk also asked Charles O. Ermatinger, an independent trader and magistrate at the Sault, to go with him to Fort William. Ermatinger also begged off the duty, although he helped Selkirk interview an aboriginal who had accompanied Lagimodière when he had been seized and stripped of his dispatches.

Ironically enough, further details of Seven Oaks arrived at the Sault in a letter from William McGillivray at Fort William. It reported that the settlement had been attacked by some aboriginals and mixed-bloods while no partner of the NWC was within miles of the incident. McGillivray also reported that Semple had been put to death despite having asked for mercy from Cuthbert Grant, a NWC clerk. Selkirk wrote to Lower Canadian governor Sir John Sherbrooke of the revelations at Drummond's Island. Unable to gain the assistance of local magistrates, he was forced to head to Fort William alone. Selkirk thus began heading into confrontation with the NWC fully conscious that he was operating at the outer fringes of legitimacy. His position could only get worse, and indeed it did. Before he was finished he would defy legal warrants of arrest and the British government itself.

One voice of caution at the outset came from Dr. John Allan, who felt strongly enough about Selkirk's decision to press forward to object in writing. Allan's reservations were on many fronts. He pointed out that the expedition had been predicated upon finding provisions at the settlement, which was likely not to be the case. Passage through the United States would not only annoy the Americans but also the British government, which was likely to be prejudiced "against everything you may do or propose." Even were Selkirk in good health, the journey would be difficult, Allan noted, "but in your Lordships state of health, it would be almost surprising if you survived it." Without Selkirk, the settlement could not succeed. Surely the British government would now act to ensure the safety of Red River, he argued.

Allan's letter indicates that Selkirk's earlier delays in getting his party heading west were caused by more than difficulties of organization. Although Allan was not precise about his patient's medical problems, they clearly were long-term and life-threatening. Selkirk was probably exhibiting symptoms of consumption. What Allan did not take into account was the possibility of a lengthy remission of the disease. This is exactly what happened, although why remission occurred can only be the subject of speculation. It may well be that the news of Seven Oaks turned Selkirk into an avenging angel, his emotions triumphing over his bodily disabilities. It is also possible that the cool dry air of the West proved a positive benefit to a man in Selkirk's physical condition. Whatever the explanation, Selkirk would thrive physically under the regimen that his physician thought would destroy him. Serious illness would not recur until after his return to Canada more than a year later.

2. Capturing Fort William:

Selkirk and his party, now accompanied by a small military escort, left the Sault on 2 August to canoe across Lake Superior. On 11 August, the Selkirk party rejoined Captain Frederick Matthey and his party of De Meurons at Thunder Bay, fifteen miles east of Fort William. The twelve canoes of the Matthey brigade contained four former officers and 100 former enlisted men of the De Meuron Regiment, still in uniform and under military discipline. A day later, Selkirk reached the Kaministiquia River and encamped a mile above Fort William, which was buzzing with activity. It would soon be time for the famous annual gathering — the rendezvous — of the North West Company. The business deliberations were designed to coincide with the arrival of fur brigades from the west and the provisions brigades from the east. Fort William was not only occupied by a substantial number of NWC partners, but hundreds of voyageurs and hangers-on as well.

On 13 August, John McNab, Captain D'Orsonnens and Captain de Lorimier went to the NWC headquarters with nine men, their weapons concealed. Calling for William McGillivray, the newcomers walked into the undefended fort through crowds of Nor'Westers. They handed the Nor'Wester partner a note from Selkirk that said as a magistrate he wanted to enquire into the causes of imprisonment of those being detained at Fort William. McGillivray denied that anyone was detained, but several former prisoners soon appeared at Selkirk's tent to swear affidavits about their treatment. McGillivray was thus summarily served with a warrant for his arrest issued by Selkirk as one of His Majesty's justices assigned to keep the peace in Upper Canada Western District and in the Indian Territories.

McGillivray accepted the warrant "as a gentleman," reported John McNab, one of those who had presented it. He asked for time to consult with his colleagues, and then he would come to Selkirk's camp to furnish bail. When McGillivray and his partners Kenneth McKenzie and John McLoughlin subsequently appeared at Selkirk's tent, the earl arrested them all. He then sent a party of 25 De Meurons commanded by D'Orsonnens and Lieutenant Fauche back to Fort William, with a search warrant. The Nor'Westers attempted to bar the gate, but the armed escort forcibly kept it open. A bugle was sounded by the Selkirk forces at the first sign of resistance, and Captain Matthey quickly arrived with reinforcements. A number of other partners of the NWC were arrested and taken to Selkirk's tent, to be released on their word that no resistance or hostile moves would be undertaken.

The surprising absence of serious resistance to Selkirk's occupation of Fort William was a product of a combination of factors. For one thing, there was the element of surprise. That Selkirk was on his way west with a large force was well known at Fort William. But the Nor'Westers had expected either that the news of Seven Oaks or want of provisions or disciplinary troubles with his forces would induce Selkirk to turn back. One Nor'Wester at Fort William wrote a friend on the Pacific Slope on 28 July that three of Selkirk's canoes had already mutinied and returned to the Sault. Selkirk had fallen victim to calamity before and certainly nobody had expected the earl to go on the attack.

In the second place, Selkirk was not leading a party of prospective settlers, but was at the head of a small private army. Many of his men were still wearing the uniforms in which they had been disbanded. They were well-armed and under military discipline, commanded by their usual officers. Selkirk's forces were only about one-third as numerous as those at Fort William, if voyageurs and aboriginals were included in the fort's population. But his men were cohesive and properly commanded.

Finally, Selkirk was a duly-appointed magistrate. He was prepared to operate at the fringes of a legality which the NWC had never expected to confront. As was true of Miles Macdonell in 1815, the NWC stood in awe of legal British authority. Operating without law as they did most of the time, the Nor'Westers did not really understand about defying warrants. Selkirk himself would adopt a different approach later in the year.

Once Selkirk had gained access to Fort William, he quickly discovered the prisoners, who had been brought from Red River. P.C. Pambrun and John Pritchard insisted that they had been confined against their will, and Pritchard was in irons. From these men and others, Selkirk learned of hostile preparations occurring within the fort. He issued another search warrant, and the subsequent search uncovered four cases of guns and 40 fowling pieces, loaded and primed, that had been concealed in a hayloft.

Selkirk then discovered that the North West partners had used their paroles to empty their files and burn a number of documents in the fireplace of the council room. Deciding that the Nor'Westers could not be trusted, the earl ordered the evacuation of all North West personnel from the fort. His people occupied it, the De Meurons encamping just outside the gates, and he began the examination of witnesses.

The ease with which he subdued the Nor'Westers was the best proof possible of Selkirk's continued insistence that a small military force of redcoats authorized by government would easily quiet the Indian Territories. Subsequent testimony by Frederick Heurter, still employed by the NWC at Red River, provided further confirmation of this assumption. When Alexander Greenfield Macdonell learned of the seizure of Fort William by Selkirk, he immediately attempted to lead a force of mixed-bloods and aboriginals to liberate the NWC headquarters. Heurter reported, "one of the Halfbreeds named Laplante spoke for himself, observing that he understood there were Kings Troops coming with his Lordship and that he would not fight them. That he would rather take a Buffalo Skin about him and live in the plains than to be guilty of such things. The others followed his example and all refused to advance."

The NWC had taken for granted that Selkirk was an effete and ineffectual member of the British aristocracy, while the earl had always held that the Nor'Westers were bullies who had never been properly challenged. Fort William proved the NWC wrong and Selkirk right.

At Fort William was a building called the council room, which only partners were normally allowed to enter. The formal business of the NWC was done there. In this room at the council table of the NWC on the 15th of August — in the presence of Captain Matthey, Captain Lorimier, Lieutenant Becher, constable John McNab, Dr. John Allan, and former Red River sheriff John Spencer (who had been freed from confinement) — Selkirk examined under oath the arrested partners. Notes were taken of the examinations by Allan and Spencer, and some of the witnesses signed them.

The Nor'Westers generally denied having participated in the events at Red River. They insisted that they were not responsible for the conduct of either the wintering partners or their servants and did not have any means of controlling them. The partners maintained they had no knowledge of property seized in Red River in 1815 and had given no rewards to any of the settlers, although some admitted they had given presents. William McGillivray admitted that Governor Semple had been killed but denied he had been murdered. McGillivray acknowledged, however, that Cuthbert Grant was a clerk in the NWC service. Allan Macdonell confessed that he had Semple's double-barreled gun and had brought it to Fort William. Most of the prisoners objected to Selkirk's use of the term "massacre" to describe Seven Oaks, altering it to "battle" or "affair." Simon Fraser was so agitated by the examination that Selkirk suggested he retire to his room and prepare a declaration in his own handwriting. Partner Daniel McKenzie's examination was postponed until another day.

On 17 August, Selkirk wrote to Upper Canada's attorney-general, D'Arcy Boulton, that he was sending to him "A Cargo of Criminals of a larger Calibre than usually came before the Courts at York." Selkirk insisted that evidence was mounting by the hour of the "most detestable system of villainy that was allowed to prevail in the British Dominions." Despite the denials of the Nor'Westers, Selkirk thought he had a case for conspiracy.

Much of the evidence was circumstantial. Twenty bales intended for the Red River department were found to contain suits of clothing which Selkirk was certain were destined for those involved in the Seven Oaks killings. In one of the NWC books was found a list of mixed-bloods who had received "habiliments" at Red River in June shortly after Seven Oaks. Names were ticked off. Thirteen names not ticked were found to correspond to the names on the suits of clothing. It was not often, Selkirk noted to the Upper Canadian attorney-general, that "Acts of public justice are executed under circumstances like the present," with his 100 effectives surrounded by 300 members of the opposition, mainly "bastard Half-Breeds."

On the same day that Selkirk wrote to York, Lady Selkirk in Montreal penned a letter to Lower Canada's governor Sir John Sherbrooke, pleading for government assistance in Red River. She had received a letter from Selkirk indicating that he intended to investigate events at the colony, she wrote. She was concerned that Selkirk's authority in the West was inadequate. "All the magistrates for the Indian Territories are equally parties interested," she observed, "& the Partners of the North West Company cannot be expected to offer themselves to justice."

What was needed was a show of proper government authority. At Fort William, Selkirk had shown authority, but as Lady Selkirk was suggesting whether it was proper was another matter. For his part, Sherbrooke refused to act. Lady Selkirk riposted with the suggestion that an impartial team of investigators be sent. She dreaded delay, she wrote, for "the necessary slow proceedings of Courts of Law, offered no remedy to such evils as now exist in that country." Sherbrooke could only lamely respond that the lateness of the season and "various other causes too numerous to mention" made it impossible for him to intervene. The failure of governments on both sides of the Atlantic to impose their authority on the Indian Territories provided the best justification possible for Selkirk's unilateral and creative use of his power.

Selkirk himself certainly realized that he had exceeded his authority. He attempted to defend his actions in lengthy letters to Lieutenant-Governor Gore of Upper Canada and his attorney-general, D'Arcy Boulton. When he received news that his colonists had been "massacred by the Half Indian Servants of the North West Company," wrote Selkirk in the first public use of the term "massacre" to refer to the events at Seven Oaks, he had decided to visit Fort William "with a force capable of making the law respected." Unable to find a neutral magistrate to accompany him, he was forced to act himself. He asked Gore to lay aside the "scruples" which would have governed him "if I had been in a civilized and well regulated country." The proof of guilt was stronger than ordinarily necessary for arresting criminals, and when the use of force became necessary Selkirk had employed it.

To Boulton also Selkirk sent the news that he had dispatched two Swiss officers east on 18 August in charge of eight arrested prisoners, mainly partners of the NWC. While the wintering partners all claimed innocence of events at Red River, pleading they had neither consented nor approved the local actions, there were presents at Fort William which had been promised the "murderers" after the event. Claims that Semple had confronted a party of innocent brûlés without provocation were nonsense, for they had taken prisoners among the settlers. The expedition from its outset formed "a series of the most undisguised violence and aggression." Along with the prisoners, Selkirk had dispatched Archy McDonald to deliver papers and other evidence to the lawyers in Montreal.

Selkirk understood from the beginning his legal excesses. Nevertheless, he expected to be supported by government because —

as he observed to Sir John Sherbrooke on 23 August — the North West Company was "not to be restrained from crimes by anything less than a striking example of the Vengeance of the Law."

Selkirk also appreciated full well the problems of proving charges of conspiracy, one of the most difficult claims at law to justify. But he defended such an approach to the HBC legal counsel in Montreal, James Stewart, on the grounds that it was the only way to get all the evidence in front of the public. Whether his basic assumption was accurate — that the behaviour of the North West Company was so awful that both government and public would react against it once the "facts" were put before them — was a question that did not occur to Selkirk for a moment. Here was a principal disadvantage of being an interested party: an inability to assess accurately the way in which the situation would be viewed in the court of public opinion, particularly when the counter case had been presented, as it would be in the autumn of 1816.

Archdeacon John Strachan commented in early September on a general feeling at York that the controversy "appears to be a mercantile quarrel and people here have not sympathy with a Peer of Great Britain turning fur Merchant and applying the power which an ample Inheritance gives him in destroying a trade which has given bread to them for two centuries." Strachan, an acknowledged NWC supporter, admitted that both sides had taken "great liberties with Justice." He could see little to choose between them in moral terms.

With the culprits in the Semple business arrested and sent east, Selkirk turned to dealing with the NWC's operations, which his seizure of Fort William had halted. The remaining senior clerks at the post, J.C. McTavish and J. Vandersluys, pressed for permission to ship trade goods west and peltries east without any settlement of the differences between Selkirk and the NWC. They argued the larger issues should be settled in the courts.

On any considerations of fair play, Selkirk should have conceded this point. But he had control of the NWC's economic lifeline, and he was understandably reluctant to let go. The earl thus insisted that there should be some indemnification for his losses suffered at the hands of the NWC before he would release either goods or furs. He proposed an investigation and arbitration by two neutral parties at London of all acts of aggression by either the NWC or himself for the past four years, with the principals liable for damages. The furs would be sent to the arbitrators in London as sureties, and until a decision was reached, the needs of his party would be met from NWC stock at Fort William at current prices. The clerks declined this proposal, which obviously would have left Selkirk in a commanding position.

In an unsent draft letter to Sir John Sherbrooke, Selkirk justified his actions in halting the trade. The goods heading west would have supplied "a band of Miscreant Halfbreeds" in a state of "nothing less than open rebellion against His Majesty's Government," while the furs were being held as a pledge for the restoration of his property and to force an arbitration. An injured party taking the property of a wrong-doer in order to obtain satisfaction was a principle of English law, he maintained, although not often employed in "the well regulated parts of the Empire." But in the western interior there was no regulation whatever, and Selkirk invoked William McGillivray himself in asserting that the only defence of property in the wilderness was retaliation. The letter eventually sent Sherbrooke on 3 September continued to defend the halting of western supplies, arguing that Red River was in a "state of rebellion," occupied by a "Banditti, who avow their determination to set the laws of their Country at defiance." But there was no mention of furs or retaliation. Instead, Selkirk advocated the appointment of a commissioner to sort out the controversy, insisting on his pleasure in being relieved from his present load of responsibility.

While Selkirk was establishing his position at Fort William, further loss of life in early September occurred outside his control. One of the canoes dispatched eastward with prisoners, including NWC partner Kenneth McKenzie, capsized in a sudden storm on Lake Superior with all its passengers lost. The NWC would make much of this mishap, claiming that the canoe was overloaded and Selkirk's people failed to take proper precautions. Archy McDonald would find some of the victims on his way east and bury them. When McDonald reached the Sault, he was dismayed to discover that Simon McGillivray had con-trived to send an express canoe to Montreal with his own version of Seven Oaks, the events at Fort William, and the canoe mishap. Thus Canada heard first of the events of 1816 from a Nor'Wester source.

To the west of Fort William, on 11 September, one of the HBC's agents, Owen Keveny, was brutally murdered by a Métis named Mainville and Charles de Reinhard, formerly a sergeant of the De Meuron Regiment but now in the employ of the NWC. Keveny had been arrested on 16 August under a warrant issued by Archibald McLeod and sent eastward to Fort William. The canoe in which he was travelling had turned back when word reached it that Selkirk had cap-tured the Fort. Keveny, who was quite ill, was probably killed because his captors did not want to free him and increasingly found him a bur-den, particularly given his caustic tongue. The murder of Keveny while under arrest would be used to justify several defiances of simi-lar warrants by Selkirk while he was in the West.

3. Consolidating the Position at Fort William:

In September, Selkirk consolidated his position by several acts of calculated aggression against the NWC. The earl's associates, headed by Dr. John Allan and Miles Macdonell, had been leaning heavily on Daniel McKenzie, the one NWC partner remaining at Fort William, over his culpability in the events in Red River. McKenzie was not well. He had to be allowed to make notes to himself over a period of several days in order to produce any coherent statement of his activities. He was afraid he would be left holding the bag for Red River, and Selkirk's people did not disabuse him of his concerns.

Selkirk and McKenzie came to an agreement on 19 September to send Selkirk's grievances against the NWC to two or more arbitrators chosen by the Lord Chief Justices in King's Bench and Common Pleas, Westminster. The parties were to indemnify each other for damages, with a decision to be reached by 1 December 1819. This was a reasonable way to settle the dispute between Selkirk and the NWC, and it would later be recommended by the commissioners of investigation. Whether McKenzie was the appropriate person to make this agreement was another matter. Even more dubious was the consignment by McKenzie to Selkirk of all furs and the sale of all property at Fort William. In return, the earl conveyed an estate worth £3,000 yearly to be held in trust. £50 in cash was handed on 19 September to McKenzie.

On Daniel McKenzie's behalf, Miles Macdonell wrote to the wintering partners of the NWC reporting the arbitration arrangement and asking them to consign this winter's furs to a neutral house in London. By English law, Miles argued, each partner had the right to act for the partnership at large. Meanwhile, Selkirk forwarded the documents in the McKenzie negotiations to his lawyers in Montreal. McKenzie was not a retired partner, he insisted, although he admitted the papers had been drawn up without legal advice. The lawyers would be suitably appalled at Selkirk's actions.

In the course of the examination of Daniel McKenzie, a good deal of other evidence relating to NWC activity against Red River was uncovered. McKenzie himself called attention to a locked press in a corner of the council room, where he said he had seen stored a parcel of letters taken from Jean-Baptiste Lagimodière at Fond du Lac. Dr. Allan forced the lock, and found inside wrapped in birch-bark most of the letters and papers entrusted to the courier, including warrants for the arrest of some of those active in the destruction of 1815. The packet was small and placed on a back shelf among loose wrapping papers. In Archibald McLeod's room was also found a meteorological journal

Simon McTavish

William McGillivray

Freighters leaving Fort William

kept by Peter Fidler which had been taken from Fidler after Seven Oaks. On 10 September one of the voyageurs confessed that he had been at Seven Oaks and had participated in the shooting. All this information was forwarded to Montreal.

Daniel McKenzie might not have been technically retired, but he was probably not sufficiently in command of his mental facilities to understand what he had done, even without his subsequent claims of inebriation, bad treatment, and intensive interrogation. In truth, being forced to dry out was probably the most severe pressure that could possibly be placed upon him, and Dr. Allan had advised against it. Such questions did not initially bother Selkirk. When Allan pointed out that buying furs and goods from McKenzie might be viewed as misrepresentation, Selkirk replied, "it would be absurd to abstain from doing anything merely to avoid being misrepresented by the NWCo. who had already misrepresented his best actions, and would invariably misrepresent his conduct however unimpeachable it might be."

Selkirk went beyond this argument — that he might as well be hung for a sheep as a goat — when he wrote to one legal acquaintance in London, "I flatter myself that the step which I have taken, tho' perhaps unusual, is not so far out of the common path, as to be in any degree improper." Indeed, had McKenzie been more responsible, it would have been a complete stroke of genius. As it was, by it, Selkirk exposed the weakness of the corporate structure of the NWC, completely disrupting its trade. The chaos he created would take years to undo. It could be argued that the Nor'Westers never did recover from this act of corporate guerilla warfare, particularly when it was combined with a complete takeover of the NWC posts on the canoe routes between Fort William and Red River.

P. C. Pambrun, Michael McDonell, and William Laidlaw had been dispatched to Fond du Lac with warrants for the arrest of the partners residing there for the robbery of Lagimodière. Laidlaw returned to Fort William in early October with James Grant and William Morrison, who readily admitted the robbery. They produced a letter from Archibald McLeod ordering them to do so. Grant said that he was in the council room when the packet of letters from Lagimodière was brought in with the seals still intact. Nobody would break them. The next day, however, the partners were reading them and handing them around. When one partner expressed surprise that the letters had been opened, another suggested that perhaps they had been opened by mice.

On 10 and 11 September, two divisions of De Meurons had been dispatched up the Kaministiquia to rendezvous at Lac la Pluie under the command of Captain Proteus D'Orsonnens. Four weeks later, on 9 October, D'Orsonnens reported that he had occupied Fort du lac la Pluie in the name of the HBC, using warrants issued by Selkirk. The Meurons had been forced to break down the gate of the fort, but had met little resistance within. A number of Nor'Westers had been put under arrest. Selkirk's aims, which were to re-establish the Old Grand Portage along the proposed international border and to control the canoe routes to the interior, had now been achieved. Whether D'Orsonnens could carry out his ultimate ambition, which was to send a winter expeditionary force to retake Fort Douglas at Red River, was another matter.

Selkirk spent a busy autumn in 1816, issuing orders to his forces in the field, both with an eye to reconquering Red River and to reopening the western trading routes to the HBC. He took advantage of a late express to the East not only to write to Sir John Sherbrooke, but also to his friend, hydrographer William Fitzwilliam Owen, about western surveys and boundaries. The earl noted that David Thompson's "survey on a large scale is hanging up in the great Hall of this Fort." Thompson's "neat drawing, the minuteness & apparent care bestowed on his plans" had impressed people, Selkirk asserted, but governments should not be deceived by a "piece of quackery." Everything on this survey was incorrect. To the Hudson's Bay Company committee he reported that he was making settlement headquarters at Lac la Pluie until Red River could be taken in the spring.

Meanwhile, in the Canadas, Selkirk's enemies and the colonial authorities were busy as well. Sir John Sherbrooke revoked the earl's commissions as magistrate and justice of the peace in the Indian Territories as part of a general process of cancellation of all commissions for the region. Instead, Sherbrooke appointed W. B. Coltman and John Fletcher as magistrates in the Territory, and as special commissioners to investigate the recent events in the West. A warrant was sworn against Selkirk at Sandwich in Upper Canada for forcible entry and detainer. An Upper Canadian constable named Robinson, a former sergeant-major, left Sandwich for Fort William with the warrant on 30 October, while Sir John Sherbrooke wrote to Lord Bathurst of the appointment of Messrs. Coltman and Fletcher. The entire western territory was up in arms, said Sherbrooke, and both sides in the fur trade struggle claimed they wanted the law properly introduced into the region. Selkirk had hoped the capture of Fort William would have produced moderation in the NWC, but instead it only seemed to excite them to desperation.

On 12 November, Selkirk sent off a special express with letters to Lieutenant-Governor Gore in Upper Canada and Sir John Sherbrooke in Quebec. To Gore he reported that a canoe had arrived at Fort William with two NWC clerks accompanied by a man who claimed to be a constable with warrants for his arrest. The warrant was irregular and full of perjuries, and the man carried no credentials. Since Selkirk could not conceive that Gore had ordered the arrest of one of his magistrates without reasons by a man lacking proper identification, he decided to regard the man as an imposter. He refused to accompany the man across Lake Superior under conditions probably "irregular & surreptitious." His determination was strengthened, he wrote, by learning that the Nor'Westers had sent a force of canoes to recover Fort William "either by strategem or by force, by legal pretexts or open violence."

Whether or not Selkirk was being disingenuous in his protestations, the fact was that the constable was quite genuine. A deposition about Selkirk's treatment of the Upper Canadian legal officer and his colleagues was sworn at York on 17 December. According to Robert McRobb, a clerk of the NWC, when the small party of officials had arrived in Fort William, the constable had gone to Selkirk's room and arrested him. He had subsequently also arrested Captain Matthey and John McNab. The Upper Canadians were told by Matthey to depart the fort, replying that he had no power to enforce his orders. Matthey answered, "that he should then make use of the means in his power to enforce obedience to his orders." The law officers were then guarded by seven armed Meurons in uniform until their forced departure from Fort William on 9 November. Selkirk had in disobedience found another way to short-circuit the NWC abuse of legal warrants. He would always claim, with some legitimacy, that he might have lost his life had he allowed himself to be arrested. But he would ultimately pay a heavy price for this defiance of the authority of the Crown.

4. The Athabasca:

While Selkirk was completely in control of the western route and the fur trade around Fort William in the autumn of 1816, John Clarke continued to be pushed around in the Athabasca country by the Nor'Westers, using the pretence of the law. Clarke had returned to the region in September of 1816, shadowed by Archibald McLeod, who was still sporting a red coat and a long sword to awe the First Nations. On reaching Fort Chipewyan, McLeod wrote to a colleague that he would expel the HBC totally from the region, adding, "it was ridiculous to be scrupulous in driving them out and destroying their posts, and he would stand at no trifle." The NWC man seized one of the HBC servants, claiming he was still engaged to the NWC, and threatened to take others as well. He made prisoners of several of Clarke's assistants as a justice of the peace, and refused to release them until "credible security" was given for their keeping the peace. McLeod's men also captured aboriginals who traded with the HBC.

Clarke wrote McLeod complaining of his behaviour, but the Nor'Wester answered verbally "that he was justifiable in all his actions and would let me know he was not come here for trifles."

After the arrival of a large brigade of Nor'Westers in early October, events turned from bad to worse at Fort Wedderburn. A red-faced Irishman named Hector McNeill was encouraged by the NWC to parade ostentatiously in front of Fort Wedderburn, and in the ensuing melee several men were wounded. Archibald McLeod summoned the HBC men to attend court at Fort Chipewyan, and when Clarke refused to appear, a party of armed Nor'Westers seized his people fishing above Fort Wedderburn. They were released only after swearing that they would not take up arms against British subjects for two years and after Clarke had appeared in the court. As soon as he entered Fort Chipewyan he was arrested and imprisoned. His assistants were also taken prisoner. Clarke found a Nor'Wester to act as his security only by giving him a large quantity of HBC property. This legal bullying was conducted in front of the local aboriginals, who were thus persuaded that the HBC could not protect them.

At Great Slave Lake, Archibald McLeod took advantage of a quarrel between two of the HBC traders to issue more warrants. Between arrests for breaking the peace and seizures of HBC servants on the grounds that they were still legally engaged to the NWC, McLeod soon completely dominated his rivals. He threatened to keep his prisoners in irons for the winter unless they swore allegiance to the NWC. He eventually forced Clarke to forfeit all the goods he had brought to the Peace River. Clarke would later insist that he was badly outnumbered in the region, the NWC having 7 partners, 12 clerks, and nearly 300 men in the Athabasca. The HBC could procure its share of the trade only "with an equal or something like equal force," he maintained. His subordinates would complaint about his mismanagement. About the only good news Clarke could report in December of 1816 was that he had recently learned that Selkirk was in control of Fort William and its surrounding territory.

The situation was little better at Ile-à-la-Crosse. On 11 January 1817, Peter Skene Ogden with six armed Canadians assaulted three of the HBC's servants conveying letters between Green Lake and Ile-à-la-Crosse, escorting them and their sledges to the house of John Thompson. A few days later, Ogden and Samuel Black headed a party of 30 Canadians and mixed-bloods which stopped another HBC express. According to John McLeod, when he had complained, Ogden had attacked him with a pistol, desisting only when McLeod drew his weapon.

Nevertheless, McLeod was taken to Thompson, who forced McLeod to bind himself for twelve months to keep the peace. He told McLeod that "he was obliged to act as he did." McLeod argued that the Red River people were the chief troublemakers, adding "If it was only the Masters we had to contend with, it would not be a hard matter, for their Bodies are not made of Iron more than ours." Rumours would circulate in the spring of 1817 that McLeod was still held prisoner. James Bird, acting governor of the HBC Northern Department, wrote Miles Macdonell in April for a force of men to meet the NWC canoes at the Grand Rapids, where the prisoners being taken east could be liberated.

5. The Reconquest of Red River:

On 2 December 1816, Selkirk wrote a lengthy letter to Captain D'Orsonnens at Lac la Pluie. The earl wrote of the "old contests between the Engl Colonies & the French of Canada," in which winter marches had been common. It was impossible to reinforce D'Orsonnens, and for him to pull back would be a "retrograde" step. Since government intervention could not yet be trusted and the wintering partners of the NWC were getting desperate, the best step might be to anticipate everybody by a winter march to Red River, capturing the artillery and dispersing the rebels. Unlike Miles Macdonell and Robert Semple, Selkirk argued that scruples had their limits. By concerting with the Indian chiefs it would be possible to march on snowshoes through the woods. He hoped the boredom of his people could be altered by "some brilliant pictures . . . from Red R to revive them & warm their imaginations westward."

At Lac la Pluie, Captain D'Orsonnens had considerable difficulty in responding to what appeared to be more than a suggestion but less than a order. Most of those under his command were opposed to the adventure. Their arguments were many. They pointed out that the distance was too great for men to carry a sufficient quantity of supplies, and the hunt was too precarious. The presence of Miles Macdonell at the fort advocating the scheme was no help, since many argued that Miles was desperate to redeem himself from his earlier embarrassments. Word from aboriginals that Fort Douglas had been taken by men from York Factory — it proved erroneous — seemed to make the attempt unnecessary. In the end, D'Orsonnens insisted that his party could not remain until spring at Lac la Pluie because of a shortage of provisions. He held out to his De Meurons and Canadian voyageurs the promise of feasting on the smoking limbs of fresh buffalo meat if they could reach their destination.

The difficulties of supply were to some extent resolved by forming a depot about halfway between Lac la Pluie and Red River at an NWC trading post at the southwest extremity of Lake of the Woods. A small party with four sledges drawn by most of the horses at Lac la Pluie set out for this depot with supplies of flour, wild rice, and a keg of spirits. Concerns about getting lost in the snow-covered winter conditions were obviated by the unexpected appearance of a qualified guide who knew well the territory between Lake of the Woods and the Red River. This was a man named John Tanner, who had lived among the aboriginals for many years and was known as "the American." Tanner had been captured as a child in Kentucky by a war party of Ottawas, and raised as a native at Michilimackinac. He had later followed his people to Lake of the Woods. Tanner could no longer speak English, although he had some memories of his childhood and wanted to visit his natural family again. Like most of his band, he did not like the abuse of the NWC. He offered to guide the expedition to Red River in return for eventual conveyance to Michilimackinac, where he could begin the quest for his origins.

The party of 25 De Meurons and a slightly larger number of Canadians set off on foot on 10 December. Each man had snowshoes, but there was not yet enough snow on the ground to justify their use. The weather proved extremely co-operative, with bright sunshine, moderate frost, and little wind. Every two men were allotted a hand sledge, on which they could carry their baggage and provisions. The rations were quite spartan, consisting of 30 pounds of bread per man baked into three–pound loaves, plus virtually unlimited wild rice and Indian corn. The expedition carried only 15 pounds of meat and a small quantity of rum. Three draft oxen were yoked to a sledge to carry the two pieces of artillery brought from Fort William. A bull, two cows, and a heifer were driven ahead by William Laidlaw. Miles Macdonell accompanied the men on a small cariole drawn by a horse, one of the few remaining at Lac la Pluie.

Traversing the ice of Lake of the Woods, the group reached the supply depot without mishap except the loss of one draft ox, which slipped on the ice and had to be killed. The bull being driven to Red River was yoked in the ox's place, although it had never been broken to the draught. The dead ox provided a welcome supply of fresh meat, which was distributed to the men in rations of 12 pounds per man. The Canadians ate their meat within two or three days, while the De Meurons managed to make their ration last for over two weeks.

The road beyond Lake of the Woods was more difficult than that leading up to it. There was more bush and trees which had to be cut down. The party of 60 Canadians and De Meurons was joined outside Lake of the Woods on 24 December by a small group of five aboriginals led by Chief Pin-panche, who acted as scouts to make sure that the expedition was not discovered by the Nor'Westers as it made its way to Pembina. A buffalo bull was shot a few miles from the Red River.

On 31 December, Fort Daer was captured by parties led by Captain D'Orsonnens and Lieutenant McDonald. The little army had demonstrated that winter weather, while formidable, need not prevent all military activities. They found no Nor'Westers, and only a handful of Canadian freemen and their families occupying the buildings. On the other hand, all the buildings at Fort Daer were full of piles of frozen buffalo meat. The little army feasted, and consumed the two kegs of rum which Miles Macdonell had carried on his cariole. Miles was happy to find that Fort Daer was fairly intact, with only its floors, doors, and windows having been taken away. There were, however, no fresh horses to be found anywhere in the neighbourhood.

On 2 January D'Orsonnens set off for the Forks, still accompanied by "the American." He would have to act quickly, since the presence of such a large party of men could not for long be kept secret. Weather conditions quickly deteriorated, as an extreme storm blew in from the northwest with snow and wind of intense cold. While the weather proved an obstacle, slowing the party to the point that it took over a week to made the 70 miles to Fort Douglas, it was a blessing as well. The Nor'Westers were not likely to be out and about in such conditions, nor would they expect to be attacked.

At the Rivière Sale (the La Salle River), the party were welcomed by Chief Peguis and nine members of his band of Saulteaux, who startled the Meurons. Only with difficulty did D'Orsonnens prevent his men from firing. He had just as much trouble preventing Peguis from discharging his firearms in a salute to the newcomers. Either action might have given the alarm to the opposition. The men ate that evening the last of their provisions, plus a few buffalo tongues furnished by Peguis, and warmed themselves at the fire. Miles managed to find a bit of spirits which "afforded an encouraging dram to all hands." Unfortunately, many of the Meurons, inexperienced with such winter conditions, thawed their shoes and socks in front of the fire. The footgear was wet when put on the next morning. As a result, 17 Meuron plus several Canadians experienced frostbite. These were the only casualties of the march, however.

D'Orsonnens led his men up to Fort Douglas in the dark winter morning at six a.m. on 10 January. They could hear the barking of dogs and could see sparks from the chimneys within, indicating that fires were being supplied with fresh logs. At the last moment, it was discovered the scaling ladders that were brought to the walls proved not long enough. The ladders had been made hastily by cutting a tree trunk with the limbs left long enough to step on. While the invaders were attempting to sort this out, Seraphim La Mar, whose house was close to the walls, came to his door and called out, "Who is there?" "It is I," replied interpreter Louis Nolin, in French. "But who are you?" said Mr. La Mar. "It is I," again answered Nolin. "But who are you?" queried La Mar again. By this time, "the American" had scaled the walls and unbarred the gate. Nolin brandished his pistol at La Mar, forcing him inside his house.

D'Orsonnens and Miles Macdonell headed to the quarters of Mr. McLellan, whom they met trouserless outside his bedroom. McLellan complained that the intruders had entered the fort like robbers. D'Orsonnens replied that Macdonell certainly had a right to enter his own house and asked McLellan how he justified his possession of the property of others. The Nor'Wester replied that he was only a lodger and the fort was actually in the possession of the mixed-bloods. McLellan was the partner who had been involved in ordering the murder of Owen Keveny, and a number of incriminating documents were found in his quarters. According to John Tanner, McLellan was at first thrown out into the snow, but was later brought inside to prevent his becoming frozen. McLellan, Seraphim La Mar, Soussants Voudrie, and François Mainville were kept under confinement. Joseph Cadotte was released after making a "very humble and submissive apology for his conduct," immediately heading off to collect a band of mixed-bloods to menace the fort.

Fort Douglas contained very little provisions and was devoid of tools and agricultural implements. It did house several pieces of colonial artillery and a quantity of small arms. Some of the invading party was sent back to Fort Daer to live off the buffalo. Those left at the Forks scavenged for food from the surrounding trading posts of both the NWC and HBC.

Sleds sent from Bas de la Rivière with food intended for the Nor'Westers was welcome, as was the news that only six men were at the post. Mr. Laidlaw and a small party subsequently captured the fort at Bas de la Rivière without any resistance, finding more guns than food. A group of mixed-bloods led by Cuthbert Grant arrived in the area shortly after the seizure of Fort Douglas. They killed some of the cattle in the settlement and imprisoned some Canadians returning to the Fort with provisions. But despite a numerical advantage they did not attack the forts, probably in part because the invaders brought with them copies of the proclamation of the Governor-General calling for the laying down of arms by all participants in the fur trade wars. In the course of an interchange of correspondence with Grant, Miles Macdonell had sent him a copy of the proclamation. Grant is supposed to have thrown a copy of the proclamation in the fire, saying "voilà encore une de ces sacres proclamations." But he likely was influenced by it nonetheless, as well as by an awareness of the risks of violence. When Joseph Cadotte advocated a raiding party against Fort Daer, Grant rejected the idea out of hand, saying "We are not barbarians."

Not all of Selkirk's military initiatives were as successful as the reconquest of Red River. Lieutenant Antoine de Graffenreid with 22 De Meuron soldiers and a handful of Canadians had gotten lost in the woods while attempting to reinforce La Pluie. When their provisions were finished, Graffenried reported, they were forced to boil and eat their snowshoes and one of the dogs with them. Finally finding the fort and getting food from it, Graffenreid's men did "nothing but cook and eat all day." When they finally arrived at Lac la Pluie on 27 January 1817, the men found the fort stripped bare and virtually empty. His men could not follow D'Orsonnens to Red River, wrote Graffenreid, and he himself felt "the want of liquor more than I could believe." Graffenreid subsequently got lost again while trying to get from Lac la Pluie to Fort Douglas. Such experiences only demonstrated how fortunate the Red River expedition really had been, particularly in the employment of "the American" to guide the way.

Isolated as he was at Fort William, Selkirk would not learn of the success and failures of his little army until the spring of 1817. The rush of mail as the lakes and rivers opened would bring some good news and much bad. But the reoccupation of Fort Douglas undoubtedly represented the high point of Selkirk's military adventuring. By late 1816, the governments in Canada and in Britain had finally stirred themselves to become involved in events in the West. In part they were spurred by Selkirk's unilateral actions. The appointment of the Coltman Commission in 1817 would mark the beginning of a new phase in the fur trade wars — one that would prove even more costly and debilitating for Lord Selkirk than the violence of the previous two years.

~9~

The Coltman Commission

With the appointment in October 1816 of the commission of investigation headed by William Batchelor Coltman, the fur trade wars moved into a new stage. Both the NWC and Selkirk were calling for an impartial investigation, but initially Sir John Sherbrooke had despaired of finding anyone credible enough to serve. His colleague in Upper Canada, Lieutenant-Governor Francis Gore, was unable to help. Both officials found the influence of the NWC pervasive. At the last moment, two candidates emerged.

William Coltman had been born in England, but resided in Quebec from 1799. He operated with his brother John as a merchant, but was not closely associated with the NWC. His subsequent work as commissioner demonstrated that he had some legal training and experience, although we know nothing about this side of his life. He did not claim to be a lawyer. Coltman was appointed a justice of the peace in 1810, and had been made an executive councillor of Lower Canada in 1812.

His junior colleague in the commission, John Fletcher, was also born in England and had made a reputation as a brilliant attorney in London before coming suddenly to Canada in 1810. There is a whiff of scandal, probably involved with excess consumption of alcohol, but nothing is definite. Fletcher certainly had a reputation for being eccentric. He had served as an officer in the militia during the War of 1812, and he was compulsively fascinated with matters military. Like Coltman, he was not closely associated with the NWC, although there were rumours he had been employed by the Nor'Westers. In any event, Fletcher would prove less neutral than his senior commissioner. He was intended to provide legal expertise, but never advised Coltman.

Indeed, the two men never worked together at all in the interior. Both men were not only given commissions as justices of the peace for the Indian Territory, but were given military commissions in the Indian Department. Coltman was commissioned a colonel and Fletcher a major. Coltman was also to be richly remunerated for his efforts, being given a bonus of 750 guineas, a salary of £1,800 per annum, and all contingent expenses.

The commission had attempted to begin executing its mandate in the autumn of 1816, but it was unable to get beyond the Nottawasagua and turned back. While in the West Coltman and Fletcher took many depositions from NWC employees. It would take some months for word of the commission's appointment to percolate into the interior. During this period, the Selkirk forces had made considerable gains, including the reconquest of Red River. Moreover, during the winter of 1816-17 the British government became more actively involved in affairs in the West. Lord Bathurst issued a series of controversial orders to the governments of the Canadas which would greatly affect the treatment given to Lord Selkirk and certainly led colonial officials (and Selkirk's friends) to believe that the Colonial Office had taken the side of the NWC in the dispute. By the spring of 1817 and the opening of transportation to the West, all sides — but especially Lord Selkirk — were placed in a defensive position.

As events unfolded in 1817, it became increasingly apparent that one of the most serious issues of the controversy to be resolved involved legal jurisdiction in western British North America. Jurisdiction in some senses overlapped and in other senses did not exist. The matter was never totally settled when the Coltman commission was appointed. The commissioners had in theory replaced all previous legal authority in the Indian Territories, but the jurisdiction of Upper Canada was never completely eliminated. Moreover, it was not entirely clear that the commission could supersede the power of the HBC within the territory of its charter. Some of these questions would be fought out between Coltman and Selkirk at Red River, and then taken to the courts of the Canadas.

1. The Maneuvering of the Winter of 1816:

The winter closure of the lines of communication to eastern Canada spared Lord Selkirk the horrified negative reactions of his Montreal advisors to his decisions until the spring. Samuel Gale, for example, wrote that Selkirk's proposals to the NWC clerks Vandersluys and McTavish — well-publicized in the local press — were considered an offer "to compound felonies murders & other crimes."

Worse still, the arrangements with McKenzie were improper since he was not specifically authorized to do such business. These transactions, Gale insisted, only provided an excuse for other charges against the earl. His lawyers would have much preferred Selkirk under their watchful eye. Samuel Gale advised the earl to return to Montreal unless he found it "expeditiously necessary" to remain with the commissioners headed west. He reported that the NWC would probably attack both Fort William and York Factory in the spring.

Selkirk spent the winter sketching, relaxing, getting outside, and writing letters to his people scattered in the interior. In one letter to Michael McDonell in Wisconsin, for example, he warned that the NWC would likely try to use American warrants against him. He advised McDonell to sit tight and remember that his location was still territory disputed between the United States and Britain. In another letter to Donald McPherson, the earl enclosed extracts from three different books with directions for brewing beer from wild rice. Presumably the books were in the NWC library at Fort William. To Captain Graffenreid, Selkirk wrote that he had forwarded a keg of rum which had been rectified to a high alcoholic content for easier transport by Dr. Allan and Captain Matthey. Some of his sketches have survived and demonstrate that he was a competent watercolourist, as were most British travellers in the age before the camera.

In England, Henry Goulburn at the Colonial Office responded to a letter from HBC governor Joseph Berens providing news of the "most savage massacre" at Seven Oaks by observing that the situation had changed from a dispute of "conflicting claims of two Mercantile Companies" to one exchanging outrages which each blamed on the other. The courts would now settle the questions of culpability and jurisdiction in the West, Goulburn added, "it being the only justification of some of the late Acts committed."

A few days later, the London agents of the NWC proposed to the HBC that because of the "continuance of disputes and cabals in the Indian country," all the property and posts seized be restored without prejudice to the recovery of damages, the issues resolved by a competent tribunal in London. Had requests from both sides for government intervention been met, they added, much of the mischief could probably have been prevented. Selkirk's actions had certainly contributed to, and probably forced, the NWC to look for co-operation with their rivals to resolve the controversies.

The search for co-operation did not mean that the NWC gave up its own efforts in the corridors of power. The deposition by Robert McRobb accusing Selkirk of resisting a legal warrant, which had been sworn in Montreal in December of 1816, was in Lord Bathurst's hands in early February of 1817. It did not get there through government channels. On learning of Selkirk's capture of Fort William at the head of a force of mercenary soldiers, the Colonial Secretary had earlier urged the earl's return to Britain to substantiate the charges of murder he had made against those he had arrested. He also instructed the HBC that His Majesty's government wished the directors to order Selkirk home and to dismiss him if he failed to comply. The HBC directors replied that they had no control over Selkirk.

To Sir John Sherbrooke, an angry Bathurst responded to the McRobb deposition by writing of his concern for Britain's commercial and political interests following Selkirk's "admission of foreign influence over the Indian Territories," ostensibly to end the violence which had too long prevailed. By resisting warrants for his arrest, Bathurst added, Selkirk had made himself doubly amenable to the law. The government would enforce the law against him. Sherbrooke was instructed to prefer an indictment against Selkirk and to arrest him, even if it was necessary to do so under the Canada Jurisdictions Act. These categorical instructions of Bathurst would influence the actions of colonial officials in Canada for several years, since they could be interpreted as an official repudiation of Selkirk's conduct. Sherbrooke was also instructed to inform Selkirk of the substance of his instructions, if not the actual text. For some reason, the Lower Canadian governor did not do a very good job of this communication.

Why Bathurst responded with such vehemence to the accounts of Selkirk's behaviour presented to him by the NWC has never been entirely clear. In principle it was certainly true that the British government could not condone a peer of the realm leading a private army and resisting legal Crown warrants. But this response ignored the fact that the government had resolutely refused for years to intervene in the fur trade dispute in order to bring law and order into the territories. Selkirk's people were certain that Henry Goulburn and probably Bathurst himself were entirely too friendly with Edward "Bear" Ellice and other NWC people in Britain. It was certainly true that the NWC had a much easier access to the ear of the minister than did the officials of the HBC, but what this meant is less certain. The question of access may simply have reflected the willingness of the NWC representatives to press for personal meetings with the colonial secretary. The HBC's correspondence with the Colonial Office gives the impression of a reluctance to soil its hands over the business.

Most probably, Bathurst's reaction was simply visceral and ill-considered, ignoring the possibility that there might be another side to the story. The colonial secretary might well have been aggravated by a realization that Selkirk had forced the government's hand. For years

Bathurst had resisted involving the British administration in the question of the HBC charter. He was now prepared to sponsor legislation defining the limits of HBC territory as the "mode most likely to prevent the recurrence of those mischiefs which had taken place." To some extent, this determination reflected a recognition that there was some uncertainty over whether the British government had direct authority over the territory claimed by the HBC according to its charter. The HBC itself backed off a confrontation on this point, and agreed that its people in North America would recognize the Coltman commission without prejudice to the larger issue.

In the West, Lord Selkirk was away from Fort William when the first canoes of the spring arrived in 1817. One canoe contained some of Lady Selkirk's letters. In one of these she noted that the cost of Selkirk's actions was mounting. Lady Selkirk added, "And it really will be little short of ruin if you go on with your own private funds. I acknowledge I cannot swallow the exchange of St Mary's Isle for your kingdom on Red River."

A later canoe brought the official announcements about the Coltman commission and the revocation of all other commissions. Another canoe also brought a deputy-sheriff, William Smith, from Upper Canada to arrest Selkirk. The earl pointed out to this individual that all commissions west of the Sault had been revoked by government, although it was not clear that this applied to warrants issued in the Western District of Upper Canada. Selkirk would later complain to Lieutenant-governor Gore about the behaviour of Smith. The deputy-sheriff continued to hang around the fort, then kept attempting to execute his warrants. Selkirk tried to throw him out, then placed him under armed guard within the fort, giving yet another example of resistance to authority, however dubiously legal.

Others in Selkirk's entourage became implicated in this resistance. Smith complained in writing to A. B. Becher, who wrote to Selkirk as an "impartial person in the service of His Majesty" to enquire about the law officer's treatment. Selkirk responded that with the appointment of the Coltman Commission came the revocation of all commissions of peace west of the falls of St. Mary. Smith should have known about this revocation before proceeding. Nobody would interfere with his liberty if he were not so insistent about executing his illegal writs. Smith would subsequently protest to Sir John Sherbrooke about his treatment at Fort William, adding that Selkirk's military escort had not only failed to respond to his appeals for assistance, but had rescued several individuals whom he had apprehended. Smith noted that he carried a military order to Sergeant Pugh of the 37th which Pugh refused to receive until he had consulted Selkirk.

As Sir John Sherbrooke would observe to Selkirk of the sergeant, "the poor fellow has certainly been placed in a situation of great difficulty."

In early April, Selkirk learned of the reoccupation of Fort Douglas. A few days later, a rush of mail assured him that his family was flourishing in Montreal. A girl had been born to Lady Selkirk without incident on 4 January. She would be named Katherine Jean and Lady Sherbrooke would be the godmother. Fortunately the news was positive on the personal front, for what Selkirk learned from his business correspondence was hardly encouraging. His Montreal attorney, James Stuart, was even more brutally critical of the deal with Daniel McKenzie than Samuel Gale. There was no legal way to make the furs answerable for Selkirk's claims, Stuart insisted. Moreover, McKenzie could not bind his co-partners to arbitration, which was allowing him more latitude as a partner than did either English or Canadian law. While the sale of goods could be claimed as valid by Selkirk, Stuart frankly doubted its legitimacy, and recommended that the earl leave all remaining goods when he departed the fort. In conclusion, Stuart observed that the warrants against Selkirk were all quite legal, and he could only hope that his client was beyond their reach by the time they were served, preferably re-establishing the power of his government at Red River.

Selkirk never expressed any regrets over defying the law officers, but he did write in chastened tone to his wife about "my wretchedly ill-judged conduct in September." He added that he had written Sir John Sherbrooke apologizing for the September actions, thinking "it was better to take the responsibility frankly on myself than to attempt to evade it and hope that my letter would at least show that my error was rather an exception than a specimen of my general conduct." Heeding Andrew Stuart's warning, he ordered only necessary supplies and his own goods packed for the journey to Red River.

In letters to William Coltman dated 28 April, Selkirk apologized for not remaining at Fort William to greet the commissioners. He also apologized for exposing himself to misrepresentation "through my own imprudence" in dealing with Daniel McKenzie. He further noted that Messrs. Spencer and McNab were named in the warrants carried by Deputy-sheriff Smith, but Selkirk was sure that the commission would not sanction those documents. On 1 May, his party — including his manservant William, Captain de Lorimier, and William Laidlaw — left Fort William. Dr. Allan would follow later. John McNab was left in charge of Fort William, with orders to hand it over to the commissioners or persons authorized by them when they arrived. The journey to Red River went exceptionally well, although not swiftly. To his wife, Selkirk reported, "I never was in better health, and in fact have enjoyed a vigour of health since I have been under my tent, such as I hardly knew when living in a house." The group would arrive at the Forks exactly seven weeks later, on 21 June.

2. The Coltman Commission Heads West:

T he party containing the Coltman Commission was not the only one organizing in Lower Canada to head west in the spring of 1817. The Nor'Westers had been collecting men all winter for what was widely rumoured to be a major attack on Selkirk at Fort William in the spring. A brigade sent in the autumn of 1816 had foundered in the gales of Lake Superior, and had been forced to turn back. William McGillivray himself personally led the NWC force from Lachine by the first canoes possible. McGillivray had plenty of incentive for his haste. Selkirk was in occupation of the entire western canoe route from Lake Superior to Fort Douglas. He had seized and arguably purchased about £100,000 worth of furs, the proceeds from which were absolutely essential to keep the NWC solvent. To make matters worse, John Jacob Astor was asserting American rights south of the 49th parallel.

At the same time, Lady Selkirk had personally recruited another body of De Meuron soldiers, who would serve in the dual capacity of settlers and defenders of the settlement. The Selkirk/HBC party gathering at Lachine consisted of 48 De Meurons, 45 wives, and 55 Canadian voyageurs and fur traders. She wrote her brother, "I plume myself much on them as they are my throw entirely," and would make "a very effective addition to the Posse comitatis of Red River." Lady Selkirk put the De Meurons under the command of Archy McDonald. She had also persuaded Samuel Gale, one of Selkirk's attorneys, to accompany the party west, principally to provide legal advice to her husband in his dealings with the Coltman Commission. Gale was a small timid man, the son of Loyalists. He was more than a bit of a hypochondriac. A bachelor in his thirties, he worshipped Lady Selkirk. This canoe journey to Red River would be the great adventure of his life. Gale was accompanied by John Pritchard as his assistant.

After the Nor'Wester brigade had set off, Major John Fletcher was the next to depart Lachine for the West. He left with his corpulent body attired in full military uniform, accompanied by a guard of 14 soldiers. William Coltman remained behind, apparently concerned about the intentions of the Meurons. The Nor'Westers appeared at Lachine with depositions that the De Meuron party was armed to the teeth and determined to fight. As a precaution, Lady Selkirk already had sent a list of the entire cargo of the canoes sworn before a magistrate to avoid charges that they were carrying war stores.

Nonetheless, Coltman ordered the Prince Regent's proclamation about all military persons leaving the service of either party read to the De Meurons. When the reading was over, a Canadian in the HBC party stepped up to Coltman and asked, "Est ce tout Monsieur?" Surprised, Coltman responded, "Oui Monsieur." The Canadian answered, "Eh bien si cela est tout, vive Lord Selkirk." All the De Meurons took off their hats and cheered, "Vive Lord Selkirk!" Coltman took oaths from the entire Selkirk party, and finally permitted them to depart. He would not admit Samuel Gale into his canoe, reported Lady Selkirk to her brother, but she had anticipated this and provided one for the lawyer, with "as many comforts as I could procure for my champion, and a little flag which he demanded with the arms and motto which had taken his fancy amazingly when he saw them on the seal." She added, "It is bad to go on, but worse to go back, that is all I can say."

Trouble resurfaced at the Sault, where Samuel Gale's canoe caught up with those of the commissioners. Major Fletcher objected to Gale's presence at the investigations, saying it did not seem proper to adopt suggestions or put questions "proceeding from an advocate when there was an advocate on one side only." This attitude bothered Gale, for if the commissioners ignored him, there would be the appearance of legal counsel for Selkirk but not the reality. The lawyer was even more disturbed when he learned that Colonel Coltman was departing alone for Fort William, and had invited Gale to join him in his canoe. Gale learned that Major Fletcher was not going on immediately to Fort William, but was remaining behind with his soldiers. Gale was convinced that Fletcher's job was to delay and deter the Meurons from joining Selkirk. In his cups, Fletcher later told a British officer (who told Gale) that Coltman had left to avoid being implicated in the proceedings, leaving Fletcher to "get through the affair as well as he could."

Even Samuel Gale had to admit that Major Fletcher's behaviour at Sault Ste Marie was ludicrous and would have been amusing had the stakes not been so high. "Sometimes the occurrences of the last fortnight have produced melancholy, at other times indignation, and at other times it has been impossible to avoid laughter." Gale's reports of Fletcher's buffooneries were confirmed by depositions from British officers who were equally offended by them. Fletcher was a drunkard who consumed alcoholic beverages from morning to night but somehow continued to function. He was also a man fascinated and obsessed with military drill, in which he could engage with his little detachment for hours. He ingeniously combined these two penchants to frustrate and aggravate the party being led west by Archy McDonald. Samuel Gale recognized the danger perfectly well. If any of Selkirk's party lost their temper, Fletcher would have an excuse for further action. Gale advised McDonald's people to meet every act of aggression with Christian forbearance. He was prepared to allow that Colonel Coltman was a neutral, but obviously had considerable doubts about Major Fletcher.

Fletcher seized the eight cases of trading guns from the HBC canoes and refused to listen to Gale's legal objections. "I act *en militaire*," he proclaimed at one point. As the Montreal lawyer well knew, Fletcher was quite correct in his assertion that "there were no great Chams of Tartary in this part of the world" but the commissioners, who "might do as they chose with anything." On 9 June, Simon McGillivray arrived at the encampment. Gale described a meeting with McGillivray at Fletcher's tent. The Nor'Wester was "armed with a pair of hair trigger duelling pistols, a fowling piece with a Spanish barrel, and Egg's waterproof lock, and a coteau de chasse."

As for Major Fletcher, in the presence of Gale and McGillivray he ostentatiously loaded his pocket pistols and his double-barreled fowling piece with ball cartridge, three balls per cartridge. Although Gale insisted that there was no law prohibiting the Selkirk party from proceeding, they were not authorized to depart. Frustrated by the delays, Archibald McDonald wrote a letter of protest and announced his intention to proceed regardless. The Major met Archy's canoes at the first portage with his detachment of soldiers, arms at the ready. He ordered the men to drop their packs and took McDonald into custody, subsequently releasing him. Not until 20 June were McDonald's canoes allowed to proceed to the entrance to Lake Superior. There they paused for several days before Fletcher allowed them to enter the lake and proceed with him to Fort William. By this time, it was certainly too late to get any of the party to the Athabasca.

3. The First Restoration of Property:

Whatever the other intentions of the commissioners, the effect of their actions was to allow the Nor'Westers to re-enter Fort William uncontested. John McNab had been left by Selkirk on 1 May in charge of the fort, with orders to give it up peaceably to the commissioners when they arrived.

William McGillivray with a large number of men in six canoes arrived on 29 May at Fort William. He immediately demanded all the keys. He placed John McNab and John Spencer in adjoining apartments under the watchful eye of a constable. John Spencer reported that a guard accompanied McNab and Spencer everywhere, even "to the necessary." McGillivray admitted that he had no authority and denied that McNab was his prisoner, insisting that he had been committed under the authority of Deputy-sheriff Smith. In any event, McNabb and Spencer were taken under custody from the fort on 2 June, while the Nor'Westers got on with the task of assessing the damage done to the fort and the NWC by Selkirk's occupation. A few days later the Selkirk men met Commissioner Coltman travelling west. On 13 June they were reporting to Gale and Major Fletcher at the Sault, on their way to Sandwich to answer charges of having forcibly entered Fort William. On that same day, two NWC canoes arrived at the fort at Lac la Pluie. Deputy-sheriff Smith advanced with a piece of paper (it was the proclamation) in his hands, demanding admittance. When refused, he called for an axe. A number of Nor'Westers cut their way into the fort without the proclamation ever having been read. The HBC men occupying the fort were quickly sent packing.

On 20 June, the Selkirk entourage met NWC partner Angus Shaw on the Red River. Shaw asked Selkirk whether he had seen the Red River proclamation. Selkirk said he had not. Shaw said that he had come directly from England, where he had confidential communications with His Majesty's ministers. He added that the proclamation he handed to Selkirk demonstrated that the HBC and Selkirk had no more right to the country than anyone else. The proclamation ordered a mutual restitution of all property. Shaw demanded that Selkirk send an order to Bas de la Rivière to surrender the fort. Selkirk replied that he had already given such an order. Captain de Lorimier then informed Selkirk that Deputy-sheriff Smith was in the canoe with Shaw.

Dr. Allan and Lord Selkirk, accompanied by Sergeant Pugh and his military escort, arrived at Fort Douglas on the evening of 21 June. Two days later, Lieutenant Graffenreid arrived from Bas de la Rivière. He had opened the gate on being shown the Prince Regent's proclamation by Angus Shaw and Deputy-sheriff Smith, he reported. The latter, claiming it his duty, had seized the furs of the HBC. On 24 June, Shaw and Smith also arrived at Fort Douglas. Smith was immediately arrested by Governor Macdonell as a disturber of the public peace. The next day, John Shaw requested an interview with Selkirk. He demanded the return of the furs and other property of the NWC which had been in the fort when Captain D'Orsonnens had taken pos-

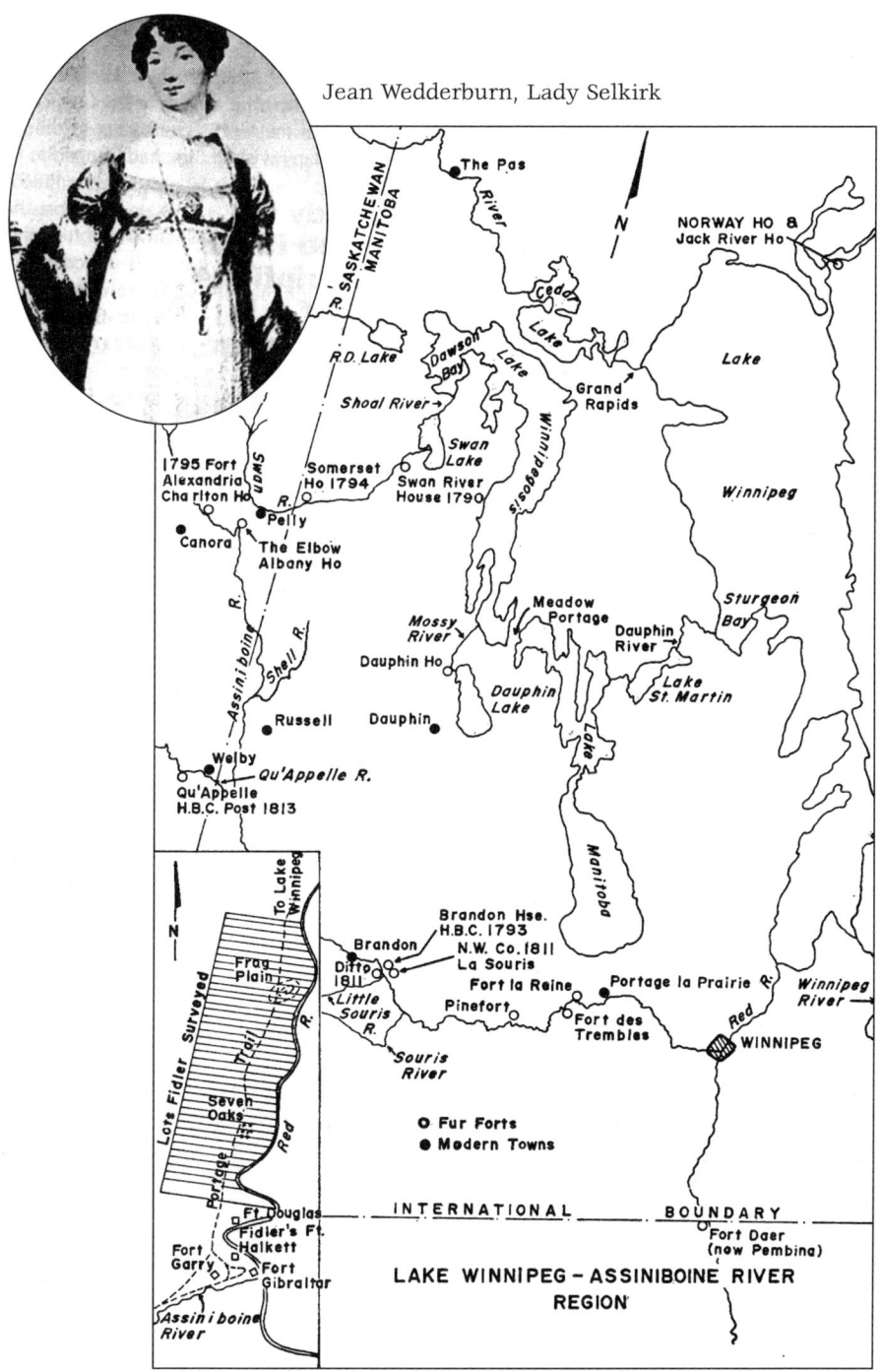

Jean Wedderburn, Lady Selkirk

LAKE WINNIPEG – ASSINIBOINE RIVER REGION

session of it. Selkirk replied that Shaw could take everything that could be ascertained to belong to the NWC except two brass cannon, which would be delivered up to the King's commissioners. Shaw insisted that the mixed-bloods were not under the control of the NWC. They were regarded by the Nor'Westers as was any other band of aboriginals. He extended this declaration to Cuthbert Grant, Alexander Fraser, and Roderick MacKenzie, and later told Selkirk that he considered his own son William as "merely an Indian."

On a more positive note, Selkirk met John Tanner at Fort Douglas. "The American" had spent the remainder of the winter and spring of 1817 hiding with the aboriginals from the wrath of the NWC before taking refuge with Selkirk's people. The earl was not only grateful to Tanner, but quite fascinated with his story. He promised to assist the American to return to his relations, and would keep his word. In his later memoir, Tanner related that Selkirk became "very impatient" waiting for Commissioner Coltman. This was quite understandable, since Selkirk's reputation and the future of his settlement both depended on the commissioner's adjudication of the dispute and his eventual report.

The impatience was not reduced by news coming to Selkirk from all quarters that the Nor'Westers were behaving in their usual arrogant fashion. Nor was it helped by a letter from Sir John Sherbrooke brought by an express, which alluded to certain measures for the due execution of the law which the governor wrote he had received in instructions from the British government and was entrusting to the commissioners. Sherbrooke noted that the measures would seriously affect Selkirk, but he did not fully explain them, thus ignoring his explicit instructions from Lord Bathurst. Unfortunately, Samuel Gale was not yet on hand to provide calming advice. Delayed by Major Fletcher, Gale was only making his way to Fort William during the period Selkirk anxiously awaited Coltman at Fort Douglas.

4. Coltman at Red River:

Not surprisingly, Selkirk wrote to the commissioners from Fort Douglas on 28 June, complaining that while he was complying with the injunctions of the proclamation, the NWC was engaged in new acts of aggression. He also protested strenuously about the actions of "soi-distant" Deputy-sheriff Smith, "who has the effrontery to assume the powers of a magistrate in this territory." He concluded by insisting that the commission should be arranging the restitution, rather than one party seizing "with the strong hand what-ever they may pretend to claim as their own wherever they may have the power to enforce their claim." This would be the beginning of a long protracted series of disagreements between Commissioner Coltman and Selkirk over the role of the commission and the alleged favouritism shown to the NWC.

Colonel Coltman continued majestically beyond Fort William towards Red River. He stopped briefly at Bas de la Rivière but took no action against the Nor'Westers he found there. From the head of the Red River he wrote a letter to Selkirk stating that he had come on in advance of the remainder of his party in hopes of being useful. Coltman briefly outlined his plan of conduct. He emphasized that the Prince Regent's first objectives, as stated by Lord Bathurst, were the cessation of hostilities, the mutual restoration of all property, and the pacification of the country. Thus "the enquiry into & investigation of past offences will consequently stand last in point of time." The emphasis would be placed on measures for the future rather than con-siderations of the past. Such a strategy could hardly please Selkirk and his people, whose principal interest was legal retribution against those who had been harassing the settlement and the HBC for years.

At the Forks, which he reached on 5 July, Coltman pointedly ignored Selkirk's salute and ordered his four canoes paddled about a mile above Fort Douglas. Here he pitched his tent and dined with part-ners of the NWC. The corpulent Coltman also dined with Selkirk and his "gentlemen" the following day, successfully reassuring the earl that he was impartial.

Selkirk was considerably less convinced that the commissioner really understood the situation, however well disposed he might be. Selkirk tried to explain the problem as he saw it to Coltman in a letter of 7 July. Most of the disorder resulted from the habit of the Nor'Westers to take the law into their own hands. If Selkirk's people had responded in kind, it was because there was no alternative. The NWC had ignored the Prince Regent's injunction to abstain from vio-lence in every case where they had the advantage, such as at Fort William and Lac la Pluie. Coltman would accomplish little if Selkirk's people and the HBC could "see no check put on outrages which have thus been committed almost under your eye." The Nor'Westers need-ed a practical lesson about the impropriety of their conduct, which implied legal action against their excesses.

Meanwhile, Major Fletcher and Samuel Gale, arrived at Fort William on 4 July. Gale immediately sat down to write a letter to Lady Selkirk reporting with considerable indignation on the outrages of Major Fletcher. "Does it not seem probable" he speculated, "that orders have been received from England for something like a hunt against the E of S thro the influence of the under friends of the NW's at home?" Two days later, the Selkirk brigade commanded by Archibald McDonald also arrived. Archy and Colonel Robert Dickson (the war hero and Indian interpreter who had joined the Selkirk party at the Sault) went to visit at Fort William. They became involved in what Dickson described as a "waubano," or general drunk. They ended up in Major Fletcher's tent, where the major sat at table with a number of Nor'Westers, surrounded by decanters of shrub, spirits, and brandy.

The major boasted of his absolute power and turned unexpectedly to McDonald to say that he could cause the visitor to be hanged in an hour. McDonald made some answer and was accused of impudence. He was taken into custody and told by Major Fletcher, "I can hang you in an hour, sir, after you are in custody, upon a gallows eight feet from the ground, I can have you shot, I will put you in irons, and I will have you tied hand and foot and flogged seven dozen with all the good humour imaginable, in the true camp style with the strap of a musket." When he ordered McDonald tied down to "give him two dozen," Dickson protested and was supported by one of the British officers present, Lieutenant Austin. "What, sir," asked the major, "do you say I am wrong?" Dickson responded, "Yes sir. You are damned wrong." Fletcher backed off and ordered a guard to take McDonald away. The guard asked where he should be taken. "Take him to hell," replied the major. Archy was given a bed for the night by one of the Nor'Westers. He would be released in the morning. He was so shaken by his experience that he accepted Samuel Gale's advice to leave the brigade to their own leaders and return to Montreal.

At the Forks, Lord Selkirk was quickly disabused of any hope he may have had that Colonel Coltman would move to investigate the outrages committed against his settlement in 1815 and 1816 by immediately calling witnesses and hearing testimony. Instead, the earl found himself haggling over the restoration of property and other matters he regarded as peripheral, while individuals who had played a leading role at Seven Oaks were allowed to come and go as they pleased. Worse still to his mind, he learned that Coltman in effect was granting immunity to most of the mixed-bloods in return for their evidence. Conscious of his heavy losses in the Athabasca district, Selkirk understandably wanted a simultaneous restoration of all property throughout the Indian country.

Simon McGillivray insisted that restitution start immediately with Red River. Selkirk maintained that only property illegally seized should be returned, while the Nor'Westers wanted everything included since to make inventories of what belonged to each company was a "manifest absurdity." The NWC also insisted that all servants hired by either party while still under contract to the other be restored. This was actually a quite one-sided demand, since all the servants thus hired, including Frederick Heurter, were defectors from the NWC. Coltman added insult to injury by refusing to take Heurter's evidence on the grounds that he had left the NW service and was not a neutral witness.

Both Selkirk and Coltman quickly discovered that their respective high expectations for the commission were not to be met. If Selkirk had hoped for a full investigation of the violence in the West, Coltman had hoped that the termination of the immediate state of hostilities between the parties in his presence would end "the misconstructions of each other's proceedings so naturally arising out of the jealousies and suspicions incident to a state of hostility." Instead, the commissioner found all the elements of the confrontation being continually played out in the negotiations themselves, making it increasingly unlikely that he could ever effect a genuine pacification.

Selkirk blamed everything on NWC predilections for violence. The NWC, in its turn, insisted that "the origin of all disturbances which have taken place is the assumption of territorial rights and independent Jurisdiction by the servants and Grantees of the HBC." If trade had not been interrupted, the fatal contests on the plains would never have occurred. In any case, only the NWC seemed to be getting what it wanted — a return to the status quo ante bellum — from Coltman's presence.

After many days of bargaining and the exchange of numerous letters, Coltman managed to arrange with Selkirk the return of all contested property to the NWC. Coltman and Selkirk exchanged over 50 letters and memoranda between July and September 1817, most of them in the first half of July. Selkirk fought fiercely to have the question of the property purchased from Daniel McKenzie adjudicated in the courts, but eventually surrendered the point. The order on restitution was signed by the parties on 15 July. On that same day, Coltman reported in a letter to Sir John Sherbrooke that the proof was decisive that Selkirk obeyed "legitimate authority."

The earl had also demonstrated his peaceable intentions by his refusal to interfere with NWC canoes bound for the Athabasca, despite many rumours of violence committed against HBC traders in that western region. Coltman added that he was not clear whether Selkirk's reasons for refusing to obey the earlier warrants were "well founded," but "with his Lordship's views of the character and proceedings of his opponents, they were not unnatural, and must I think be allowed considerable weight in extenuation on a future bona fide surrender." Taken in conjunction with the commissioner's own refusal to recognize the authority of Deputy-sheriff Smith, this judgment went a long way to exonerate Selkirk from charges of the flaunting of legal warrants.

Selkirk did not make much progress with the commissioner on the matter of legal action for earlier depredations against the settlement. Coltman did meet on 10 July with a delegation of Métis to retrace in situ the movements of 19 June 1816. He had Peter Fidler a few days later draw up a map reflecting the testimony of the participants. In an affidavit sworn before Coltman, Fidler managed to make an editorial comment on his map and the Métis testimony, noting that there were no natural impediments to the mixed-blood party making a wider sweep around Fort Douglas than they had done.

Coltman also took many depositions from the Métis and Canadians. Samuel Gale would later complain that the Commissioner allowed the witnesses long preambles of "mitigation and extenuation of the atrocities committed in Red River." The Selkirk people were continually upset by Coltman's refusal to detain legally any of those involved in the violence. Both Selkirk and Captain D'Orsonnens offered to execute the warrants already outstanding against the culprits, but were refused by Coltman. The commissioner's rationale for this tolerance of lawbreakers was twofold. In the first place, he would not have had the co-operation of the Métis in his fact-finding investigations had he gone around arresting them, either before or after they had testified. Secondly, he truly believed — and would repeat many times — that most of what had happened, while horrible, was not really actionable in the courts.

On 27 July, the very day Samuel Gale and Colonel Dickson arrived at the Forks, Coltman issued a public letter to the "respective proprietors, governors, factors, agents, servants or adherents of the Hudson's Bay and North West Companies." The letter in many respects anticipated Coltman's ultimate findings on the dispute. It called for obedience to the Prince Regent's proclamation. It noted that one of the great legal questions of the dispute between the two companies related to whether the charter to the HBC had been earlier breached by non-use. It described the violences in the western territories as resulting from one party's assertion of the rights of the charter before they had been confirmed in the courts and the other's retaliation on principles of self defense "in a country distant from the customary protection of the law" which was "a plea inadmissible by any government."

Coltman's letter further observed that the proclamation "appears to treat these violences rather as acts of private hostility or war, than as robberies, felonies, or Murders, in the usual acceptation of these words, and it is fairly presumed that Judges and juries will hereafter be inclined to look upon them in a similar view." Those involved in the violence could look for lenity, said Coltman, if they had "not participated in deliberate murder or been the primary cause or instigators of the offences at large."

5. Selkirk and the Settlement:

Lord Selkirk did succeed in getting Coltman to attend a two-day conference with a number of aboriginal leaders from the Red River region who were at the Forks. He also managed to convince the commissioner to discuss with the chiefs the question of a land concession to the settlement. On 17 July, Coltman wrote to Selkirk, "It appears to me as far as I can see that the Indians wish the Settlement for their own advantage & would scarcely require any consideration for allowing to the Settlers an exclusive possession of a reasonable portion of land." He added, "something will however perhaps be expected as the subject has been so much talked of & certainly an annual present seems best, as it is evident that the interests of the Colony would require the Indians' friendship to be ensured in this manner, even if they gave up their lands voluntarily."

Coltman promised to get the aboriginal sentiments "faithfully recorded," but understandably wanted nothing to do with the negotiations concerning any deed of land. These negotiations were carried out independently on 18 July by Selkirk and a number of officers from the settlement with five of the Saulteaux and Cree chiefs who were attending the conference, including Peguis. In return for an annual quit rent of 200 pounds of "good merchantable tobacco," the chiefs granted to the King an area extending six miles in all directions from Fort Douglas all the way south to Fort Daer at Pembina, as well as land extending two miles from the banks on either side of the Red and Assiniboine Rivers. This land was to "have and to hold forever" and was for the use of Selkirk and the settlers he established on these lands. Whatever other effect the transaction had or would have, it made clear that the resident aboriginals were in 1817 well disposed to Selkirk's settlement.

Despite the frequently annoying presence of the commission, Selkirk did succeed in putting his settlement back on its feet, particularly after the settlers had returned to the Forks on 19 July and after the arrival of Samuel Gale a few days later. Gale took over much of the detailed negotiation with Coltman, casting a suspicious eye on most of the commissioner's activities. Alexander Macdonell recorded the meeting between the founder and his people laconically: "about 11 o'clock forenoon he came to the Frog Plains and conversed with the settlers." As well as arranging the treaty with the aboriginals, Selkirk allocated land for a church and a school. He also announced that those loyal settlers who had suffered in the recent depredations — 24 families — would have their land forever free in any debt to him. Land surveys of Peter Fidler, which allowed farm lots of 220 yards along the river and 1980 yards back from it, were confirmed by the earl, and lots given to the De Meurons. Ten thousand acres of land was set aside for the Roman Catholic Church, a substantial amount given the nature of the aboriginal cession.

Selkirk also negotiated with the HBC for the establishment of a company store at Fort Douglas. The earl was under no illusions about what he had done. While he had some hopes for the future, he wrote Lady Selkirk that "we are thrown back into all the difficulties of the first stage of a settlement." All the work and expense of the past six years were lost. There were few tools and not even a dependable supply of provisions.

The founder's presence and actions in the summer of 1817 acquired the status of mythology in the settlement, as Alexander Ross would record in his history published nearly 40 years later. Despite the exhilaration of dealing in person with his colony, Selkirk could spend little time with his settlers. It was necessary to return east to deal with a myriad of problems there. Selkirk fought unsuccessfully to prevent the Nor'Westers from continuing to hold Fort Gibraltar within gunshot of the Forks, arguing to Coltman that without the elimination of the NWC, it would be most prudent to remove the settlers across the American boundary to Pembina, "where at least they will not have to apprehend hostility from subjects of the same Government and where if they be liable to be attacked it will not be considered an offence to be prepared for resistance."

6. Winding Up at Red River:

Samuel Gale accompanied Commissioner Coltman to Bas de la Rivière in mid-August. There the NWC canoes for the western interior were stopped, the Prince Regent's proclamation was read to the voyageurs and traders, and some depositions were taken. Gale was not happy with the time spent collecting information on what had happened in the Athabasca, arguing that what had occurred earlier at Red River was "the cause and sole justification for any of the measures at Fort William." Coltman stayed up all night to take the depositions, in order not to delay the brigades unnecessarily.

In late August Selkirk was forced to put on his HBC hat and deal with the fur trading part of the brigade which had come west in 1817 and had been delayed for so long by Major Fletcher at the Sault. He determined to winter the fur traders at Lac la Pluie rather than send them late in the year into the Athabasca, where they would probably have only experienced another disaster. But it meant that the proper restoration of property in the Athabasca and the resumption of competition in that region would not occur until 1818.

Commissioner Coltman was quite unsympathetic to Selkirk's plan to return to Canada through the United States, apparently feeling he would be charged with having allowed the earl to escape out of the jurisdiction of the Crown. Selkirk's advisors insisted that he ran the risk of being arrested and returned to Montreal in chains if he passed through NWC territory. They were probably right, since Miles Macdonell was arrested in August near Fort William and taken to Canada under heavy guard.

Officially, Selkirk's reason for his decision was the need for canoes (and voyageurs to paddle them) to take witnesses to Montreal. Selkirk's entourage would have consumed too many canoes needed for other purposes. Coltman eventually decided he did not have the authority actually to prevent the earl from his proposed American route. Instead, he tried deterrence, insisting upon a heavy bail for Selkirk and his Fort William associates, to guarantee that they would appear for court appearances in Canada. This bail — £6,000 for Selkirk and two sureties of £3,000 each, and half that amount for Dr. Allan, Captain Matthey, and Captain D'Orsonnens — was of an unprecedented size. Selkirk and his attorney questioned Coltman's competence to exact such bail for offences allegedly committed within the jurisdiction of Upper Canada. Gale further complained of the legal absurdity of the process, in which "a magistrate for the Indian territory, for offences charged to have been committed in the Western District of Upper Canada, took bail for the appearance of the parties in the district of Montreal in the province of Lower Canada."

As time went on, Selkirk and his people would become increasingly critical of Coltman's performance at Red River The taking of bail was only one of the principal subjects of their objection. Selkirk himself, who had held his temper with Coltman over most of the summer and continued to do so until his departure, later turned livid with rage whenever he contemplated this affront to his honour, particularly when it was combined with a refusal on the commissioner's part to hold those acting for the NWC to a similar requirement. Newspapers in Canada and Britain, in subsequently reporting the huge amount of the bail, often observed on the enormity of the crimes that must have brought it about.

On 9 September Selkirk departed Red River, riding south on horseback to the St. Peter's River and carrying on by boat to the Mississippi, arriving in St. Louis on 27 October. William Coltman left the Forks in the other direction two days later, with Samuel Gale and his canoes of witnesses not far behind. Gale's passage east was broken by continual controversy with the NWC at each of the stopping points before Lake Superior. The little lawyer became increasingly less sympathetic to Coltman on his journey east, partly because he saw the amount of time the commissioner spent in convivial company with the Nor'Westers, and partly because he had time to brood on the events of the summer.

Sitting in his canoe for hours on end, Gale became persuaded that Coltman's insistence on benevolent neutrality was really quite detrimental to Selkirk and the HBC. As the lawyer wrote Lady Selkirk from the Sault, Coltman "took it for granted that Government looked upon all parties in almost the same light, which he deemed likewise to be apparent from the Proclamation of the Prince Regent, and like a good subject he has labored to fulfil what he believes to be the wishes of Government."

Gale's conclusions from his ruminations were critical, for they helped determine the future course of the controversy. He did not expect much vindication from Coltman or his commission. "I look for no justice save only what we can force from persons in power, through fear of disgrace," he wrote Lady Selkirk. Only publicity about the outrages of the Nor'Westers would have any effect on the outcome of events. "Our cause is happily one which may be so managed as to excite sympathy and it should be our endeavour to create a universal interest. No set is so humble as to be unimportant, nor ought we to consider any so exalted as to be beyond our reach." The management of Canadian public opinion was for Gale the key to ultimate success.

Selkirk was guided through the Sioux country by Colonel Dickson, accompanied by Messrs Matthey, D'Orsonnens, Heurter and Allan. Selkirk chafed at St. Louis until early November. He finally got horses and set out for Pittsburgh. The party bogged down in Vincennes, Kentucky, in mid-month. Despite bad weather and much aggravation, Selkirk was able to report to his wife, "with all this somebody keeps his health perfectly." A few days later, in Lexington, Kentucky, his group decided to continue via Virginia instead of Pittsburgh. On 16 December Selkirk was able to write Lady Selkirk that he had arrived in Washington, where he was well received by the American administration. He reached New York on 28 December. As he moved closer and closer to Canada, his thoughts turned increasingly to the legal battles upcoming in the Canadas and to the public presentation of the evidence. For it was into the courtrooms and into the newspapers that the fur trade wars would now be transferred.

~10~

The Campaigns at Law, 1818-1819

*I*n 1818 and 1819, the antagonists in the fur trade wars shifted their conflict into the courts, mainly those of Upper and Lower Canada. A year of virtually non-stop legal activity followed, with suits, countersuits, and the expenditure of thousands of pounds by the parties involved. For the enormous outlay in energy and money, the concrete results — particularly on the criminal side — were puny. One NWC employee was convicted of the murder of Owen Keveney. Several individuals were awarded damages for abuse done them by Lord Selkirk, but this was in a civil case heard under curiously political conditions. In the criminal prosecutions against Selkirk for his treatment of Crown officers, the cases were dismissed. The larger issues, particularly the claims by the Hudson's Bay Company under its charter, remained unresolved by any court in either Britain or North America.

The reasons for the lack of criminal convictions were extremely complex. Lord Selkirk's defenders blamed the poor results on a combination of Lord Bathurst's ill-considered instructions to the Canadian governments early in 1817 and the favouritism shown the NWC by the Colonial Office and colonial officials in both Lower and Upper Canada. Both these factors undoubtedly had some effect. In truth, however, the legal problems involved in the criminal trials of 1818 and 1819 went well beyond Bathurst and Canadian support for the NWC.

Legal events in the Canadas demonstrated conclusively that the Canada Jurisdiction Act of 1803, which transferred criminal trials from the Indian Territory to the courts of the Canadas, was badly flawed. The legislation simultaneously left jurisdictional holes and produced overlaps, both of which could easily be manipulated by the lawyers on either side. The existence of the district around Fort William as an anomaly of imprecise jurisdiction did not help matters. Moreover, even if the 1803 legislation had been well-drafted, long-distance justice simply did not work very well. The use of the Canadian courts to try criminal offences in the West might have been proved acceptable in isolated instances, but not in these cases involving literally dozens of defendants and witnesses, all of whom had to be brought east and housed there for considerable periods of time.

Attempts by both Selkirk and the NWC to convict the other side of conspiracy only showed how difficult conspiracy was to prove, especially thousands of miles from the event. Indeed, many of Selkirk's prosecutions were extremely abstract, even abstruse, in nature. They involved attributing criminal motives to events which were much easier to understand as spontaneous. The earl's efforts to convict the Red River settlers who left the colony in 1815 of felonious behaviour were particularly dubious, as were the Nor'Wester prosecutions of colony officials in the pemmican business. Even without the manipulations of the Crown against Selkirk's attempted prosecutions, most would probably have resulted in acquittals.

The reluctance of Canadian law officers to allow Selkirk's lawyers to participate in the prosecutions they had brought, as would have occurred in England, produced considerable criticism among the Selkirk people. Selkirk's defenders insisted that the Crown did not understand the cases his lawyers had constructed, and was not eager to pursue them in any case. There was some evidence of direct favouritism as well, with NWC lawyers allowed to lead in ways denied the HBC forces.

The simple fact was that Crown officials in British North America did not believe in private prosecutions. Moreover, they were hamhanded lawyers to boot, easy for a defence which had sympathy from the bench to out-maneuver. In this and in other respects, the trials demonstrated that criminal proceedings in British North America were not mere imitations of British justice. British North America was not Great Britain. Selkirk's Canadian lawyers seriously contemplated pleading his privilege as a peer to escape from the Canadian court cases against him, for example, but were told by English counsel that in Canada Selkirk "has no privilege or rank but by courtesy."

The court cases of the fur trade wars were not simply legal proceedings, of course, which could be adjudicated strictly on their merits. They were also matters of high politics in both Lower and Upper Canada, particularly in the latter. The cases became inexorably intertwined with local political infighting. Given the Selkirk apprehension that colonial governments and officials were hand-in-glove with the Nor'Westers, it is not surprising that the earl's people should seek support from the ranks of political opposition to the elites. In Lower Canada, the Selkirk people sought to identify with French-Canadian interests in the legislature. This identification was not especially natural and was not carried very far.

In Upper Canada, however, Selkirk had formed a firm if informal alliance with the developing popular opposition to John Strachan and the Family Compact, which in the period of the trials was associated with the Scots-born critic Robert Gourlay. This alliance was aided by the fact that Selkirk had long done his business in Upper Canada with the Lowland Scots who were now employing Gourlay as a stalking horse in the province. The Lowlanders had joined with the American critics of the government. The developing opposition critique in Upper Canada saw the influence of the NWC in government circles as one more illustration of the conspiracy between Crown officials and anti-democratic forces in the province.

Lurking behind all the very real legal and political difficulties were two general apprehensions. One was that what had occurred in the West was well beyond the law. Both sides had committed reciprocal atrocities in the absence of a proper legal structure, akin to some sort of struggle between feudal barons, and the sooner the whole business was ended and forgotten the better. This was certainly the position of William Coltman, the commissioner who had investigated the disputes in 1817. The second apprehension was that the court cases were show trials, designed for publicity purposes rather more than for the accomplishment of true justice. Such a view was to some extent unfair. Both sides truly believed that the other had been guilty of great enormities that deserved punishment. In the case of the Red River settlement, particularly, the charges resulted from considerable loss of life, and Selkirk and his supporters genuinely and legitimately sought legal retribution.

At the same time, public opinion was always an important consideration in the legal maneuvering. Lord Selkirk was conscious that his credibility had taken quite a beating in the earlier course of the conflict, and he sought a full exposure of events to vindicate his honour. The Selkirk forces took for granted that they and the HBC started with public sympathy, at least in Canada, against them. From this perspective, the trials and their surrounding publicity — whatever the outcome — could only rebound to Selkirk/HBC advantage. The Nor'Westers could be charged with a good many more serious criminal offences (including murder) than could the HBC and the settlement. From the Nor'Wester perspective, much of the legal maneuvering was purely defensive, designed to prevent Selkirk and the HBC from gaining too many advantages from their assumed position as innocent victims of NWC violence.

Lord Selkirk may not have won in the courts of the Canadas, but he would eventually win the battle of public relations. He and his supporters even managed to turn the failures in the Canadian courts to their advantage in the subsequent war of words. Undoubtedly the biggest mistake of the NWC in the entire dispute was in taking too much advantage of its political connections in 1818 and 1819 to persecute its adversaries and to avoid prosecution itself. The Nor'Westers thereby exposed themselves as easy targets for HBC propaganda, which helped Selkirk's people win the battle of the press. These victories, in turn, had enormous implications for the future of the fur trade.

Following the complicated legal proceedings is no easy matter. Bills of indictment were filed against most participants, and not all indictments resulted in prosecutions. Trials were removed from one province to another and postponed from one term to another. Samuel Gale wrote of the business as "perfect chaos," and he was almost correct. Nevertheless, it is possible to bring some order out of confusion. For convenience, the court battles of 1818-19 can be divided into three categories. First, there were the prosecutions instituted against Selkirk and those who had accompanied him into the interior. Second, there were the proceedings by Lord Selkirk and his people against the NWC and those held to be its accomplices. Finally, there were the prosecutions instituted by the NWC against persons employed at or belonging to the Red River settlement.

The unfolding of these legal battles occurred against an obbligato of other developments. These included the continued investigations and eventual completion of the report of Commissioner William Coltman, increasing evidence of Selkirk's mortal illness, and the agreement by the British and American governments on the joint occupation of the Oregon country.

1. The Early Prosecutions against Selkirk and his Associates:

As we have seen, several warrants had been obtained by the NWC against Lord Selkirk, which his opponents had tried to execute at Fort William and Red River. Selkirk had refused to accept these warrants on site on a variety of grounds, including his understanding that Fort William was not in Upper Canada. He and his leading associates had been forced by Commissioner Coltman to supply an enormous bail to guarantee that they would answer charges involving them and the resistances to them in the courts of Lower Canada. Selkirk and his legal advisors were so concerned about dealing with these Upper Canadian charges that the earl (accompanied by Dr. Allan and Captain D'Orsonnens) rushed off straight to York in

Upper Canada upon his arrival from the United States at the end of 1818, instead of heading to Montreal to be reunited with his family and see the daughter born in his absence.

Upon his arrival at York, Selkirk immediately called upon Chief Justice William Dummer Powell and then on the solicitor-general D'Arcy Boulton in an attempt to sort out the cases. Selkirk had met Powell on his Upper Canadian tour in 1804, and had done Powell a favour in London a year later; he doubtless hoped for some reciprocation. The earl offered to surrender himself and give bail to answer the charges against him, but Powell claimed he could not interfere, since there were officially no charges before him.

A day later, Boulton informed Selkirk that he had orders from Lord Bathurst to prosecute criminally for the earl's refusal to accept the Upper Canadian warrant originally served on him at Fort William. Boulton further suggested that if the case were brought officially before him he would have to arrest Selkirk on a charge that was not bailable. The solicitor-general suggested, apparently seriously, that Selkirk and his associates immediately flee to the United States to escape his jurisdiction. Colin Robertson would later take similar advice and cross the border.

Selkirk refused to take such a step at this time, arguing instead that he was already under bail ordered by Coltman to answer these charges in Lower Canadian courts. Boulton insisted that Coltman had no power to take such a bail, a position with which Selkirk privately concurred. But it was agreed that the Coltman bail eliminated the need for Boulton and Powell to act. In reporting all this to his wife, Selkirk appeared surprised at the revelation of the Bathurst order. Lady Selkirk was not surprised. She and Samuel Gale had suspected its existence for nearly a year.

Unsatisfied at York, Selkirk and his companions — accompanied by Boulton — headed off for Sandwich, the seat of the court of quarter sessions for the western district of Upper Canada which had issued the original warrant for felony. This was the warrant which Selkirk had rejected at Fort William. The Selkirk party found the session of the court just ended, but the chief magistrate obligingly called a special session. Sandwich was not far from Selkirk's Upper Canadian settlement at Baldoon, and he had a good deal of public sympathy in the district. Selkirk testified that the NWC clerks had perjured themselves by saying that they had been shown no search warrant, and another affidavit by Vandersluys was produced which totally contradicted the one on which the warrant had been based. The court set this warrant aside and discharged the parties from it.

The discharged warrant was not the only one that had been issued, however, and Boulton soon produced another one charging

Selkirk with committing a riot at Fort William and forcing the gates. Selkirk maintained that he was acting as a magistrate and there had been unlawful resistance. He challenged Boulton to prove that the force used to carry the arrests was excessive. The court insisted on witnesses, which Selkirk did not have present, and he was put under bail — a small one — to answer these charges at the next meeting of the court.

Boulton then brought still another warrant, which he said he was officially directed to prosecute. This one was for refusing to submit at Fort William to the original warrant for felony (which had already been set aside by the court). Selkirk again explained his actions, and the court demanded witnesses. Boulton insisted that this resistance was not a bailable offence, but the court disagreed. Selkirk and his associates were bound over on a small recognizance on this charge, as well as on another of resisting in March 1817 the warrant of Deputy-sheriff Smith. These indictments would hang for several years before they were settled, with the Crown on several occasions postponing prosecution and once quashing an indictment, although Selkirk had transported his witnesses to Sandwich at great expense.

With the Upper Canadian warrants dealt with for the moment, Selkirk and his companions rushed off for Lower Canada to meet the recognizances which Colonel Coltman had demanded before they had left Red River. This proved a real legal quagmire, since Coltman had required appearance at a court in Lower Canada for offences committed in Upper Canada. The attorney-general of Lower Canada admitted that he could not institute proceedings against Selkirk for the alleged offences. But instead of discharging the recognizances, the attorney-general moved for new ones guaranteeing that Selkirk would answer the same charges before a special court of oyer and terminer to be held in the upper province. The attorney-general acknowledged that he took this action because of his interpretation of the Bathurst dispatch of 11 February 1816. Selkirk's lawyers argued unsuccessfully that this action was both illegal and vexatious, since the cases were already being heard in the Upper Canadian courts, where bail had been given in far lesser amounts.

2. The Early Prosecutions against the NWC:

One of the first attempted prosecutions against a Nor'Wester involved Duncan Cameron, the partner who had been involved in the removal of the Red River settlers in 1815. This case demonstrated the legal complications involved in prosecuting for crimes committed in Red River. It also illustrated the maneuvering which went on between the British government and the HBC over its charter "rights". Cameron had been arrested by Colin Robertson at Fort Gibraltar in March 1816. He was sent to York Factory, where he was held for a year before being sent abroad for trial. Part of the reason for the delay was the failure of the HBC ships to arrive in the Bay in 1816. Instead, Cameron was eventually sent overland to Montreal, where a grand jury of the Court of King's Bench had charged him with arson, theft, and "malicious shooting" in the unorganized "Indian Territories" of the West. This was part of a large package of indictments against the NWC and its associates obtained by Selkirk and the HBC in Lower Canadian courts in 1817.

At this point, the HBC ran into a series of legal catch-22s. The company in 1814 had obtained an unofficial legal opinion from a team of distinguished lawyers which said that the Canada Jurisdictions Act of 1803 did not extend to the territories granted the Company under its charter. With typical caution, however, the lawyers had warned that while the HBC charter granted it powers of civil and criminal jurisdiction which could by extension be passed on to the colony, it would be singularly unwise to employ these charter rights in the midst of a violent dispute over jurisdiction with the NWC. So Cameron could not be returned to Red River for trial (even if there were courts there).

Sir John Sherbrooke had accepted the petitions of the NWC that all the prosecutions of individuals for which Selkirk was committing magistrate, and some other cases, be transferred to Upper Canada for trial, on the grounds that party spirit ran too high in Montreal between the two companies to find an impartial jury. Cameron was not actually one of these people, having been arrested under a Red River warrant. The solution adopted for Cameron was to send him to England. This was done. Cameron was taken to England without a formal warrant, however, and the HBC was thus forced to apply to the Crown for a warrant so that he could either be tried in England or taken back to Canada for trial.

Further complicating legal matters, there was a general consensus among the lawyers that only the criminal offenses enumerated in 33 Henry 8 (1541) c. 23 extended to the overseas empire. All other offenses were the responsibility of the criminal code of the local colony. Thus only treason, manslaughter, or murder could be adjudicated in an English court. Since Duncan Cameron had been arrested on charges which were all felonies, they were not actionable in England. So the Colonial Office informed the HBC.

The Crown's legal officers went further, however. They also advised that Cameron could not be carried back to Canada under the Habeas Corpus Act of 1679, which allowed a person arrested in England to be returned to the "foreign plantations" for trial. Habeas corpus applied only when an offense had been committed in an overseas jurisdiction of His Majesty, and Cameron was charged with offenses in the Indian Territories, "which is not within any dominion or foreign plantation of His Majesty" in which he could be tried. The Canada Jurisdictions Act gave jurisdiction in Rupert's Land to the courts in Canada, further opined the Crown officers, but did not permit the Habeas Corpus Act to be employed on charges of crimes committed out of His Majesty's jurisdiction. The HBC protested that its territory was part of the British dominions overseas, but this argument was refused. Duncan Cameron thus was freed. He would eventually return to Canada to sue Colin Robertson for false imprisonment and be awarded damages of £3,000.

The transfer of Duncan Cameron to England for trial had seemed to accord with the thinking of the Colonial Office in early 1817. On 17 January of that year, Lord Bathurst had written Sir John Sherbrooke that justice could be done only if those individuals arrested and accused by Lord Selkirk were brought home and tried in England. Lord Bathurst eventually changed his mind, however, and authorized the trials to be held in Canada.

3. Commissioner Coltman:

While Selkirk and his attorneys were preparing their court cases against the Nor'Westers, William Coltman continued the investigations and interrogations that would lead to his final report. In late January of 1818, after Lord Selkirk had made his first visit to Sandwich but before the opening in Lower Canada of the trials against the NWC and those connected with it, Commissioner Coltman attempted to arrange an out-of-court agreement among the contending parties. By this time Coltman had finished the first draft of his report on the violence in the Western Territories, but had not yet submitted it to the authorities. From the beginning of his appointment, and certainly from his arrival at Red River, Coltman had taken the view that there was nothing to be gained from attempting to assess culpability in the conflict. He had made this clear to Lady Selkirk and to Selkirk's lawyers. With few exceptions, Coltman viewed the violence in the West as beyond the capacity of courts to adjudicate. What was more important, he thought, was the restoration of stability for the sake of the colony, and the resumption of the western trade for the sake of the companies.

As evidence of his eagerness to promote stability, Coltman assisted Samuel Gale and the Selkirk forces early in 1818 in arranging for the establishment of a western mission by the Catholic Bishop of Quebec. Lady Selkirk used her wiles to help bring about Coltman's cooperation. The commissioner agreed with Gale that the presence of priests might well meliorate the present wildness of the Métis and the freemen, which could only work to the advantage of the settlement of the Red River region. He went so far as to take a subscription list for the clergymen to the Nor'Westers.

Coltman made his overtures through Colin Robertson, who appeared in Montreal to make his deposition before the commissioner at the end of January 1818. In their informal conversations before Robertson began officially testifying, Robertson later reported, he remarked that the best ways to secure peace in Red River were through the establishment of priests — a project by now set afoot — and by establishing a hundred-mile cordon sanitaire around the colony free from either trading company. Coltman, who had been in continual contact with both sides since returning from Red River, responded that he thought the NWC would not disturb the colony again and might agree to abandon Red River altogether if Selkirk would cease the prosecutions currently pending.

Robertson wondered how Selkirk was to be reimbursed for the two successive destructions of his colony. Coltman answered that he thought William McGillivray so tired of law that he might waive his demands for damages at Fort William and allow Selkirk damages for what had taken place at Red River. McGillivray thought, said Coltman, that Selkirk by now must realize he could make nothing of the charge of conspiracy. Minor prosecutions might be withdrawn, leaving the Crown to prosecute criminal cases at its discretion, especially the murder of Keveny, which was distinctive from the other transactions in the Indian Territories. Robertson observed that the personal feelings of Lord Selkirk had to be taken into account. But Coltman remarked that expenses were enormous for proceedings at law, and Selkirk's feelings could be satisfied by allowing the government to decide the legal issues based on three reports: one by Selkirk, one by the NWC, and a third by the commissioner.

Robertson asked whether he could communicate these thoughts to Selkirk. Coltman said yes, and repeated the substance of his statement. Robertson reported that Lord Selkirk had insisted that he could not drop the criminal charges and was averse to discussing matters verbally. In fact, later in February proposals in writing were exchanged between William McGillivray and Selkirk through the medium of Commissioner Coltman. On behalf of the NWC, McGillivray proposed that the HBC withdraw from the Athabasca and the NWC would pay for the goods left there. In return the NWC would withdraw from Red River, although it would continue to hold the upper part of the Assiniboine. Civil damages were to be submitted to intelligent merchants two for each side, and in case of a disagreement to an umpire. Criminal charges were all to be waived. For his part, Selkirk denied that he had anything to do with the Athabasca. He further insisted that any limitation of criminal prosecutions would, in his view, appear to compound the crimes.

Coltman subsequently reported to Lord Selkirk that his intervention had made matters worse. The commissioner added that the NWC's terms for Red River were "so unreasonable that there is no hope of anything being done unless by the influence of government." Coltman told Colin Robertson that "there was more difficulty than had been imagined in the way of the proposed arrangement." He added that he was sorry the matter could not be settled, since he was of the opinion that Selkirk might not have another opportunity for so advantageous an adjustment.

However sensible an analysis of the situation Coltman might have, he still had not appreciated the true nature of the controversy or the stubbornness of its chief protagonists. The NWC's concerns were to recover its monopoly of the Athabasca and to free itself from criminal prosecutions, although it was unwilling to give up completely on the Red River region. Selkirk's concerns were to protect his settlement and to obtain "justice" for those settlers who had been killed or otherwise abused by what he still regarded as an NWC conspiracy. Coltman's involvement in these "negotiations" further confirmed Selkirk's suspicions that Coltman was really a tool of the NWC. As for Samuel Gale, he was convinced that "trumped-up" charges against Lord Selkirk was one of the NWC's major weapons for forcing a settlement between the parties.

4. The Prosecutions Against the Nor'Westers Continued:

One of the major weaknesses of the Canada Jurisdiction Act was that it allowed venues to be transferred by the order of the governor-general, but did not specify in detail the legal processes to be employed in so doing. The government of Lower Canada had argued in 1817 for a North American venue, but it also determined that while indictments could be generated in the province, it did not want — perhaps could not manage — to hold the actual trials. Thus Selkirk not only found the cases of those people he had arrested transferred within courts in Lower Canada, but from Lower Canada to Upper Canada.

Moreover, the two provinces disagreed over the legal instruments to be employed. Upper Canada would not accept the documents prepared and sent it by Lower Canada executing the transfer. The Upper Canadian law officers, headed by John Beverley Robinson, insisted that the crimes to be tried had to be specified in detail. Many defendants were released in the process. Samuel Gale protested the policy of simply letting those arrested go, arguing with Robinson that "if the provisions of the act of George III, be really inadequate to the purposes of securing offenders who have committed crimes in the Indian territories, as you have supposed, the sooner their insufficiency is established by legal determinations the better for the ends of justice."

Transferring venues meant that witnesses had to be transported from one place to another at great expense, and given the distances involved, would often not be available to testify in all venues unless proceedings were carefully co-ordinated. Selkirk understandably wanted all the charges of crimes committed in the Indian Territories tried at the same place and at the same time.

The Court of King's Bench in Montreal proved quite incapable of dealing with almost any of the cases, since two of its justices declared in open court late in 1817 their connections with the NWC at a time when there were only three justices sitting on the court. As a result, Sir John Sherbrooke issued a commission that in effect created a special court of oyer and terminer which opened at Montreal on 20 February 1818. This court quite promptly found a number of bills of indictment on evidence provided by the Selkirk forces. The total included bills of indictment against 15 NWC partners, 12 NWC clerks, and 15 NWC servants, for principals or accessories to murder; bills of indictment against 2 partners, 6 clerks, and other others for arson; and bills of indictment against 6 partners, 11 clerks, and 16 others, for robbery.

As well, another bill of indictment was found against 20 partners, 11 clerks, and 12 others, for a conspiracy to destroy the Red River Settlement. Every individual sent east to Lower Canada under warrant of Selkirk was indicted with at least one offense. Indictments are not the same thing as convictions, of course, but the actions of this special tribunal should have got Selkirk off the hook as far as the Colonial Office was concerned. His activities at Fort William had, after all, resulted in "true bills". The special court was then forced to adjourn because of the opening of the Court of King's Bench.

The scene now shifted to Quebec City, where the trial of Charles de Reinhard and Archibald MacLellan was to be held for the murder of Owen Keveny. Before that case opened, however, attorney-general Norman Uniacke handed Lord Selkirk two hastily bundled lots of papers relating to the forthcoming business. In one of them Selkirk found in the handwriting of the advocate-general a copy of a dispatch dated 11 February 1817 originally sent by Lord Bathurst. This finally explained much of the behaviour of the colonial officials which had been long suspected. When Uniacke discovered that Selkirk had made a copy of this copy, he demanded it back. Selkirk refused to comply.

Sir John Sherbrooke found it necessary to write an abject apology to Lord Bathurst for allowing the document to get into Selkirk's hands. Since Bathurst had intended Selkirk to know its substance, he must have been surprised at the tone of Sherbrooke's dispatch, which merely confirmed that Sherbrooke's paralytic stroke, suffered on 6 February 1818, had rendered him ineffectual. The first trial of MacLellan and de Reinhard was broken off in mid-hearing. In the process, MacLellan (and a number of other indicted individuals, including Cuthbert Grant) were released on bail, immediately departing the province. The dispersal of the prisoners meant that they might not all be present at the same time for trial, further complicating matters for the maintenance of witnesses.

At the beginning of the trial for the murder of Owen Keveny, the law officers of the Crown in Lower Canada announced unexpectedly that they were solely responsible for the management of all the trials relating to offences committed in the Indian country. Selkirk's lawyers were surprised by this news. They had been allowed to participate in the grand jury proceedings, and they thought they had an agreement with the attorney-general relating to the trial of de Reinhard that they would do most of the examining and cross-examining. Selkirk and his attorneys protested this decision in vain, pointing out that they had better command of the "facts and the evidence" than did the Crown's officers and a better familiarity with the colloquial French employed by many of the witnesses.

Such arguments only aggravated these officers, who insisted that they were fully capable to conduct the prosecutions. Why the Lower Canadian legal officers took this step was never clear, although it seems likely that they disliked being treated as inferiors by Selkirk's legal team, who plainly saw them as incompetent blunderers. Selkirk's people understandably saw it as part of the conspiracy against them.

The trial of de Reinhard and MacLellan ended in June with the conviction of the De Meuron sergeant but the acquittal of the Nor'Wester. William Coltman took the occasion of the MacLellan acquittal to reiterate to Lord Selkirk that his earlier proposal for settlement was still a good one. On the other hand, Samuel Gale wrote Lady Selkirk that the whole business only confirmed that the law "is rather a labyrinth of technicalities and subtleties whereby the guilty escape from punishment, than a direct and open path by which the innocent arrive at justice."

A further blow for the Selkirk prosecutions came in October of 1818 at York. These trials had been several times postponed over the summer of 1818. In the dock were François Boucher and Paul Brown, charged with the murder of Governor Robert Semple. Selkirk himself was ill and was not present. Instead, Samuel Gale and Dr. John Allan observed the conduct of the trials by Upper Canada's law officers, John Beverley Robinson, assisted by Henry John Boulton. On the bench was Chief Justice William Dummer Powell, D'Arcy Boulton, and Mr. Justice Campbell. For the defence stood Samuel Sherwood and his brother Livius, both highly experienced defence lawyers. Despite his inexperience at criminal prosecution, Robinson refused adamantly to take advice from Gale, who recommended that the charge be revised from the murder of Semple to the murder of Captain John Rogers. Gale argued that Semple's death was less clear-cut than that of Rogers, who had been cut down while on his knees pleading for mercy.

Robinson was from beginning to end totally out-lawyered by Samuel Sherwood. As the attorney-general proceeded with his examination of witnesses, Sherwood used all the techniques of the successful defence lawyer. When he could not shake the witnesses' testimony through cross-examination, he discredited them through ad hominem arguments whenever possible, as in famous cases of our own time, and in the process building an alternative case. Michael Heden, who insisted that the two shots that killed Lieutenant Holte and Robert Semple had come from the mixed-blood party, for example, was accused of having improperly seized lands in Red River. The settlement was not a proper one but only a thinly disguised trading post and a camp for hunters. The implication was that the mixed-bloods had a legitimate case.

Sherwood finally unveiled his chief argument, which like most of his arsenal had come from a careful perusal of the Coltman report. Red River was in a state of private war such as had prevailed at the time of Edward I between the Earls of Hereford and Gloucester. What happened at Seven Oaks was not murder, but only a great riot, for which the mixed-bloods had considerable justification. Sherwood focussed attention on the question of who had fired the first shot as if this were all that mattered. Robinson in his turn failed to elicit from the witnesses evidence that whoever fired the first shot in this encounter, the mixed-bloods had congregated looking for trouble — rigged out in war paint, fully armed, and taking prisoners. The defence witnesses finished the job. Two provided an unchallenged alibi for Paul Brown, and two others testified that Michael Heden had told them, "We cannot blame the half-breeds, we fired first, and if we had got the better we would have served the half-breeds the same." It was a perfect way to close.

Chief Justice Powell ordered Brown acquitted. The jury itself acquitted Boucher in 15 minutes, before the judges had time to leave the court-house. In a letter to Lady Selkirk, Samuel Gale provided his analysis of the trial. "Relations, only on one side, of irritations caused at distant times and at different places are produced combined and confounded together. Dates are confused, hearsay is brought forward where facts are deficient, the charges from the bench increase the confusion till all becomes perfect chaos. In a case of doubt the jury are bound to acquit. It must certainly be a case of doubt where all is unintelligible." Not long after the trial, Samuel Gale was attacked in the streets of York by Archibald MacLellan wielding his cane. MacLellan was later sentenced to six months imprisonment and a fine of £100 for his actions.

The same session of oyer and terminer which acquitted Brown and Boucher also tried John Cooper and Hugh Bannerman on charges of stealing cannon in a dwelling house of the Earl of Selkirk at Red River and putting its inhabitants in bodily fear for their lives. The law officers of the Crown prosecuted, and Mr. Sherwood represented the defendants. Attorney-general Robinson insisted that the jury had nothing to do but decide on the innocence or guilt of the two men before the court. "It is, gentlemen, no matter where the crime has been committed, so that we prove it was within your jurisdiction that it was perpetrated."

From the beginning of the cross-examinations, Sherwood ran rings around Robinson. Sherwood insisted that what had been done was at most a mere trespass. Mr. Justice Boulton in his charge to the jury agreed, labelling the present trial "another of the trials resulting from the misunderstanding, and a very unhappy misunderstanding it is, of these two rival companies." The jury returned a verdict of not guilty. The attorney-general then explained that he had more cases to bring, but could not because of the defective instruments prepared in Lower Canada.

In a later report to Sir Peregrine Maitland, lieutenant-governor of Upper Canada, John Beverley Robinson insisted that the evidence against the mixed-bloods in the Seven Oaks trials "must be considered fairly to justify the Earl of Selkirk in imputing the charges to them, and taking any necessary measures to bring them to trial." Robinson was not impressed with "the extraordinary claim set up by [the] half-breeds to be considered as an independent nation." The trials may have demonstrated the absence of "any premeditated guilty design," but Selkirk was in no position to know this.

5. The Later Proceedings against Selkirk:

Selkirk and his family sailed for Sandwich by steamer in late August of 1818, so that the earl and Captain D'Orsonnens could answer the charges laid against them in the Sandwich court. As the steamer landed on American soil, the sheriff of Wayne County boarded the vessel and served Selkirk with a writ issued on the complaint of Nor'Wester James Grant, charging that the earl had caused his fur-trading post at Fond du Lac (in Wisconsin) to be pillaged of goods to the amount of $50,000.

The American authorities were slightly embarrassed by this act of legal harassment, and with the assistance of a prominent local attorney, Solomon Sibley, Selkirk was quickly released on bail. When the case was subsequently tried, the judge dismissed it on the grounds that the writ had been improperly served on the Sabbath. His decision, based on citations from the Bible, Coke, Blackstone, and William Wilberforce, was in manuscript 20 pages long, and filled several columns in the Detroit newspapers.

Freed from American custody, Selkirk was able to appear before the Sandwich court in September of 1818. Chief Justice Powell was himself on the bench. Here Selkirk began by answering the charge of resisting legal process at Fort William, the case which had led to the Bathurst dispatch. Much contradictory evidence was heard, and this bill of indictment was thrown out by the Grand Jury.

Selkirk was finally legally vindicated. The Upper Canadian court had not sustained the charge about which Lord Bathurst had responded so angrily in early 1817. For Selkirk's supporters, this merely demonstrated the extent to which the colonial secretary had shot from the hip, acting on the basis of information from only one side in the dispute. In fairness to Bathurst, he had only insisted that Selkirk be prosecuted, not that he be necessarily found guilty. The dispatch had emphasized "upon a true bill being found," and this had not occurred. The true meaning of the original dispatch of Bathurst and this vindication of Selkirk was considerably obscured, however, by the actions at this point of Upper Canada's attorney-general John Beverley Robinson. These actions had precious little to do with Lord Bathurst's instructions and a great deal to do with Upper Canadian politics in 1818.

In his earlier visit to Upper Canada in 1804, Selkirk had developed an understandable hostility to the elite which ran the province like a feudal fiefdom. He had employed a member of this elite, Alexander Macdonell, as his agent at his Baldoon settlement. Macdonell proved both incompetent and unable to cut through the obstacles placed upon land development by the Upper Canadian bureaucracy. Selkirk had naturally turned for assistance to the critics of that elite bureaucracy, who also happened to be Lowland Scots from the earl's own region of Scotland around Dumfries. This cadre of Lowlanders included the Dickson brothers (Thomas and William), Thomas Clark of Niagara Falls, Robert Nichol, and Robert Hamilton. By 1818, the elite had not changed their attitudes, although they now had a leader in the person of Dr. John Strachan, the Aberdeen-born rector of the Anglican Church at York.

Strachan was connected by marriage with the NWC, and as early as 1815 had declared himself on Selkirk and Red River by writing a pamphlet which denounced Selkirk as an unscrupulous emigration promoter and his settlement as inimicable to the interests of Upper Canada. Strachan was genuinely appalled by the stories he was told about Selkirk's recruiting in Sutherlandshire by the Highlanders who were carried by canoe to Upper Canada in 1815 after the NWC dispersal of the settlement, although he might have appreciated a bit more that these people had to make a case to justify their abandonment of Red River. He was equally appalled by the overstatements about the climate and fertility of the soil at the Forks which he found in a promotional brochure conveniently circulated in Canada by the NWC although it had never actually been published by Selkirk, who had quickly come to realize its excesses.

Not only did Strachan have a longstanding antipathy to Selkirk, but he believed there was a close connection between the earl and Robert Gourlay, the latest critic of the Upper Canadian elite. Gourlay, who was himself from the Dumfries area, had come to Canada in 1817 and was encouraged by those same Lowlanders who were associated with Selkirk and who formed the backbone of the popular hostility to the elite in the legislative assembly. In early 1818 Gourlay had sent out his notorious 31 questions on the state of Upper Canada, and he had also published a letter in a local newspaper which had blamed Seven Oaks in part on John Strachan's pamphlet. Gourlay spent most of the year 1818 escalating his critique of what was now emerging as the "Family Compact" and being systematically hounded in the Upper Canadian courts for his pains.

By the time of Gourlay's third address to the people of Upper Canada in April 1818, which called for "a radical change of system in the government of Upper Canada," most of his earlier Scottish allies had disassociated themselves from his cause. The government had ordered attorney-general John Beverley Robinson to prosecute Gourlay at the first opportunity, and he was charged with seditious libel in several cases. The trials occurred in August in Kingston and in Brockville, and in both instances he was acquitted by the jury.

During the summer of 1818, at the same time that the government was attempting to use the courts to suppress Gourlay, Lord Selkirk was gearing up for his defence in those same courts. He had considerable difficulty in finding legal counsel. Most of the best Upper Canadian lawyers, including John Beverley Robinson, had accepted fees from the NWC. Selkirk's Lower Canadian lawyers were not members of the Upper Canadian bar, and were not likely to be allowed to become so. On recommendations from his Scottish friends in Upper Canada, Selkirk retained Daniel Washburn of Kingston, a known radical reformer, as one of his attorneys, knowing full well that this action meant that he was really introducing Barnabas Bidwell into the cases. Bidwell, an American who had been attorney-general of Massachusetts and an ardent Jeffersonion, had come to Canada in 1810 to escape prosecution for malversation of funds. He was not a member of the Upper Canadian bar, but worked as a law clerk in Washburn's office. Bidwell's very existence sent the Family Compact into paroxysms of rage.

One of the tasks Bidwell took on in 1818 was to investigate the possibility of suing John Strachan for libelling Selkirk in his pamphlet. Neither Bidwell nor Washburn was in Sandwich in September of 1818, but the government must have been aware of their involvement in Selkirk's legal affairs. There were certainly rumours circulating of the possible law suit against Strachan, and Strachan himself had been privately advised of the possibility in early September of 1818. Thus Selkirk had managed to associate his cause not only with Robert Gourlay but with the notorious "Alien Question" revolving in part around Americans like Bidwell. Both Gourlay and the "Alien Question" themselves were connected back to Selkirk's Scottish friends, who were land speculators anxious to be able to sell their lands to incoming American settlers. Indeed, Selkirk himself held Upper Canadian lands that he had been advised would be attractive only to Yankees.

John Beverley Robinson was the son of an American Loyalist. He had been literally brought up and educated by John Strachan at his boarding school in Kingston, and Strachan always regarded Robinson as his best pupil, still in some ways in tutelage to the master. Robinson had spent much of the summer of 1818 — when he was not prosecuting Robert Gourlay and attempting to keep out the Americans — closeted with Nor'Westers preparing for the prosecutions of Selkirk. When the Grand Jury failed to find a true bill against Selkirk on the charge of resisting arrest, Robinson postponed the other actions he had pending. Instead he brought forward a bill of indictment which charged Selkirk and his companions with conspiracy to injure or destroy the trade of the NWC. This indictment epitomized the Nor'Wester case against Selkirk. Chief Justice Powell warned the attorney-general against this strategy, pointing out the difficulty of proving conspiracy. But Robinson had forty NWC witnesses who could testify to Selkirk's behaviour at Fort William and elsewhere. By this time William Coltman had issued his report, and Robinson was able to take advantage of its testimony. Unfortunately, the attorney-general ignored Coltman's careful analysis, which was that there had been no conspiracy on either side.

In the Sandwich courtroom, Robinson went so far as to propose that Simon McGillivray be admitted into the jury room and allowed to examine the witnesses. When this was denied, Robinson insisted on doing all the examination himself, on the grounds that the complexity of the testimony could not be made intelligible to the Grand Jury unless "properly marshalled." Two known NWC agents were on the Grand Jury, but Chief Justice Powell refused to order them to step down, saying he was sure they would withdraw if they thought it "proper." Robinson took three days to examine witnesses, and the Grand Jury itself deliberated for several days, recalling several witnesses in the process and making clear that it was having trouble reaching a decision.

The court met again on a Monday morning, with 15 of the 17 Grand Jurors assembled separately in the Grand Jury Room. Before the Grand Jury could report that they had been unable to find a true bill, Chief Justice Powell addressed the bar complaining of the conduct of the Grand Jury. He then declared the court adjourned *sine die*. Having recently lost two libel cases against Robert Gourlay, the Upper Canadian oligarchy could hardly afford another acquittal in a highly publicized political trial. Selkirk immediately protested this action to the lieutenant-governor of Upper Canada, writing "My conduct has been misrepresented & my character traduced in the most infamous manner & by this mode of proceeding I have been deprived of the opportunity of exposing the calumnies against me."

The next scene in the legal history of the prosecution of Lord Selkirk came in November of 1818 in the legislature of Upper Canada. Attorney-general Robinson (and probably John Strachan) was convinced that both Selkirk and Robert Gourlay had escaped judicial punishment in the Upper Canadian courts because they had been tried in venues which were friendly to them. Use of judicial persecution in the courts to deal with individuals disliked by the Upper Canadian oligarchy was at its height at this point. Legislation in the form of the Sedition Act of 1804, never before used against a British subject, was available to employ against Gourlay. This gadfly was ordered out of the province in January 1819; when he failed to comply he was put in jail to await trial.

Robinson had to create new legislation to deal with the Earl of Selkirk. He introduced a bill into the House of Assembly which made it possible for trials of crimes and offences committed in the province but not committed "within the limits of any Township or County" to be tried in any judicial district of the province. Fort William was notoriously outside the limits of any township or county, and Selkirk's supporters immediately suspected that the legislation was directed against the earl, the more so when it was rumoured that the government would apply the legislation retroactively. The opposition in the House of Assembly was unable to prevent passage of the legislation, claiming that it was adopted before the rural representatives, especially those from the western district, had arrived to attend.

The final court cases resulting from Selkirk's activities in the West came in the spring of 1819 at the York Assizes, after the earl had gone home to continue the fight to clear his name. Selkirk had been again tried in Sandwich on 12 January 1819 — in absentia — for an assault and false imprisonment of William Smith. Through his attorneys, the earl pleaded not guilty and was found not guilty by a jury. Later in the month, in York, John Beverley Robinson acted on behalf of deputy-sheriff William Smith and Daniel Mckenzie, who sued Selkirk in civil court for false imprisonment. Dr. John Allan was the only witness for the defence, and Robinson insisted that his testimony helped prove the charges.

While Selkirk's detention of McKenzie may not have been criminal, it was clearly coercive, particularly when combined with the purchase from McKenzie. Much was made of this purchase of goods by a magistrate from a person he held as prisoner under a felony charge. Miles Macdonell was the person who actually did the coercion, although Selkirk was held to have authorized it. Chief Justice Powell told the jury that the only limitation upon its award was "the amount of the defendant's fortune." The jury found for the plaintiffs, and awarded substantial damages. The only property which Selkirk was known to hold in Upper Canada was attached for these awards, but they did not otherwise affect Selkirk or his estate.

At a subsequent session of oyer and terminer held at York on 22 February, Selkirk and all his major associates in the West were indicted, in absentia, for a conspiracy "to interrupt and abstract, and to put a stop to and ruin the Trade and business of certain persons trading under the name of the North West Company." This oyer and terminer was held under the recent legislation allowing criminal proceedings resulting from crimes in the Indian Territories to be held in any court in Upper Canada. John Allan was the only person indicted who was actually present, and he put up a spirited defence, submitting a lengthy affidavit telling the entire Fort William story from his perspective. Attorney-general Robinson said that he could not see the point of the affidavit, and Allan's attorney answered in three words several times repeated: "mitigation of bail." Bail was taken. Allan described the entire incident to Lady Selkirk as representing a "New era in British Judicature" in which British legal rights were trampled upon by the state. Perhaps not surprisingly, this business ended with Allan charged with assault following a visit to his quarters by the acting solicitor-general, who was armed with a cane.

6. The Legal Proceedings Initiated by the NWC:

The NWC had used legal warrants from 1815 onwards against the officers of the Red River settlement. Sheriff John Spencer and Governor Miles Macdonell were both arrested at Red River in the spring of 1815 under a warrant issued by Norman McLeod for breach of the peace, although not for seizure of pemmican. Spencer was held in custody for nearly a year at Fort William before he was released by the Earl of Selkirk. Left by Selkirk in charge of Fort

William in the spring of 1817, he was rearrested when the NWC reoccupied the fort, and was sent east in irons.

As for Macdonell, he was in 1815 taken to Montreal, where he was again arrested on a felony warrant, this time for the pemmican. The NWC informed Lord Bathurst early in 1816 that legal opinion indicated that it was doubtful Spencer and Macdonell could be prosecuted further for their part in the pemmican affair, since they had acted under a misapprehension of authority without any felonious intent. The criminal warrants were not rescinded, however. Macdonell and Spencer both appeared in court in Montreal in 1816, but only to have their bail extended. Trial proceedings on the pemmican warrants finally occurred in September 1817, by which point both men had been served with warrants in other matters.

John Spencer appeared before the Court of King's Bench in Montreal in September 1817, and he was joined by Colin Robertson. Two justices of the court declared their interest for the NWC, and said they could not proceed in the cases. Without a quorum, neither Spencer nor Robertson could receive a trial, but simply had their recognizances again extended. The prisoners petitioned Sir John Sherbrooke for a commission of oyer and terminer, which was granted. This tribunal opened on 21 February 1818. Seven bills against Spencer, Macdonell and Robertson were preferred before the Grand Jury of this court, but only one — against Robertson and others for riot and pulling down Fort Gibraltar in 1816 — was accepted. An attempted indictment against John Pritchard and two other settlers who had survived Seven Oaks was also dismissed; the charge was murdering the one Métis who had been killed that day.

A subsequent session of the Court of King's Bench in Montreal indicted the Red River people under many of the same charges, however. On this occasion many of the grand jurors were connected to the NWC. The sheriff testified that he had been told that no fur trade business would be done by this court, or he would not have summoned such a jury. Selkirk was unable to get the Lower Canadian law officers to drop the charges, and his people were required again to give bail to appear in court in September 1818. At this point the individuals involved protested their "perpetual recognizances," indicating a willingness to go to jail if they were not tried immediately. The charges were finally abandoned. In the end, all of the criminal charges brought against Selkirk's settlers for the events of 1814-1816 were dismissed by magistrates, thrown out by grand juries, or abandoned by the law officers of the Crown.

The departure of Lord Selkirk from Canada in November of 1818 brought to an end any serious efforts to bring Nor'Westers to "justice" in the Canadian courts. Most of the initiative had come from Selkirk acting as a private prosecutor, and the law officials of the Canadas were happy to be done with the cases.

Getting free of them was not as easy as it might seem, however. At least one court — the commission of oyer and terminer in Quebec City — resolutely refused to discharge any indictments which it had not issued. Selkirk's lawyers also refused in his absence to appear in court to prosecute. The result was that indictments hung over the heads of many of the Nor'Westers, especially the freemen and mixed-bloods, for years. Some of them — such as the murder indictment of Cuthbert Grant — may never have been formally discharged. Thus the lengthy and expensive Selkirk legal wars ended in confusion and uncertainty rather than with substantial court decisions.

~11~

Merger

y 1819, both the North West Company and the Hudson's Bay Company recognized that their fur trade competition was becoming prohibitively expensive — and deadly. Negotiations between the companies to end the fur trade wars had occurred sporadically over the years, but neither was willing to make the necessary concessions. By 1819, however, a union of the companies was recognized by all parties as the best solution. Union would eliminate costly competition and stabilize prices in the fur trade. The resultant monopoly might not be in the interests of the First Nations, but it was regarded as ideal by everyone else.

The final agreement in London in early 1821 followed protracted discussions beginning late in 1819. The understanding reached in 1821 had to be accepted by the British government and translated into legislation, which took another year. Much of what happened during the final months of heated bargaining remains undocumented and undocumentable. We can see the basic outline, but not all of the details. Not only were the discussions sporadic and protracted, but they were punctuated by a series of other important developments, such as the restoration of Fort Astoria, the death of Lord Selkirk, and the mission of George Simpson in America. There was thus no direct line of development from 1819 to 1821.

1. Astoria and Anglo-American Diplomacy:

On 6 October 1818, a curious ceremony was held at Fort George (formerly Fort Astoria) on the Columbia River. In the presence of Captain Frederick Hickey of HMS *Blossom*, American plenipotentiary John B. Prevost, and NWC officer James Keith, the fort's British flag — which had flown since 1813 — was lowered. The American flag was hoisted in its place, and Captain Hickey fired a responding British salute. Documents of transfer were subsequently signed officially restoring Fort George to the United States. Then Prevost, on behalf of the American government, agreed to allow the NWC to continue to occupy the post. This ceremony was the result of a disjointed chain of events which had begun in 1813, shortly after the earlier sale of Astoria to the NWC.

In the preparations for peace negotiations after the War of 1812, the American government had assumed that Fort Astoria had been captured by the British (rather than sold by the Americans to the NWC before being captured). The American negotiators were instructed to have the post returned, while rejecting all British claims to territorial sovereignty on the Pacific Slope. Meanwhile, John Jacob Astor tried desperately to obtain information from Donald Mackenzie about what had happened on the Columbia, finally succeeding in a meeting in New York late in 1814. He was understandably not happy at the news he received. Nevertheless, upon the signing of the Treaty of Ghent on 24 December 1814, Astor began to agitate for Astoria's return in accordance with Article 1 of the treaty, which called for the restitution of all land captured. The problem, as Astor well knew from his conference with Mackenzie, was that Astoria had been sold, not captured.

The American government, responding to Astor's insistence, pressed for the restoration of Astoria. It expected no difficulty. The British chargé d'affaires in Washington, Anthony St. John Baker, wrote to Canada looking for information on what was going on in the far North West. His query was passed on to William McGillivray, who handed it over for answer to his brother Simon McGillivray. As a result, Baker got more than he expected. Simon used the occasion to assert NWC and British sovereignty to the entire Pacific Slope by right of discovery and occupation. The Nor'Wester also emphasized that Astoria had been legally sold rather than captured. He did not point out that the captain of HMS *Raccoon* had subsequently engaged in a formal ceremony of conquest at Astoria, however, claiming the entire country by right of capture. The Americans ultimately discovered this fact. Unfortunately, despite an active campaign with the Colonial Office in London by the NWC on behalf of the Pacific — in between its lobbying about the fur trade wars — the British government was not persuaded that the Columbia River served any advantage to the Crown. This provided another example of the relative diffidence with which the Colonial Office dealt with British territorial expansion in the early years of the nineteenth century.

Washington was more interested in the Columbia District than was London. The American government made plans as early as 1816 for an official naval voyage that would assert American sovereignty over the Pacific coast of the continent. That voyage began on 4 October 1817, when the USS *Ontario* — an ironic name for a vessel of American imperialism — under the command of Captain James Biddle sailed from New York for the Pacific. Accompanying Biddle was Judge John B. Prevost, whose orders included the injunction "to proceed to the Columbia River with a view to assert there the claim of sovereignty in the name and on the behalf of the United States, by some symbolical or other appropriate mode of setting up a claim to national authority and dominion."

The departure of the *Ontario* was kept a secret from the British government, although British ambassador Sir Charles Bagot heard a rumour of its mission and notified the Canadian government. In turn, Simon McGillivray warned Bagot that the Americans wanted to "seize or destroy the Establishments and Trade of the North West Company" on the Pacific Coast. When confronted with this charge, the Americans denied any designs on the NWC trade. But Secretary of State John Quincy Adams insisted that Astoria had been captured during the war and ought to be restored. The entire Northwest belonged to the United States, he claimed.

The British government in London did not accept the larger American claims, but in its policy of entente with the Americans, it decided to return Astoria as an informal part of the eventual 1818 settlement that resolved outstanding border questions, including the border as far west as the Rocky Mountains. The NWC was so informed in late January 1818. The British naval commander in Chile was ordered to make a peaceful restitution of the post to the United States. The larger issue of sovereignty would be settled by later negotiation.

This strange tale did not quite end with the 1818 ceremony of restitution. As British ambassador in Washington, Sir Charles Bagot was ordered to "assert in suitable terms the claim of Great Britain to that Territory upon which the American settlement must be considered as an encroachment." Unfortunately, Bagot did not make this reservation formally in writing, but only orally in conversation with John Quincy Adams.

Even more unfortunately, those who participated in the ceremony at Astoria did not properly understand Lord Bathurst's order that the post be restored to the United States "without, however, admitting the right of that Government to the possession in question." This reservation should have been expressed in writing, or at least verbally. Instead, the document signed at Astoria restored the post unconditionally, and there was no reservation whatever. British claims to the Columbia were thus severely weakened, which would ultimately have a great effect on the disposition of the territory by the diplomats. In the meantime, of course, the NWC remained in effective control.

2. The Return of Lord Selkirk to England:

At about the same time that Astoria was restored to the Americans, Lord Selkirk decided to leave Canada and return to England. His acquittal in Sandwich on charges of resisting arrest had been one of the few bright spots for Selkirk in the year 1818. Although he had returned from the West the picture of good health, he was soon spitting blood again. Lady Selkirk and Dr. Allan blamed the illness on the stress connected with the legal struggles, combined with the need to spend too much time indoors at his desk.

In truth, the fortuitous remission in his consumption which Selkirk had enjoyed while in the interior could not have been expected to continue forever. He was exhausted, having spent most of the year travelling to or from a court hearing, appearing in court, or writing to the authorities attempting to achieve what he regarded as justice. The thwarting of his singleminded quest for justice increasingly frustrated him, but was hardly his only problem.

Caught as he was in the throes of the Canadian legal system, Selkirk had to fight in absentia in 1818 for re-election to the House of Lords as a representative peer. The Duke of Buccleuch probably spoke for many of Selkirk's colleagues in the Scottish peerage when he wrote that despite his goodwill for Selkirk, "I must fairly confess, that his Lordship's constant absence from Britain, as also the probability of its increased continuance, precludes me from giving him my vote at the ensuing election." The government's Scottish manager Lord Melville refused to lean heavily on his colleagues to vote for Selkirk. Moreover, Melville probably sealed Selkirk's fate by ruling that since the earl was abroad and not on His Majesty's service he could not vote himself. Selkirk took the defeat badly, convinced that the government had made it impossible for him to appear in person and then condemned him for his absence. He insisted with some legitimacy that his enemies interpreted the defeat as another sign of the government's hostility to his cause.

However tempted Selkirk might have been to abandon his 6,000 pound recognizance, it was clear that he could not afford to do so. He had spent recklessly to re-establish his settlement and to challenge the

Nor'Westers in the Athabasca. He was now spending equally recklessly to battle the NWC in the courts. There were constant cash flow
problems, which resulted in mortgage after mortgage to stave off
bankruptcy. Worse still, his estates in Scotland were in as much financial trouble as the rest of Britain after the conclusion of the
Napoleonic Wars. Letters from his Kirkcudbright estate manager were
hardly encouraging, with rentals down and expenses considerably up.

Selkirk could not even find solace in the re-establishment of Red
River, now that it had been brought back from the brink of extermi-
nation. The news from the settlement in August of 1818 was extremely discouraging. The enemy was no longer the NWC, but the grasshopper. Acting governor Alexander Macdonell reported in mid-August
that a plague of grasshoppers had invaded the crops. Much of the barley and potatoes were gone. The crop of 1818, which had seemed so
promising and had been expected to make the settlement self-sufficient in foodstuffs, was now going to be a disaster.

Finally, in November of 1818, Selkirk gave in to the pressures and
determined to return to Britain.

3. The Renewal of Trouble in the Athabasca:

The Athabasca humiliations of John Clarke had not been immediately answered by the HBC for reasons beyond its control.
Fort Wedderburn had been seized again in January of 1817, and
Clarke again arrested. He was not released until later that same year,
his reputation badly damaged. He was asked to resign by James Bird
at the end of 1817, Bird reporting to the London committee that "he
will never conduct a large and complicated Business advantageously."
Only François Decoigne kept the HBC banner flying in the region. His
contract was renewed by James Bird at a salary of £300 per annum.
The brigade intended for the region in 1817, led west by Archibald
McDonald, was delayed by Major John Fletcher so long that it was
forced to winter east of Red River. Thus no trading goods reached
Decoigne, who spent a very unproductive winter of 1817-18 at
Athabaska Lake. About the only good news for the HBC traders in all
this disaster was that the London committee had decided that all losses up to June 1817 would be the responsibility of the Company rather
than charged partly to the resident traders.

By the spring of 1818, rumours swirled everywhere regarding a
settlement between the NWC and HBC; William Coltman had already

attempted his conciliation in February of that year. The HBC was eager to return to the Athabasca, increasingly seeing the territory as a major counter when peace was finally negotiated. For reasons best known to himself, Colin Robertson agreed to return to the West to lead the 1818 HBC expedition to the Athabasca. This was probably his last chance at a major personal coup that would enhance both his reputation and his pocketbook.

Lord Selkirk had accepted that Robertson was the best candidate for the job, if his qualities could be harnessed to the task. By early October of 1818 Robertson was at Athabaska Lake with 27 canoes and 190 men. John Clarke, in a subordinate capacity, was sent up the Peace River.

The NWC did not hesitate for a moment. On 11 October Robertson was arrested by a party headed by Simon McGillivray and the "enforcer" Samuel Black. The charge was that the HBC man had brandished a pistol at the Nor'Westers, and Robertson himself admitted that a pistol had mysteriously gone off in his pocket in the course of the scuffle. None of the HBC people came to Robertson's assistance, and he ended up in a NWC canoe on his way to Fort Chipewyan, where partner J.G. McTavish sheltered him from further intimidation. McTavish had little but contempt for Black, whom he described as "certainly a desperate character."

Robertson would spend the winter under confinement in a room connected to the post's privy. He was able to read, and using a cypher, he corresponded with his men continually. The cypher was transmitted inside the bung hole of a small keg filled with rum. The hardest part, wrote Robertson later, was finding a way to get his colleagues at Fort Wedderburn to open the keg upon its first appearance. The shipment of the keg back and forth became so regular that on one occasion Simon McGillivray himself sealed it up. As a result, the winter of 1818-19 saw the most successful trading ever done in the region by the HBC. The cypher was eventually discovered but was not intelligible to the opposition. Observing the NWC from the vantage point of his tiny prison, Robertson also came to appreciate the further deterioration of relations between the NWC merchant aristocracy and the wintering partners.

At the Peace River over the winter of 1818-19, John Clarke succeeded in gaining some revenge on the Nor'Westers. Clarke was short of provisions and had to survive through hunting. His subordinate Jacques Chastellaine at Smoky River was forced by the NWC at Vermilion to give up his trade goods in return for food. Unlike 1815, Clarke did not simply let this indignity pass. He marched to Vermilion, occupied the post, and seized the trade goods.

Robertson escaped from his captors in June of 1819. He was being transported out of the interior under both a guard and a parole based on his word not to escape. At a portage on the Saskatchewan, he was nearly drowned when his canoe overturned while running some rapids. He managed to survive by clinging to the gunwales of the canoe, but remembering Owen Keveny, seriously wondered whether the accident was deliberate. That two voyageurs lost their lives in the mishap suggests an absence of intent.

When Robertson dried off from the near disaster, he found his papers, including his journal, were missing from his jacket pocket. After he raised a fuss, they were mysteriously found in Mr. McTavish's basket. It was a mark of Robertson's power to mesmerize his opponents that they had allowed him to keep his papers in the first place. Robertson violated his parole shortly after at Cumberland House. He had nodded his head rather than actually giving his word when asked whether he could be allowed to visit the HBC post while under arrest. This action he described as "not very agreeable to my feelings," but it did not pain him for long.

The new feistiness of the HBC was further underlined by the actions of recently-appointed HBC governor-in-chief William Williams at the Grand Rapid in June of 1819. Williams was not a professional fur trader. He had served previously in the East India Company and was a bluff sailor. He had been hired to give some backbone to the HBC in the West. Selkirk had forwarded various warrants issued by a grand jury in Lower Canada to Williams, who decided to use them. Williams expanded his warrants by issuing his own as a magistrate of Rupert's Land, although he had no authority for offences committed in the Athabasca.

The governor visited Red River and organized a spring action in coordination with De Meuron Captain Frederick Matthey. The HBC well knew that the best place to effect a capture of Nor'Westers was at the Grand Rapid, and the idea had been discussed several times in the past although never pursued seriously. With 20 of Matthey's De Meurons among his party of 30 constables, Williams carefully planned the action. He placed artillery at the bottom of the rapids. The unsuspecting Nor'Westers walked along the banks of the Saskatchewan while their canoes shot the rapid — two miles in six minutes — and at the bottom they were summarily arrested. The haul included partners John Duncan Campbell, Benjamin Frobisher, William Connolly, John McDonald (le Borgne), John Angus Shaw, John George McTavish, and William McIntosh, as well as a number of voyageurs.

Williams' arrests were of dubious legality. Most Canadian warrants did not apply at the Grand Rapid, and certainly Williams had no right to issue warrants for crimes committed in the Athabasca. Mr. Shaw protested the arrests, and Williams replied, "the judges, juries and crown officers of Canada are a set of d—— rascals, and for our part, we shall act independently of the rascally Government of Canada."

The arrests were in many ways an embarrassment to the HBC. They demonstrated a visible renewal of the earlier exchanges of legal harassment, and much was made of their illegality by the NWC. Worse still, Benjamin Frobisher died of exposure in the course of attempting to escape from his captors, becoming the second NWC martyr to the fur trade conflict. Shaw, McTavish, and Campbell were sent to England for trial, and were released as had been Dugald Cameron earlier, for want of English court competence to try felonies committed in the HBC territories. Those Nor'Westers subsequently brought for trial in Lower Canada were released for want of prosecution. It could be argued — and was — that such behaviour was counter-productive at a point when the two companies were involved in negotiations toward a settlement.

Certainly the Grand Rapid business belied the old claim of the HBC to be the passive and innocent victim of NWC aggression, as well as brought into question the HBC claim for sole jurisdiction over the Indian territories. An English legal opinion on the cases talked of the need to concede a "concurrent jurisdiction over the Company's territory" to the courts of Canada. Samuel Gale tutted and officially the London Committee of the HBC was quite critical of Williams. Gale insisted that the action was too strong for a legal maneuver and not strong enough for a military one.

Fear that Williams would be arrested and taken out of the country for his actions would lead to the HBC's dispatch of George Simpson in February 1820. At the same time, the arrests proved that the successful exercise of force was still the best strategy to employ in the interior of the continent. Like the earlier Fort William occupation of 1816 by Lord Selkirk, the Grand Rapid arrests totally disorganized the NWC in the West. The action also sent a message to the Athabasca, especially to the First Nations, that the HBC was now a force to be reckoned with. In the complex negotiations that led to the resolution of the fur trade wars, the events at Grand Rapid ultimately strengthened the HBC's bargaining position. It was certainly not the last act of legal retaliation in the fur trade wars, however, much less the last act of violence.

Colin Robertson returned to the Athabasca in 1819 after his escape from captivity. He headed further into enemy country than ever before, this time going to the Peace River, where he established Colvile House. In the spring of 1820, Robertson ordered a party led by Ignace

Giasson over the mountains into New Caledonia, thus confronting the NWC directly in their Pacific territory. On the eve of his exodus from the far interior in 1820, he warned William Williams, "Our opponents are either totally disconcerted, and find the Game up, or they are meditating some grand 'Coup de main,' there is nothing but expresses flying in all quarters." Williams escaped seizure by avoiding Grand Rapid.

Not surprisingly, the "coup" was against Robertson himself. Robertson was unable to find a guide for an alternate route, and, characteristically, gambled that he could get through on the Saskatchewan. On 28 June 1820 Robertson was arrested by the NWC, which had gathered to ambush him at Grand Rapid. Eight partners, six clerks, and 50 engagés assembled to deal with Robertson. The arresting party included John George McTavish, who had been sent to England for trial and from whose custody Robertson escaped in 1819, as well as Cuthbert Grant. When Robertson observed that he had been captured by the same men who had murdered Robert Semple, Grant responded by dragging out his pistol and saying, "Don't insult the halfbreeds or I'll shoot you!"

The HBC man later insisted no actual warrant was ever produced for his detention. When Robertson demanded of his captors to be shown some written authority, he was told, "To be plain with you, against superior force there is no resistance." Robertson was eventually taken to Lower Canada. Upon his escape from captivity, he went into brief exile in the United States before departing for England.

4. The Death of Lord Selkirk:

After his return to England late in 1818, Lord Selkirk, visibly declining in strength, became obsessed with obtaining something from the wreckage of his North American activities. Under the constant care of a physician, he worked hard preparing a series of statements defending his conduct. A death among the representative peers of Scotland opened another opportunity for Selkirk to run for Parliament. Despite the assurances of some of leaders of the government, who told him that they had no idea of the Bathurst order of 11 February 1817, he was not officially supported in the election, apparently on the grounds that he might again depart for America. He was hardly likely to reassure the electorate by pointing out that he lacked the strength to cross the Atlantic again. Unable to appear in

Edinburgh personally for the vote, Selkirk was easily defeated by a government candidate.

Despite warnings from friends and family alike about the dangers of overexertion and emotional upset, by the spring of 1819 Selkirk was in a recurring pattern of hemorrhage and recovery familiar to readers of nineteenth-century novels. A paragraph in the London newspapers referring to more Canadian trials set off another hemorrhage. According to his sister, "from that time forward, we had nothing but anxiety, sorrow, labour of body, and heart break."

Lady Selkirk finally came home in June, just in time to be present when Sir James Montgomery, in what was undoubtedly the finest speech he ever made — William Wilberforce described it as "singularly attic, simple, and clear" — called successfully for the tabling of the relevant Colonial Office papers on the Red River settlement. Wilberforce and Selkirk, old allies in the war against slavery and for the improvement of the treatment of aboriginals, were reconciled in the earl's final months.

Selkirk revised his will in August of 1819, as he prepared on medical advice to head to more southern climes. Medical wisdom at the time was that the Mediterranean was a good place for consumptives. Before he left England for the last time, Selkirk made clear to his brother-in-law Andrew Colvile his determination to fight on. "My honour is at stake in the contest with the North West Company and in the support of the settlement at Red River," he wrote. "Till that can be fairly out of danger and till the infamous falsehoods of the North West Company are finally and fully exposed, expenses must be incurred which it is utterly impossible to avoid, and to which it does not depend on me to put a limit."

This characteristic obstinacy persisted until Selkirk's death, making it impossible for his colleagues to complete satisfactory negotiations with the NWC. The earl and his family left England in September 1819, travelling as far as the foothills of the Pyrenees when winter came. The Selkirks settled into a villa in the French town of Pau.

Selkirk had done what was almost unforgiveable in a nineteenth-century family of landed aristocrats. He had virtually pauperized his heir. But he still would not agree to settle the conflict which was draining his estate. On 8 April 1820, Lord Selkirk, founder of the first European settlement in the Canadian West, died. He was buried in the nearest Protestant cemetery at Orthez. With his death, a settlement between the warring companies was finally possible.

5. Peace Overtures:

Both fur trading companies, as well as Lord Selkirk, had been reeling for years from the costs of maintaining the conflict. In the end, the winner was likely to be the party with the most dependable line of credit with the bankers. The HBC overdraft at the Bank of England was £75,000 in 1820, with unpaid bills representing an additional £30,000 of indebtedness. But the directors of the Bank of England had considerable confidence in the ultimate success of the HBC, despite its lack of government support.

Maintaining the loyalty of those employees in the interior was also critical, and here the HBC also seemed more successful than its rival. The credit crisis and the loyalty crisis were for the NWC closely connected. Alexander Ross later insisted that the cost of the trials in the Canadas to the NWC was over £50,000, and for the most part the money was found by not paying the wintering partners.

Dissension in the ranks of the NWC, which had been going on for years, reached a peak in the summer of 1819 at the annual meetings at Fort William. Many of the partners had been arrested at Grand Rapid on their way to this gathering. The firm was desperately short of working capital. William McGillivray tried to convince the wintering partners to promise continued support for McTavish, McGillivray and Company but he met with only limited success. A few partners agreed to give their powers of attorney to McGillivray, but most did not. John McLoughlin actually proposed that the winterers approach the HBC to become their agent if the engagement of 1804, due to come up in 1822, could not be renewed.

Despite the overall dissension and disruptions caused by the HBC at the Grand Rapid, the Nor'Westers confirmed their trading structure in the Athabasca. George Keith was continued in charge. Colin Robertson, who had been imprisoned by Keith at Fort Chipewyan, admired Keith's "firmness of character" and his refusal to waltz "to any tune the McGillivrays chose to strike up." Keith was to be assisted by Simon McGillivray and Samuel Black.

As a result of this meeting, Samuel Gale was approached informally about negotiations with the HBC by an unnamed wintering partner of the NWC, actually John McLoughlin, through third party George Moffatt. Would the HBC supply goods to the wintering partners who could not get their money from the Montreal houses? Gale thought it would be possible to work with all but the worst criminals.

In London, Andrew Colvile concurred that most of the winterers were not involved in the disgraceful acts of the war, although a few would have to be excluded. But Colvile did not see how the HBC could act as a supplier to its competitors. His alternative was "that the whole trade of these countries, both what is comprised within the territories of the Company, and what is beyond its limits, is to form one concern, that a certain number of the servants of the Company are to be joined with those persons now wintering partners of the North West Company, and thus form a united body of managers resident in the Hudson's Bay or interior country, whose time and attention shall be wholly devoted to the management of the trade of the concern."

Colvile recognized that this arrangement could not be brought into effect until the termination of the present partnership of the NWC in 1822, by which point the rights and privileges of the HBC under the charter would have been determined either by the Privy Council or Parliament. But many of the old HBC servants were on the eve of retirement to Red River, and there would be plenty of room for Nor'Westers.

Andrew Colvile in December of 1819 certainly preferred the possibility of a merger to the alternative he and Lord Selkirk had been discussing for some months with Edward "Bear" Ellice, under which Ellice would purchase the HBC stock held by Selkirk and his friends at a liberal price, indeed, at their holders' own valuation.

Ellice was the London agent for the NWC and an important Whig politician, who had married in 1809 the youngest sister of the second Earl Grey. Lady Selkirk had long suspected his hand in the support of the Colonial Office for the NWC. The arrangement would involve guarantees for the continuation of the Red River settlement and the abandonment of all civil actions and damage claims by the NWC. Selkirk did not like this proposal, which both he and Lady Selkirk saw as "merely a question between money and principle." The earl was unwilling to give in to what he described as "a set of unprincipled miscreants" on the basis of an acquiesence in the equality of "faults on both sides."

6. The Mission of George Simpson:

As Selkirk lay dying in France, the HBC made one of its most important initiatives of the fur trade wars. The London committee determined to send George Simpson to British North America. Simpson had been born on the wrong side of the blanket in the parish of Loch Broom, Ross-shire, sometime in the late 1780s. His father, George Simpson, was the son of a Presbyerian minister, and the Simpson family had brought up young George. He had then removed to London and found employment with a firm of sugar merchants which was subsequently dominated by Andrew Wedderburn-Colvile.

Simpson had no experience in the fur trade, but plenty of background at efficient business administration. He also had considerable intestinal fortitude. He stood five feet seven inches tall and every inch displayed the characteristics of the determined, courageous, even pugnacious, Highlander. Colin Robertson was unavailable, William Williams might well be removed from action at any moment, and Alexander Macdonell at Red River had no obvious successor. Andrew Colvile recognized the need for new leadership for both the company and the settlement. Given Colvile's business inclinations and the situation at the time — negotiations with the NWC pending but temporarily stalled — the new leader would have to be an efficient and ruthless administrator who could manage men. Colvile thought Simpson the ideal candidate, and time would prove him correct.

Simpson left London on very short notice, sailing to New York from Liverpool on the *James Monroe*. He carried a dispatch from Lord Bathurst ordering both the HBC and the NWC to desist from further violence and retaliation, and had contingency orders from the HBC to replace William Williams as head of the Northern Department should Williams be arrested or otherwise removed from the interior. His plans were otherwise uncertain, and he expected to be back in London within a few months. He did not tarry long to enjoy the social life of Montreal.

From the beginning of his lengthy North American residence, Simpson insisted on pressing ahead to his next destination, ignoring personal inconvenience and hardships. He was soon wending his way west by canoe. Even before his departure, he had begun a journal to "give an accurate and unbiassed report of the principal Occurrences that may take place within my observation."

The "Journal of Occurrences in the Athabasca Department by George Simpson 1820 and 1821" not only told the story of Simpson's adventures in the western interior, but was an extremely revealing document of his development — and limitations — as a fur trader. From the outset, Simpson's gaze was focussed on ways to be more efficient and to save money. The very first page of the journal discussed ways of reducing the salaries of the inland servants he was in the process of engaging.

Upon his arrival at Fort Wedderburn, Simpson soon stood up to the NWC "bullies." True enough, the Nor'Westers were considerably less confident than they had been in 1815, but Simpson was prepared to take full credit for any lack of aggression. When the Nor'Westers began to build a watchhouse very near the HBC fort, Simpson ordered a fence constructed between the NWC building and Fort Wedderburn. He calmly informed Simon McGillivray that he was "determined to maintain our privileges with firmness," and he subsequently had one of his clerks execute a warrant for the arrest of the Nor'Wester.

Simpson claimed he had not ordered the arrest, but he did not release McGillivray either. Instead he encouraged the Nor'Wester's family to join the prisoner at Fort Wedderburn, and routinely opened all his correspondence. It was not long before Simpson came to perceive that the entire Athabasca operation was conducted without system or concern for the profit sheets of either the HBC or the NWC. The year at Fort Wedderburn confirmed his belief that economy was the key. When Simpson emerged from his year of seasoning in the interior, he discovered to his surprise when he arrived at Lake Winnipeg in June 1821 that the two companies had been successfully amalgamated.

7. The Final Coalition:

The 1820 meeting of the wintering partners at Fort William was as full of controversy as its predecessor in 1819. Old William McGillivray understood full well the threat to his authority represented by the wintering partners. McGillivray was convinced that John McLoughlin and other dissidents were meeting privately behind his back. On the eve of the summer gathering, McLoughlin was summarily transferred out of Fort William, to be replaced by John George McTavish.

At the annual meeting, the criticisms of the Montreal merchants were openly expressed. McGillivray's explanations of the problems caused by Lord Selkirk and the HBC no longer satisfied the complainers. The wintering partners again refused to renew their agreement with the merchants.

Eighteen partners authorized McLoughlin and Angus Bethune to travel to London in order to deal with the HBC on their behalf. The two men sailed for England in the autumn of 1820 on the same ship as Colin Robertson. They would not be important players directly in the subsequent negotiations — McLoughlin was ill during most of his European sojourn and later insisted that he had been deliberately shut out from the discussions — but indirectly their presence was critical. Andrew Colvile always insisted that without the pressure from the wintering partners, the Nor'Wester leaders would never have come to terms. For his part, Simon McGillivray thought the parties were on the verge of an arrangement favourable to the Nor'Westers when the winterers' representatives arrived in London.

The negotiations were far enough advanced by early January 1821 for John Halkett to outline a potential settlement in some detail to Lady Selkirk. This was not the Gale-Moffatt plan, Halkett emphasized. Instead, the HBC would take on as regular partners most of the wintering agents of the NWC. Halkett did not much like it, because he still did not trust the Nor'Westers. The entire business would be divided into 100 shares. Forty would go to the NWC wintering partners and HBC chiefs and factors, five would go to the London agents, 20 to the Montreal agents, 20 to the HBC, five to Selkirk for losses suffered, and 10 as a contingency fund. A subcommittee of five would run the new concern, two from the NWC (Simon McGillivray and Edward Ellice) and three from the HBC. This might work with honest men, he thought. In this case in five years the NWC would control the company, charter and all, he warned.

A few days later, Andrew Colvile also reported on the arrangement to Lady Selkirk. What Colvile described was not appreciably changed from the deal discussed by Halkett, but Colvile was jubilant, writing "we retain the power of management and get paid for our stolen goods, and they kiss the rod in both respects." (William McGillivray would subsequently write of the agreement, "We have made no submission. We met and negotiated on equal terms.")

Lord Selkirk would get at least £5,000 per annum in dividends, beginning in 1823. The final terms had been worked out by Colvile and Simon McGillivray in half an hour. Colvile's exultation was a bit premature, for the deal subsequently came unstuck on several occasions. Part of the problem involved the demands of the NWC, part the resistance of some directors of the HBC, including John Henry Pelly. Among the debated issues was the place of Colin Robertson in the new company. Pelly wished him to be the leading Chief Factor, the NWC wanted him excluded altogether. On 26 March 1821, the parties finally signed a formal agreement. Colin Robertson was subsequently appointed a chief factor, but soon fell victim to George Simpson's enmity.

The Colonial Office was easy to win over to the new arrangement, which had the great advantage of including all of the previous antagonists. "An Act for regulating the Fur Trade and establishing a Criminal and Civil Jurisdiction within certain part of North America" passed Parliament on 2 July 1821. It permitted the King to grant exclusive trading privileges for 21 years in all parts of North America not part of the lands previously granted the HBC or embodied in a province.

This act tacitly recognized the HBC charter and equally tacitly insisted that the Athabasca, Mackenzie, and Peace basins, the Pacific

Slope, and the fur trading territory north and east of the Canadas were not part of the territorial grant to the HBC in 1670. A clause reserved American rights west of the Rockies. Courts were authorized throughout the Western Territories. Lord Bathurst on 5 December 1821 granted to the HBC and to three partners of the NWC (William and Simon McGillivray and Edward Ellice) a 21 year monopoly license in North America. The new company was, in the end, a coalition rather than a true merger. On 29 May 1822, the General Court of the new company authorized a series of ordinances for the administration of government to be submitted to the Colonial Office for approval, and they were quickly accepted by Lord Bathurst two days later as "well calculated to preserve the peace and good Government of that part of North America under the Jurisdiction of the Hudson's Bay Company."

8. Working Out the Local Arrangements:

Although satisfactory negotiations at the top, sanctioned by the British government, were obviously vital to peace in the fur trade, they did not entirely settle the business. The biggest remaining problem was the wintering partners of the NWC, whose acceptance of the new arrangement was absolutely essential. The dissenting winterers, of course, had hoped to deal directly with the HBC. Instead, the negotiations had been shanghaied in London by the merchant-leaders of the NWC. Rather than becoming partners in a loose trading association now supplied with goods by the HBC, the NWC winterers found themselves about to become profit-sharing employees of a much more centrally-organized monopoly than had ever previously existed.

This was particularly galling to the NWC traders because without them, the new company could not succeed. The leaders of the HBC knew perfectly well that most of its rank-and-file people were not equal to the Nor'Westers; Lady Selkirk once described the HBC men as "a sorry set." The Nor'Westers were essential not only because of their trading competence, but because their known predilections for violence could be fatal to the peace of the trade if they decided to mount an opposition.

The new company set out in the summer of 1821 to sell the resident fur traders of both companies on the advantages of the new organization. Simon McGillivray travelled to Montreal with the HBC's Nicholas Garry to try to settle the business. Garry, accompanied by William and Simon McGillivray, headed west by canoe for Fort

William, where the three men would meet with the bulk of the winterers of both companies at the annual summer gathering. Here the traders would be introduced to the "Deed Poll," the document which set out the terms of the agreement between the two companies and which those who would remain with the new company would have to sign within 18 months of March 1821. Here the traders would be informed of the 40 shares (out of a total of 100) in the current trade to be set aside for the wintering partners, the chief factors, and the chief traders. These shares were neither in the HBC itself nor in the land of trading. The 40 shares would be further divided into 85 parts. Twenty-five Chief Factors would get two shares each. Twenty-eight Chief Traders would get one share each. Seven shares would be held for retiring servants.

The meeting at Fort William in July of 1821 was an incredible gathering. We are fortunate to have a vivid account of its opening by John Todd. At one level there was great rejoicing that the many years of bitter rivalry were finished. At another level there was much unhappiness over the terms offered to the winterers and traders. And at yet a third level, of course, there were the smouldering resentments of men who had fought bitterly with one another for years. When a bell first summoned this group of former antagonists to dinner on 10 July, wrote Todd, they stood around on the floor of the mess-hall, uncertain about how to seat themselves. It was George Simpson who stepped into the breach, concentrating on the pacification of the Nor'Westers. A few of the former rivals shook hands and embraced one another, others continued to glare. Eventually all were seated and the dinner was begun.

Simon McGillivray and Nicholas Garry went on together from Fort William to the chief posts of the HBC to explain the new arrangement. The meeting went on to arrange the administration of the trade. Not surprisingly, given their experience, the Nor'Westers got most of the key positions. Colin Robertson, who was not very well placed, complained that "the N.W.Co. had gained a complete victory and were dictating the terms of capitulation." At the same time, Fort William was abandoned as a central supply depot in the fur trade, to be replaced by the HBC forts at the Bay. American author Washington Irving later lamented the demise of the NWC and the loss of Fort William: "The fuedal state of Fort William is at an end; its council chamber is silent and deserted...the lords of the lakes and forests have passed away."

William McGillivray stated bitterly: "the fur trade is for ever lost to Canada." That statement was perhaps a bit extreme, but it was true that the Bay — connected directly with England — would become the North American entrepôt for the trade. In this sense the HBC had triumphed. The HBC had also seen its people appointed as chief North American administrators. William Williams (thoroughly detested by the Nor'Westers) became governor of the southern department, while George Simpson took over the northern department, which ran most of the fur trade.

Not everything went smoothly. Later in 1821, John Halkett visited North America on behalf of the Selkirk estate. Halkett, of course, had been one of the most effective of the Selkirk pamphleteers and he was cordially detested by many Nor'Westers for what he had said of them in print. On 18 October, Halkett was met outside a Montreal hotel by Alexander Greenfield Macdonell and threatened with a horsewhip. Halkett had a writ issued against his assailant, but took the precaution of carrying a set of primed pistols. Later that same evening, Jasper Vandersluys (he of the Fort William affidavit) resumed the attack, striking out with a whip. Halkett fired his pistols and wounded Vandersluys, who subsequently charged him in court with "intent to kill."

The complex details of rationalizing the merger on the ground would take some time to complete. Many posts, often deliberately set next to one another, would have to be closed. George Simpson was put in charge of the department which supervised most of the fur trade; William Williams was placed in charge of the department dominated by the Red River settlement. Simpson calculated that twice as many traders were available as were needed.

Only a few of the main combatants from the NWC — men like Alexander Greenfield Macdonell and Duncan Cameron — were excluded in advance from the new company. Many others were persuaded to retire. Some went to the Canadas. Some, especially HBC employees and their mixed-blood families, were encouraged to move at company expense to Red River, where they received lots of land. Many other traders were forced out of the country or into retirement by Simpson. Lesser employees simply were not given new contracts. In 1821, at the time of the merger, there were 1,983 Company employees. By 1825 there were only 827 remaining, and wages had been reduced substantially as well. Simpson's ruthless domination of the post-merger fur trade confirmed that, in the end, the HBC had won the peace, if not the war.

Epilogue

utting the past into neat chronological compartments for analytical purposes is one of the things that historians do best. Unfortunately, the ongoing story is often difficult to contain. It keeps wanting to spill over its imposed bounds in a variety of ways. The corporate merger of 1821 does provide a relatively definitive end for the great fur trade wars in North America. But many readers may well wonder, what happened next, where did the merger lead?

In the short run, the creation of a new and unchallenged Hudson's Bay Company did not greatly change the direction of development in western British North America. Indeed, the HBC under George Simpson increasingly sought to prevent significant change in the West. At the same time, the company also took over primary responsibility for British imperial concerns in the region. It was possible simultaneously to oppose change and to defend imperial interests because Simpson's vision was exclusively that of a "Fur Trade Empire." He perpetuated the old Nor'Wester assumption that the fur trade was incompatible with settlement and agriculture. He further assumed that the best interests of the First Nations — and even the mixed-bloods — were served by a fur trade empire in British hands.

In this the British government fully concurred. Gradually forces beyond Simpson's control led to the unravelling of his imperial HBC. In 1846 Oregon was lost to the Americans. The HBC proved exceedingly unsuccessful at administering settlement colonies, and by 1858 Vancouver Island and British Columbia were both independent of the company. By Simpson's death in 1860 a new world was waiting to be born in Western Canada, although it would take more than a decade for the birth to actually occur.

1. Empire Hudson's Bay Company:

Between 1821 and 1870, the HBC enjoyed a virtual monopoly of the fur trade in British North America. Within its domain, it behaved like an independent principality, and in its relations beyond it, the company even operated its own foreign policy, especially in border areas where competition threatened the monopoly. On the borders, its principle was to stifle competition by collecting all furs possible at whatever cost necessary. High profits in areas without competition were used to subsidize its strategy elsewhere. The HBC was seldom directly instructed by the British government, and its policies were not the responsibility of any single individual within the company. But the effect was to turn the HBC into an unofficial imperial agent, for some years protecting British sovereignty in a vast section of western North America and even extending British trade to California and the Sandwich Islands (Hawaii).

The two areas of North America where the HBC was most anxious to protect its frontier were along the international boundary from Lake Superior to the Souris River in Montana, and on the Pacific Coast. In both cases the threats came from the Americans. So long as the opposition was principally fur traders, the HBC was highly successful in its policy of outbidding and stifling the competition. When the opposition came from settlers or potential settlers, principally those interested in agriculture, the company was less able to hold its own. The threat of ultimate American expansion of settlement came principally in two regions: the territory to the south of the border between Lake Superior and Pembina, and the Willamette Valley in what would become Oregon.

While American settlement moved inexorably westward in the Ohio Valley far to the south of the Lake Superior-Pembina border, the HBC concentrated on its fur trading rival the American Fur Company, originally founded by John Jacob Astor. Both companies rejected violence. George Simpson commented at one point, "There are 1,000 ways of annoying and harassing our opponents without having recourse to violent measures." In 1829 and 1830, the Americans sought a mutual elimination of the use of liquor in the fur trade, but both companies eventually agreed that such a restriction would only benefit petty fur traders. Astor himself commented of liquor regulation, "it is of no use to attempt it, as if we did the Hudson's Bay Company would hold the head of the Cow, the American Fur Company would hold the tail of the Cow, and the Petty traders would come in and milk the Cow."

The emergence of new trading competition in 1831 forced the HBC and the American Fur Company to come to terms. For some years until the 1840s, the American Fur Company suppressed competition south of the border, and the HBC did likewise north of it. Eventually the spread of settlement in Wisconsin and Minnesota made it impossible to control illicit trading on the American side. The HBC attempted to limit it by coming down hard on the traders operating out of Red River. It even managed to get the British government to send troops to Red River, ostensibly to protect the frontier from American expansion but even more to provide some muscle for control of the fur trade. After 1849, the HBC gave up attempting to regulate international trade in the Red River Valley, which indeed had less and less to do with furs.

The international boundary between Lake Superior and the Rocky Mountains had been fixed by Anglo-American agreement in 1818 at the 49th parallel. The sovereignty of the area west of the Rockies between California (which was Spanish) and Alaska (which was Russian) was left undefined for the next ten years, with settlement open to both British and American citizens. Obviously actual occupancy would be an important aspect of any final settlement. The HBC took over a series of Columbia forts from the NWC in 1821. It not only maintained them, but added to them. Its concern was not territory for the British Empire, but trade competition out of the Columbia Valley in the northern districts which would become Vancouver Island and British Columbia. Improved management actually made the Columbia posts profitable, and the HBC expanded into the Snake River District beginning in 1823.

In the Snake Country, which was regarded as the key to the Columbia Territory, the HBC deliberately adopted a policy of intensive trapping to eliminate fur-bearing animals. It appointed Peter Skene Ogden, who had been barred from the company in 1821 because of his behaviour in the Athabasca, to administer this policy. The intention was to discourage the Americans from moving westward before the question of sovereignty was decided. George Simpson wrote John McLoughlin in 1827, "The greatest and best protection we can have from opposition is keeping the country closely hunted as the first step that the American Government will take towards Colonization is through their Indian Traders and if the country becomes exhausted in Fur bearing animals they can have no inducement to proceed thither." As the unlikelihood of any Anglo-American agreement in 1828 became increasingly apparent, these policies were stepped up. Cuthbert Grant (of Seven Oaks notoriety) was ordered in the summer of 1827 to recruit a party of 25 "steady fellows" for service in the Snake Country. The boundary agreement of 1818 was renewed to continue indefinitely, with either party allowed to end it after a year's notice.

The HBC was successful in holding down the number of American fur traders in the interior of the Oregon Territory, but it had more difficulty in maintaining a maritime monopoly and in keeping settlers and fur traders out of the coastal areas. The company's local agents were charged with not being militant enough, although they insisted it was better to come to terms with the opposition than to compete with it. Chief Factor John McLoughlin, in charge of the Columbia District from 1824, reached an understanding in 1833 with the American fur trader, Nathaniel J. Wyeth, formerly head of the Oregon Colonization Society. For this agreement McLoughlin was heavily criticized by George Simpson, who reiterated the policy of "most vigorous opposition . . . even should it occasion a sacrifice of money."

In 1838 the British government agreed to extend for another 21 years the HBC exclusive monopoly for trade with the aboriginals west of Rupert's Land. In the course of petitioning for this extension, the HBC had promised agriculture, settlement, and immigration in Oregon to protect British interests there. Earlier farms to make the local forts self-sufficient led to the creation of the Puget's Sound Agricultural Company as an HBC offshoot, with ownership of stock limited to Company shareholders. The PSAC established sites on the Cowlitz plain south of Seattle and also founded Fort Nisqually. Both were successful stockraising ventures, but never attracted many settlers. The PSAC did recruit actively in Red River in 1841, and 121 people departed that June from Red River for Fort Nisqually, under the command of James Sinclair. As had been the case with Red River and would later be the case with Vancouver Island, however, the HBC could not reconcile the fur trade and settlement. As for the Americans, Nathaniel Wyeth was succeeded by the settlers of the Oregon Company, for whom fur trade competition was totally irrelevant. Nevertheless, the HBC was the sole British presence in the Oregon Territory, and its interests would have to be taken into account when the final border was fixed.

The Americans settlers in the Willamette Valley began pressing for annexation virtually before they had planted their first crops. Questions of occupancy would not be crucial in the settlement of the Oregon boundary, however. Other factors entered the mix. The British government under Lord Aberdeen did not require the Pacific Coast as a matter of great urgency to Great Britain. Territory there, which the Americans obviously desired, could be sacrificed for advantage in the

Maine/New Brunswick boundary dispute and in the interests of Anglo-American entente. Aberdeen was a bit taken aback when President John Tyler in 1843 declared for a northern American boundary of 54 degrees 40'. While the foreign secretary was prepared to compromise at the 49th parallel, he did not want to be bullied. In 1844 he dispatched a sloop of the British navy to the Columbia. George Simpson was even summoned to London to consult over Oregon, which he did between November 1844 and April 1845. Simpson was heard mainly on the issue of defence.

Simpson and the HBC were ultimately prepared to settle for concessions protecting HBC interests in the territory ceded to the United States, but their part in either the final policy-making or negotiations was very small. What did matter was that Lord Aberdeen was prepared to settle for the 49th parallel and the whole of Vancouver Island. Earlier trivialities — such as the failure to reserve British claims when returning Fort George to the Americans in 1818 — assumed new importance. The British government resolutely ignored the matter of occupancy, for if the presence of actual settlement had been taken into account, it should have insisted on retaining what is now the state of Washington. The HBC had placed almost all the settlers in the districts north of the Columbia River.

Aberdeen's successor at the Foreign Office, Lord Palmerston, noted on one document that the Oregon Treaty "gives them [the Americans] everything which they ever really wanted." A clerk in Palmerston's office minuted at this point, "Nothing to be done." And indeed there was little to do except withdraw from American territory. Because the treaty did not describe in detail every square inch of territory, there would be a subsequent dispute over the islands between Vancouver Island and Washington Territory — the so-called "Pig War" — which would be resolved by drawing a line down the middle of the Strait of Georgia. But the HBC had always planned on the surrender of the Oregon Territory and a transfer of operations to what would become Vancouver Island and British Columbia. That transfer finally happened in 1846.

2. Vancouver Island and British Columbia:

The HBC recognized from the beginning that it would eventually be required to surrender control over the Oregon country, although the extent of the loss was not certain until the end. As early as 1827, therefore, the HBC had moved its principal depot in

New Caledonia to the mouth of the Fraser River, where Fort Langley was established. Lord Selkirk's old protege, Archibald McDonald, was put in charge. As had long been the case everywhere in the fur trade, one of the most serious internal problems on the West Coast was that of provisioning. Fort Langley had access to some of the richest river delta soil in North America. In 1829 over 2,000 bushels of potatoes were harvested from 91 bushels of seed. When in 1842 it became apparent that the Columbia would be soon lost to the Americans, the company set up a new depot for the maritime fur trade on the southern tip of Vancouver Island. Under Chief Factor James Douglas, Fort Victoria was built over the next few years.

By the time of the resolution of the Oregon business in 1846, the British government had become convinced that the colonization of what remained to the British on the Pacific coast was essential if it were to be preserved. Vancouver Island would be the first district settled. Colonial secretary Earl Grey wanted to put the job of colonization in the hands of the HBC, mainly because he was adamant that settlement must not cost the Crown any money and thus must be executed by private capital. Sir George Simpson and other fur traders in the HBC, including "Bear" Ellice, opposed such a venture. They did not believe that colonization could ever be made profitable to the HBC. Considerable public opposition developed to putting Vancouver Island in the hands of the company. An alternate scheme was advocated by James Edward Fitzgerald, a keeper at the British Museum, who proposed a joint-stock company to settle the Island, selling land at a "sufficient price" to finance the process. Fitzgerald had no capital and made little positive headway with the government. But his public opposition to the HBC called into question the company's motivations.

The entire business was conducted on false premises by all parties. Colonization could almost never be made immediately profitable to its promoters, as Lord Selkirk's schemes earlier in the century had well demonstrated. Not surprisingly, his son was one of those opposed to HBC involvement in Vancouver Island. The HBC agreed to take on the job rather than have a private land company competing with it on Vancouver Island, but it never intended a full-scale immigration project. Instead, the HBC dragged its feet and placed restrictive requirements on immigration. Much of the company's energy went into the activities of the Puget's Sound Agricultural Company, which had been transferred from south of the 49th parallel. After some attempts with autonomous governors, Chief Factor James Douglas in 1851 combined the governorship with the supervision of the HBC's Western Department. Those colonists who arrived on the Island grumbled continually — both in general and about the HBC — and soon fulfilled the earlier fears of HBC officials that independent settlers would inevitably clash with the Company. In 1856 the Colonial Office ordered Douglas to call a legislative assembly, which met later that year.

The discovery of gold on the Thompson River in 1857 forced Douglas to extend the political control of the mainland to the Crown. In 1858 British Columbia was established by the British government as a separate colony. Douglas became governor of it and of Vancouver Island after he agreed to divest himself of all connection with the HBC and the Puget's Sound Agricultural Company. The HBC and the Colonial Office spent the years between 1858 and 1862 haggling over the amount of compensation to be given the company for its colonization activities, and the final surrender of Vancouver Island by the HBC came in 1867. Despite the many criticisms of the HBC over its Vancouver Island and British Columbia supervision, the Company had breached a gap until the gold rush provided both the population and the incentive for direct British colonial involvement. Given the Colonial Office's refusal to spend money on its development, there were really no alternatives to HBC control of Vancouver Island from 1848 to 1858. As in Red River, HBC rule served as a transition to full political maturity.

3. The Red River Settlement:

Lord Selkirk's colony at Red River remained in the hands of the family, ostensibly under the control of the estate executors, until 1835. Andrew Colvile attempted for several years to carry on with the expansion of settlement, knowing full well that this was the direction in which Selkirk had wished him to go. He spent a good deal of time and money in the early 1820s in recruiting new settlers for Red River, mainly from the cantons of Switzerland. Colvile had gotten into Swiss colonization through the De Meurons. He had never been happy with Highlanders as settlers, and he was easily persuaded by agents in Switzerland that high quality settlers — skilled, hard-working, highly disciplined — could be acquired in the cantons. The Swiss may have had all these qualities, although whether the people actually recruited did was an open question. But they were badly suited as wilderness pioneers and subsistence farmers.

After years of complaint and disadvantage, the great flood of 1826 convinced the Swiss — and many other settlers from Europe — that life at Red River was simply too difficult. They abandoned the settlement for greener pastures, leaving Red River populated largely by mixed-bloods and retired fur traders, although a few Scots carried on north of the Forks on the Red River. This shift in population was symbolized in 1828 when mixed-blood leader Cuthbert Grant, long since rehabilitated to the HBC cause, was given the office of "Warden of the Plains of Red River" and put in charge of policing the illicit fur trade of the region.

As Andrew Colvile and the executors gradually withdrew from the direction of affairs in Red River — none ever actually resided there for very long — Colvile's annointed agent George Simpson became increasingly dominant on the scene. In 1822, executor John Halkett, who visited Red River that year as part of his unsuccessful effort to gain legal title to lands granted to Lord Selkirk south of the 49th parallel, recognized the importance of Simpson. Spending a good deal of time in Red River in the early years of his governorship, Simpson did his best to make the settlement useful. He supported and in later years even initiated a series of business enterprises in an effort to find some exportable commodity for Red River. Over the years, the Buffalo Wool Company, the Red River Tallow Company, and the Assiniboia Sheep and Wool Company — as well as a succession of experimental farms — all failed, at considerable expense to the HBC and the Selkirk estate. It is likely that Simpson might have done more to assure the success of these ventures; he tended to allow them to be incompetently managed, apparently content that an effort was being made "for the record."

Substantial annual importations of breeding livestock in the form of cattle and sheep had not managed either to provide decent herds or a product for sale abroad. The failure to find an exportable commodity was only matched by a series of natural disasters headed by grasshopper infestation and flood. Simpson could legitimately argue that the settlement could not be made economically viable. In his heart, however, Simpson had always been a true fur trader. As early as 1822 he wrote Colvile that Red River "at this moment injures the affairs of the Company very seriously and in my humble opinion will ultimately ruin the trade if very different regulations are not pursued."

By 1830 the settlement was increasingly being perceived by the Selkirk family as a liability. Most sense of direction had by this time been lost, and attempts to encourage immigration had ended. De facto administration was in the hands of the HBC, operating with a handful of appointed advisors and constables. The mixed-bloods increasingly engaged in organized buffalo hunts — the first having been instituted around 1820 — to supply the HBC with fresh meat and pemmican. Agriculture, both grain growing and livestock cultivation, found its market only in the HBC, whose needs were distinctly limited.

Otherwise, most farming was on a subsistence basis. There had been some gains in infrastructure. Both Protestant and Catholic clergymen were well established in the settlement, although the Protestants were Anglicans rather than Presbyterians. Churches had been built and schools established.

A later writer in the newspaper the *Nor'Wester* described the population of Red River in the 1830s: "Canadians and half-breeds are promiscuously settled together, and live much the same way. . . . They are not, properly speaking, farmers, hunters, or fishermen; but rather confound the three occupations together, and follow them in turn, as whim or circumstance may dictate. . . . They are great in adventuring, but small in performing; and exceedingly plausible in their dealings." In 1833, after years of unhappiness and illness on the part of Frances Simpson, the Simpsons left Red River for England, and upon his return to North America in 1834, Simpson set up his headquarters in Lachine, Lower Canada. Simpson's disappointment at the failure of his marriage in Red River doubtless contributed to his decision.

The sixth Earl of Selkirk finally sold Red River to the HBC in 1835 for £35,000 sterling, a figure considerably less than the family's investment in it — which one source estimated at £85,000 sterling — but probably more than the property would ever have been worth on the open market. The population at the time was about 5,000. In the wake of the sale, the settlement was provided with its first constitution. The Council of Assiniboia was created as a legislative council, empowered to make both civil and criminal law, with the Governor-in-chief as president and an appointed membership of ten councillors. The council passed a number of ordinances at its first meetings. It organized a volunteer corps to serve as a police force/militia. It divided the settlement into four districts and appointed a magistrate for each, to preside in civil courts involving amounts less than £5 and in all trespasses and misdemeanors. The governor and council sat as a supreme tribunal in the colony, with all criminal cases and all civil cases over £10 to be determined by the verdict of a jury. A revenue was created by imposing import and export duties of seven and one-half percent on all goods and merchandise. One contemporary writer described this constitution as "not so comprehensive or complicated as the British original certainly; not yet so symmetrical and philosophically exact as those with which the French revolutionary leaders used to stock the pigeon-holes of their bureaus; but one comprehensive and symmetrical enough for the place, the people, and the time."

Although after 1836 the HBC in effect governed Red River, the Company continued to have trouble with the settlement right up to the sale of its territory to Canada in the late 1860s. The population in the 1840s chafed under the Company's efforts to keep Red River residents from independent trading. That issue was settled in favour of the settlers in 1849 at the trial of Guillaume Sayer, but this resolution did not satisfy everyone. In the 1850s many agitated to have the settlement transferred from the company to the British government as a Crown Colony, an administrative act which would have brought representative government to Red River. The British were not keen to convert Red River into a Crown Colony, agreeing after a parliamentary investigation of the HBC charter in 1857 that the settlement would eventually go to Canada.

At Red River, in the Oregon Territory, and on Vancouver Island, the Hudson's Bay Company had found it extremely difficult to reconcile fur trading with settlement. In a larger sense, this failure was not because the Company was attempting to establish a fur trading monopoly, but because it was a private enterprise run by businessmen and driven by the balance sheet. Some historians have argued that Western Canada's history of settlement was more peaceful than the United States largely because of this corporate rather than frontier ethic. This book shows that perception is not entirely founded in fact.

Despite its many problems, the new Hudson's Bay Company which emerged out of the fur trade wars provided a necessary transitional phase for the previously unorganized western parts of British North America. In a very real sense, therefore, Western Canada as it developed was a direct legacy of the often bloody conflict of the period 1811-1821.

Appendix:
The War of Words

*F*ew events in Canadian history, and certainly none in the first half of the nineteenth century, produced as much public controversy as did the fur trade wars. From 1816 to 1820, more than thirty books and pamphlets were published in Canada, Great Britain, and the United States by individuals involved in the controversy, and more would have appeared in 1821 and beyond had the Earl of Selkirk not died and the two fur trading companies finally agreed to merge.

There was substantial newspaper involvement as well, both in the form of news reports and letters to the editor. In the course of the public debate, a good deal of the documentary evidence was reprinted and made publicly available. Each side hired court stenographers to produce some of the earliest full trial transcripts in Canadian history. Each side employed professional journalists to assist in getting its version of the story out to the public. The expenses of such propagandizing, while hardly equal to the amounts spent on the courtroom battles, were not inconsiderable. Bills for the costs of printing alone in the Selkirk papers total over £1,000. "Spin-doctoring" was hardly an invention of the late twentieth century.

Naturally, the nature of the controversy being debated did not remain static. The earliest publications were criticisms of the other side's general record. A more specific level was reached as the combatants contended with different versions of what had happened in Red River and Fort William in 1815 and 1816. The final phase of the controversy really was over British government policy and the administration of justice in the Canadas.

Documenting any effect of the enormous quantities of printers' ink consumed by the fur trade warriors is extremely difficult, although occasionally public policy was demonstrably affected, not so much by a publication itself as by a petition or report to government that was subsequently published. Some evidence exists that the Selkirk forces did eventually make some impact on opinion among British members of parliament and the elite circles associated with political power in Great Britain with their explanations of how Selkirk and his people at Red River had been systematically victimized by Colonial Office actions and Canadian favouritism. In general, however, about all we can do with the evidence is to assess the shifting nature of the overall credibility of the arguments and evidence of the contending sides, rather than the influence of one single item or another. Each side presented its version of the general conflict and various particular events within it in a variety of forms.

In terms of overall credibility, what is plain is that the NWC increasingly lost the battle of the press. Partly this was because Selkirk's people became over time ever more conscious of the importance of the public controversy, and came to devote substantial amounts of time and money to it. But mostly the eventual "victory" of the Selkirk forces came because they were able to shift the focus of the discussion from who was responsible for what had happened in the West to who was responsible for the inability of all parties — but especially Selkirk and his settlers — to achieve any measure of justice for earlier malefactions. In the process, it became possible to portray Selkirk as an honourable man attempting to achieve justice despite the best efforts of governments on both sides of the Atlantic, overly sympathetic to the NWC, to sweep matters under the rug. The NWC could make out a decent case for its resistance in the West. There was little case to be made out for the maladministration of justice which resulted from the violence which had occurred. Moreover, when the cumulative violence was totted up, the two sides appeared not equally culpable. Almost all of the damage to persons (as opposed to property) could be laid at the door of the NWC, as Selkirk and HBC propagandists continually emphasized.

1. The Public debate opens:

Some letters to the editor and newspaper articles had appeared in Scottish newspapers in 1811. The anonymous letters of "Highlander", 'really Simon McGillivray' in the *Inverness Journal* at the time of the mustering of the first party of settlers to Red River, began the public debate. These letters produced a handful of answering correspondence at the time, but were not followed up by either the NWC or the HBC. The fur trade press controversy did not resume in earnest until early in 1816 with the publication in London of Archdeacon John Strachan's *A letter to the Right Hon. the Earl of Selkirk, on his settlement at the Red River, near Hudson's Bay.*

Strachan had interviewed a number of the Selkirk settlers who had been brought to Upper Canada by NWC canoes from Red River in 1815. He accused Selkirk of offering "generous" terms to his Highlanders which "native Americans would never accept," adding that the earl was little more than a land speculator "anxiously preparing an asylum in a distant corner of the earth" in case Great Britain should fall to the enemy. Turning to the eventual fate of Selkirk's colonists, Strachan echoed the earlier arguments of the NWC in 1811. The colony was thoroughly isolated and unable to produce for a market, which meant that the land was shamefully overpriced. The settlers recruited in Sutherlandshire had been misled by "false and delusive" promises. The archdeacon concluded by predicting that the colonists would find themselves caught in the struggle between the rival fur trading companies, a position productive of "melancholy events." He recommended that any people in Britain tempted by Selkirk's offers come instead to Upper Canada, where they could receive free land and the protection of the law.

For his part, Lord Selkirk opened his side of the controversy with publication of *A Sketch of the British Fur Trade in North America; with Observations relative to the North-West Company of Montreal.* This work was hastily written in the summer of 1815, although based on substantial earlier research into fur trade documents and history. It bore the distinct marks of the library rather than first-hand experience, being distinguished for its utter inability to recognize the existence of the mixed-bloods. The manuscript was left with an English publisher when the earl departed for Montreal in September of that year and it was published at the beginning of 1816. Selkirk used this study to condemn the NWC for its treatment of the aboriginals of North America. He insisted that the entire fur trading system of the Nor'Westers was based upon brutal violence and a "systematic violation of justice." Employing the earlier writings of Count Andreani, who had travelled in North America in 1791 and had carefully observed the North-West fur trade, Selkirk insisted that the NWC exploited its own servants and aboriginals alike.

If Selkirk had intended to produce a work as well received as his earlier book on emigration — which was quickly accepted by reviewers and politicians alike as a major theoretical statement on the subject — he was sadly mistaken. *A Sketch of the Fur Trade* was too obviously partisan. It did make an important conceptual contribution to the fur trade debate, however. It promoted Andreani's model of the systemic nature of violence in the trade, which in turn became a central ingredient of the Coltman Commission Report on the fur trade wars.

2. Documentation of the Events of 1815-16:

Both Strachan and Selkirk had produced general works rather than controversial pamphlets geared to the immediate developments in the fur trade war. Selkirk's supporters brought out under the name of Archibald McDonald the first of the attempts to spin fast-breaking events. It was entitled *Narrative respecting the Destruction of the Earl of Selkirk's Settlement upon Red River, . . .* in 1815. This account saw the dispersal of the settlement as an NWC plot, rather than a voluntary withdrawal by discontented settlers. McDonald's name was also used to refute John Strachan's "pamphlet" in a series of four letters to the *Montreal Herald*, which were subsequently collected and published as *Reply to the letter, lately addressed to the Earl of Selkirk, by the Hon. and Rev. John Strachan, D.D. &c.* The McDonald narrative in turn produced more letters to the editor of the Montreal Herald, which became *Communications from Adam McAdam, originally published in the Montreal Herald, in reply to letters inserted therein under the signature of Archibald Macdonald, respecting Lord Selkirk's Red River Settlement.*

For most of 1816, the print controversy had not reached the point of considering Seven Oaks. A series of letters appeared in the *Montreal Herald* from 28 August to 20 November 1816 signed "Mercator," a *nom de lume* for Edward Ellice, London business agent for the Montreal fur traders. These letters answered another series of newspaper letters signed by "Manlius," whom Mercator accused of being a Selkirk hiring "paid by the yard." Manlius was probably Samuel Gale. Initially intended to defend the NWC interpretation of the HBC charter, Mercator's letters developed into an ongoing commentary on events in the West as news of them reached the East. They became more and more strident and full of personal invective against Selkirk, described in an early letter as a "canting pretended philanthropist" whose colony "originated in avarice, has been prosecuted in deception and fraud, and must end in disgracing the character of a British nobleman."

The NWC produced its own version of 1815 and 1816 in *To the Right Honorable Henry Earl Bathurst, One of His Majesty's Principal Secretaries of State, . . . The Memorial of Messrs. M'Tavish, Fraser, and Co. and Messrs. Inglis, Ellice, and Co.*, printed by B. McMillan in 1816. Both sides agreed that formal statements to government ought not to be wasted in the files of the Colonial Office. Indeed, many petitions and memorials of this period were really only excuses for a publication. This memorial was sent in the names of the two London merchant firms who handled the NWC's trade. It had probably been drafted by Edward Ellice. It put before Lord Bathurst a narrative of the injuries suffered by the NWC at the hands of Selkirk, beginning with a brief account of the origins of the disputes between the earl and the Nor'westers. The pamphlet did not deny that "irregularities, or acts of violence" had been committed "by some of the numerous and mixed population in the service of the North-West Company," but it insisted that the agents and partners of the company had nothing to do with such actions. It called upon government to intervene. The usual "appendix" printed a number of documents to support its case.

Early in 1817, Lord Selkirk's brother-in-law John Halkett produced the first detailed account of the fate of the Red River settlement in 1815 and 1816, entitled *Statement respecting the Earl of Selkirk's Settlement of Kildonan, upon the Red River, in North America, its destruction in the years 1815 and 1816; and the massacre of Governor Semple and his party*. This work, which included many of the documents in the case, was printed in London, originally for "private circulation." Certainly the Selkirk forces saw to it that their "friends" all received multiple copies of this book, thus probably achieving wider circulation than simple publication could ever have achieved. Selkirk himself would later report to his wife that he had left copies of the "Statement" in New York, had sent copies to Washington, D.C., and would bring some to York as well. This narrative made a strong impression on its readers. The philosopher Dugald Stewart wrote Selkirk's sister that a friend "had got the pamphlet in Edin'r late in an Evening, & was so irresistibly carried along with it, that he read it from beginning to end before he went to bed." Stewart observed, "I heard him add, that if all the facts in it should be substantiated by proper evidence, he had not the slightest doubt that Lord S. will obtain a complete triumph over his enemy." This work was subsequently enlarged and published in London by John Murray. It now included a "Postscript" bringing events to the end of 1816. A French translation appeared in Montreal in 1818, and an American edition came out that same year. Not everyone was persuaded that publication of so many documents was a good idea. In 1818 Dr. John Allan reported to Selkirk, "We must publish no more documents. Those in the Statement have served their Lawyers as a text-book on all occasions."

The success of the Halkett pamphlet led the NWC to bring the journalist Samuel Hull Wilcocke to Montreal to head up the Nor'Wester publicity department. Wilcocke produced *A Narrative of Occurrences in the Indian Countries of North America, since the Connexion of the Right Hon. the Earl of Selkirk with the Hudson's Bay Company, and his Attempt to Establish a Colony on the Red River; with a Detailed Account of His Lordship's Military Expedition to, and Subsequent Proceedings at Fort William, in Upper Canada.* This production saw Selkirk's behaviour since 1811 as a deliberate plot against the North West Company, and appended a number of documents to support its case.

The final pamphlet of 1817, apart from the reprint of the "Mercator" letters, was Samuel Gale's *Notices on the Claims of the Hudson's Bay Company and the Conduct of its Adversaries*, which — as its title suggested — argued the charter claims of the HBC against the attacks upon it by the NWC. For Gale, the violence against the Red River settlement was only the first level of threat to the colony; more dangerous were the threats to the charter.

3. Reporting the Trials:

Attention turned to the courts in 1818, and both sides scrambled to get full trial reports of the key cases before the public. The best Montreal stenographer was reputed to be William Simpson, who was assiduously courted by both sides. Simpson told Selkirk that his rates were 5 guineas per diem and 7 pence half penny per hundred words for the copy, or 100 guineas for the duration of the job. Selkirk contemplated bringing in a stenographer from New York, but his friends were unable to find a decent candidate. Dr. John Allan was put in charge of negotiating with Simpson and dealing with his easily-bruised ego. It was no easy task. Simpson's initial notes were not regarded as sufficiently detailed to bring out the falsities in the NWC testimony at the Charles de Reinhard trial, and had to be supplemented by other material. Moreover, sensing a seller's market, Simpson's demands became increasingly extravagant. At the same time, he was very slow at producing final copy.

Allan reported to Samuel Gale that Simpson was "the most unreasonable mortal alive." He would not accept a stipend of £300 per year and all the profits of publication unless he was allowed to give away copies and received travelling expenses. Worse still, said Allan, "he talked highly of his rights as a Stenographer to publish whatever he pleased." At one point Lord Selkirk was forced to write a letter of apology to Simpson for communicating with him through third parties.

In the end, Samuel Hull Wilcocke — who probably prepared his own shorthand copy of the de Reinhard/MacLellan trials — was able to bring his version out first as *Report of the trials of Charles de Reinhard and Archibald M'Lellan for murder, at a court of oyer and terminer, held at Quebec, May 1818*. Simpson's *Report at large of the trial of Charles de Reinhard for murder (committed in the Indian Territories), at a court of oyer and terminer held at Quebec, May 1818, to which is annexed a summary of Archibald M'Lellan's indictment as an accessory* was published almost a year later. The two transcripts of the same trial mainly demonstrated how different the same original   testimony could appear in partisan hands.

Wilcocke would bring out three more trial transcripts in 1819. These included *Report of the proceedings connected with the disputes between the Earl of Selkirk and the North West Company, at the assizes, held in York in Upper Canada, October, 1818; The Trial of John Cooper and Hugh Bennerman; and finally, Report of proceedings at a court of oyer and terminer appointed for the investigation of cases from the Indian Territories, held . . . at Quebec . . . 21st October, 1819*. The first of these reports dealt with the trial which led to the acquittal of Boucher and Brown for the murder of Robert Semple. The second, at a court of oyer and terminer in York in October 1818, was one of two Selkirk settlers being accused of feloniously stealing cannon from the settlement in 1815. The jury was virtually directed by the judge to acquit, and it did so. Perhaps more than any other trial report, this one demonstrated that some of the Selkirk prosecutions were not particularly well-founded.

The final trial transcript chiefly involved the cases of a number of partners of the NWC charged with offences who appeared to demand their trials and were unable to obtain them because "The Private Prosecutor was not ready". Many of these partners were released by the court from some of their recognizances, but not all. This report also dealt with indictments against a large number of individuals employed by the HBC and Selkirk for the assault and false imprisonment of a number of Nor'Westers at the Grand Rapid in June of 1819.

The Selkirk forces gave up on William Simpson after his one publication. Instead, Selkirk brought the legal material to London and put it in the hands of the lawyer-journalist Andrew Amos, who produced *Reports of trials in the courts of Canada, relative to the destruction of the Earl of Selkirk's settlement on the Red River; with observations* in 1820. Amos arranged the complex material methodically. He was prepared to editorialize as well as transcribe. In his introduction, he described the fur trade wars as exhibiting "a state of society, of which no British colony has hitherto afforded a parallel: — Private vengeance arrogating the functions of public law; — Murder Justified in a British Court of Judicature, on the plea of exasperation, commencing years before the sanguinary act; — the Spirit of monopoly raging in all the terrors of power, in all the force of organization, in all the insolence of impunity."

In the short run, the NWC benefitted enormously from the results of the trials, as its publication of so many trial reports indicates. It was able to demonstrate that the Canadian courts would not convict, and that in at least some cases the evidence was extremely tenuous. The Selkirk forces were able to turn these legal disasters to their eventual advantage, however.

4. Influencing the British Audience:

Most of the important later publications in the fur trade wars were primarily intended for the British rather than the Canadian audience. They were mainly produced by the Selkirk side, although one of the most important items was the "blue book" published by the British government in 1819 This report reprinted the Colonial Office's papers on Red River, as well as the text of the Coltman Report. These works provided a very important perspective on the conflict, emphasizing the extent to which Selkirk and his settlers had been systematically victimized by the NWC, which was in turn supported by governments on both sides of the Atlantic. The NWC really did not attempt to compete with this spate of Selkirk-centred material. Trial reports, upon which the NWC concentrated in the later years of the pamphlet exchange, probably did not really contribute much to the British telling of the NWC story. As a result, it clearly lost the press war in 1819 and 1820, especially in Great Britain.

Before he left North America at the end of 1818, Selkirk had completed the manuscript which became *The Memorial of Thomas Earl of Selkirk to His Grace Charles Duke of Richmond*. In a letter to Richmond dated 22 October, the earl referred to this memorial, which he said would take some time to be copied out before it was submitted. A printed version of the memorial, dated 21 October, was in circulation by February 1819, for Dr. John Allan from York reported that some people had commented that Selkirk should have brought it out earlier, before he left the country. This pamphlet was Selkirk's most complete effort to provide a perspective on the fur trade wars and his participation in them. Much of it was written before he became seriously ill and while he was still in complete intellectual command of the documentation.

The narrative of events in the interior up to 1816 offered little that was new, although by this time Selkirk did appreciate that the mixed bloods (he uses the terms "half-breeds" or "Bois Brûlés") were neither aboriginals nor Canadians, but a separate group of people. At the same time, he denied that they were independent players, insisting that most were employed by the NWC. Selkirk struck out into fresh territory when he got to the appointment of William Coltman as commissioner of special enquiry. His account of his experiences with the Coltman Commission left it clear that he found Coltman part of the problem rather than part of the solution. John Allan reported from York early in 1819 that some readers were unhappy that Selkirk had come down "too heavy upon poor unoffending Coltman, a good natured Laugh and Grow fat sort of person, who had no wish but to conciliate and tranquillize all parties." But the negative consequences of this inoffensiveness of Coltman was exactly Selkirk's point. It allowed all those who had committed violence in the Indian Territories to escape punishment.

Selkirk concluded by making the point which would characterize all of the later Selkirk publications. The issue was no longer the control of the fur trade, "But whether the British Government, does or does not afford protection to its subjects" and further, "whether to promote the sordid purposes of individual gain or illegal monopoly, murder may be systematically organized, and the blood of British subjects remain unattoned, because some of those who profit by it, are members of the Executive and Legislative Councils of Lower Canada, and reputed to be under the special protection of His Majesty's Government."

The insistence that the real issue was not the fur trade but British justice was continued through a series of pamphlets published in London in 1819. Canadian official and public opinion was now pushed to the background; the British government itself — and the British "public" — was now the focus of attention. John Halkett had carried on a lengthy private correspondence with Earl Bathurst in the period 1817 to 1819 which was highly critical of both the Colonial Office and the authorities in the Canadas, who he maintained were acting in response to what they thought were instructions from London. Those letters were now collected and printed as *Correspondence in the years 1817, 1818, and 1819, between Earl Bathurst and J. Halkett, Esq., on the subject of Lord Selkirk's settlement at the Red River in North America*. One of Halkett's major theses in the letters was that many of Selkirk's legal problems had originated with the order of 11 February 1817 from Bathurst to have the earl criminally indicted, which Selkirk had subsequently found out about only inadvertently. In this dispatch, Bathurst had prejudged the earl's behaviour at Fort William on the representations of a single interested party, thus setting in motion an entire series of subsequent injustices.

Alexander Greenfield Macdonell's *A Narrative of Transactions in the Red River Country; from the Commencement of the Operations of the Earl of Selkirk, till the Summer of the year 1816* was published in London in 1819, virtually the only narrative effort by the Nor'Wester forces in this year. It was probably intended to provide an alternate narrative to those that the Selkirk forces were by this time producing in profusion for the British market. A fairly feeble effort with no new material and no discussion of the court cases, it probably had little effect on the debate.

Selkirk had hoped through private correspondence with Lord Liverpool, the head of the government and a personal friend, to induce the Colonial Office to admit its past mistakes in dealing with the fur trade wars and investigate his allegations. Not surprisingly, Lord Bathurst was unrepentant, and Lord Liverpool was not anxious to intervene. As a result, Selkirk printed the lengthy letter he had written to Liverpool, dated 19 March 1819. The earl's chief London legal advisor, Alexander Mundell, insisted that there should be no formal publication, which would make the earl eligible for a libel suit. Who would have sued is not clear. Mundell cautioned, "No copy should be given to any person, but for a purpose necessary for the prosecution of the means of redress in a legal or constitutional manner." The original letter to Lord Liverpool, as the printed version made clear, was accompanied by a copy of the Halkett pamphlet, which "will also point out the unexampled conduct of the Law Officers of the crown, and other public functionaries, in Canada; and the total perversion of justice which it has occasioned." In a much shorter compass, Selkirk concentrated here on criticism of the Coltman Commission, arguing against placing any reliance on the reports of that commission. His chief complaint was that Coltman refused to deal with the allegations made against the Nor'Westers and their allies. Instead, he offered immunity to the mixed-bloods involved in Seven Oaks while he interviewed them. "They were allowed to tell their story to the Commissioner, and then to depart, unmolested, into the plains, where there was no prospect of overtaking them; and after this, Mr. Coltman declared, that he was ready to receive evidence against them." Selkirk's old mentor, Dugald Stewart, wrote that the Liverpool letter and the Halkett correspondence "appears to me to make out so very strong a case as will render it impossible for any influence whatever to quash the investigation you solicit."

When Liverpool refused to take action, noting that the complaint did not come within his jurisdiction as first Lord of the Treasury, the Selkirk forces turned to Parliament. Such political action was dangerous, since Selkirk did not want this to become a partisan issue in the House of Commons, which would have muddied the waters. The first step, therefore, was simply to call for the papers in the case. A petition of John Pritchard for government assistance was used as the vehicle to have the papers tabled in the House. Pritchard rehearsed his own experiences, both in Red River and with the courts of the Canadas, and prayed relief from all "vexatious and harassing proceedings" by whatever means Parliament could provide. This petition was printed at the time by John Brettell. Sir James Montgomery made the request for the papers in an eloquent speech on 19 June, which was also subsequently printed. The Commons addressed the Prince Regent for the material — "copies of extracts of official communications which may have taken place between the secretary of state and the provincial government of Upper or Lower Canada, or to any complaints made of those proceedings by Lord Selkirk or the agents of the Hudson's Bay or the North-West Companies," as well as the Coltman report — on 24 June. The result was the printing by Commons order on 12 July of the blue book, *Papers Relating to the Red River Settlement*.

This "blue book" provided a sort of final vindication for Selkirk's behaviour in North America. The documentation demonstrated that he had acted as he had claimed. The papers showed that the government had refused to listen to his early pleas for intervention to protect his settlers, and this total inaction provided a context for the expedition of 1816 which ended up occupying Fort William. The corrspondence with the legal officers of the Crown revealed them as obfuscating functionaries of dubious motives. Despite Selkirk's efforts to discredit it, the written report of William Coltman further confirmed the impression that Selkirk had behaved with honour.

As might have been expected, Coltman's overall analysis was that everybody was to blame. He saw the HBC as responsible for initiating the fur trade wars by attempting to enforce a monopoly which had been allowed to fall into disuse. He was particularly hard on Selkirk's agents at Red River, especially Miles Macdonell, for the Pemmican Proclamation, which asserted a legal authority well beyond anything tested in the courts. He also admitted that there was no evidence that Selkirk had authorized such proceedings. As for the various outrages carried out in the colony in 1815 and 1816, Coltman acknowledged that here — as in the fur trade wars generally — the NWC had employed violence and intimidation as a routine part of their daily lives. But after a detailed discussion of all the available evidence in the Seven Oaks affair, he concluded that it was an inadvertent explosion rather than a deliberate action. Although he allowed that the mixed-bloods were trying to intimidate the settlers, they had not set out to murder them. Moreover, there was no evidence that the NWC had ordered such depredations. Coltman added that, given his sincere understanding of the law and his legal rights, Selkirk had never transgressed them. From the standpoint of resolving the questions of how to prevent the continuation of what had gone wrong in the West, however, Coltman's report was singularly ineffectual. He called weakly for the assumption of control of the Indian Territories by the Crown, but offered no more specific remedies.

To make sure that the right conclusions were drawn from the blue book, the Selkirk people prepared a substantial pamphlet, *Observations upon the Papers Laid before the House of Commons, relating to the Red River Settlement.* This work was published in London in 1820, printed by J. Brettell. It is possible that the author was Samuel Gale. It provided a detailed item-by-item gloss upon the documentation in the parliamentary papers, putting them all in the larger context of the story of the fur trade wars according to Selkirk.

Observations upon the Papers used the government's documentation to raise the interesting question of how the affidavit of Robert McRobb, made in York in mid-December of 1816, managed to get dealt with by Lord Bathurst on 11 February 1817. It pointed out further that not only was McRobb an NWC clerk, but that his deposition did not attempt to authenticate either the warrant or the service. Indeed, the author asserted, the evidence was that the entire series of actions of Bathurst in February 1817 were not based on "any evidence or information transmitted by the regular channel of the Provincial Government of Canada." Most of a subsequent chapter was devoted to adding an indictment of Major Fletcher to the official record. The author pointed out that Fletcher could not have advised Coltman on legal matters in the drafting of the report, although it was full of legal language. He then added, "there is not to be met with on the streets of Montreal a common Canadian voyageur who earns his bread by paddling a canoe once a year into the interior, who could not have supplied the Governor-General with better information respecting the state of the Indian countries than this Commissioner of Special Inquiry."

In his final months, Lord Selkirk prepared two further works for publication. They got as far as the printed page, but were never actually released before his death and were apparently then held back by the estate after it. In these two works, Selkirk attempted to place his experiences with Red River in the larger context. He sought — as he wrote in the opening paragraph of one of these works — to show "a consistency of view, and of conduct." He insisted he had acted under the sanction of government for an object of "national advantage" and not from petty motives connected with fur trading. In these valedictories, Selkirk saw his entire career as one devoted to encouraging and facilitating Highland emigration to British North America.

Who won the fur trade press wars? To some extent the answer depends on timing and location. The NWC probably came out ahead in British North America and before the end of 1818. But the HBC and Selkirk plainly triumphed in Great Britain in 1819, when they were able to shift the focus from Red River to the courts of Canada. Ironically, although neither side did very well in the legal battles, the NWC did far better in the courts themselves than it did in the subsequent debate over the court decisions. Certainly the Selkirk interpretation of 1818/19 — that the colonial governments and courts conspired together against Selkirk to thwart justice — became accepted by almost everybody after the event. It is still accepted by most historians today.

Nicholas Garry and William McGillivray discuss
the final merger of their two companies.

Select Bibliography

Manuscripts:

Although much of the documentation in the fur trade wars has been printed, both in the contemporary debate and in the editions and writings of subsequent scholars, much remains in manuscript form. Three collections are absolutely essential to any understanding of the conflict. The Selkirk Papers, really transcripts of Selkirk manuscripts now lost in a fire, are at the National Archives of Canada in Ottawa. These papers, running to over 27,000 pages in length, are much more than merely the correspondence of the Earl of Selkirk. They include an enormous amount of collateral material, including depositions and affidavits from many of the participants in the struggle and a good deal of scattered North West Company material. The Selkirk Papers must be supplemented by the material in the Archives of the Hudson's Bay Company in Winnipeg. The HBC has over the years really won the fur trade wars by preserving its papers with singular meticulousness. As a result, the best evidence for almost any point of the fur trade comes to us from the HBC perspective. Finally, for the Canadian trials and their context, the material in Colonial Office 42 — the official papers of Upper and Lower Canada, the originals of which are housed in the Public Record Office in London — is absolutely indispensible. Other useful material can be found scattered in a variety of repositories, most notably: the Provincial Archives of Manitoba, the Provincial Archives of Ontario, the Provincial Archives of British Columbia, the Toronto Public Library, the Scottish Record Office, the Scottish National Library, and the British Library.

Primary Printed:

Contemporary Debate: Probably no Canadian event of the nineteenth century produced as much printed documentation as the fur trade wars. Both sides reprinted affidavits, depositions, and other documents on a regular basis. The publicity war between the companies even ran to competing trial transcripts!

Amos, Andrew, ed., *Report of Trials in the Courts of Canada, Relative to the Destruction of the Earl of Selkirk's Settlement on the Red River; with Observations* (London: John Murray, 1820).

Atcheson, N., *On the Origin and Progress of the North-West Company of Canada, with a History of the Fur Trade, as Connected with that Concern* (London, 1811).

Boucher, François Firmin, *Relation donneé par lui-même des événements qui ont eu lieu sur le territoire des sauvages depuis le mois d'octobre 1815, jusqu'au 19 juin 1816, époque de la mort de Mr. Semple, avec les détails de son long emprisonment, jusqu'à son jugement* (Montreal: n.p., 1819).

Brown, Robert, *Remarks on the Earl of Selkirk's Observations on the Present State of the Highlands of Scotland, with a View of the Causes and Probable Consequences of Emigration* (Edinburgh: John Anderson, 1806).

Correspondence in the Years 1817, 1818, and 1819, between Earl Bathurst and J. Halkett, Esq., on the Subject of Lord Selkirk's Settlement at the Red River in North America ([London]: J. Brettell, 1819.)

[Ellice, Edward], *The Communications of "Mercator", upon the Contest between the Earl of Selkirk and the Hudson's Bay Company on One Side, and the North West Company on the Other* (Montreal: W. Gray, 1817).

[Gale, Samuel], *Notices on the Claims of the Hudson's Bay Company and the Conduct of its Adversaries* (Montreal: William Gray, 1817].

[Gordon, James, of Craig], *Eight Letters on the Subject of the Earl of Selkirk's Pamphlet on Highland Emigration; as They Lately Appeared under the Signature of Amicus in One of the Edinburgh Newspapers* (London: Longman & Co, 1806).

[Halkett, John], *Statement Respecting the Earl of Selkirk's Settlement of Kildonan, upon the Red River, in North America; Its Destruction in the Years 1815 and 1816; and the Massacre of Governor Semple and his Party* (London: J. Brettell, 1817).

[Halkett, John] *Postscript to the Statement Respecting the Earl of Selkirk's Settlement upon the Red River* (London: John Brettell, 1818).

McAdam, Adam, *Communications from Adam McAdam, originally Published in the Montreal Herald, in Reply to Letters Inserted Therein under the Signature of Archibald Macdonald, Respecting Lord Selkirk's Red River Colony* (Montreal: W. Gray, 1816).

McDonald, Archibald, *Narrative Respecting the Destruction of the Earl of Selkirk's Settlement upon Red River, in...1815* (London: John Brettell, 1816).

McDonald, Archbald, *Reply to the Letter, Lately Addressed to the Earl of Selkirk, by the Hon. and Rev. John Strachan, D.D., &c. Being Four Letters (reprinted from the Montreal Herald), Containing a Statement of Facts, Concerning the Settlement on Red River, in the District of Ossiniboia, Territory of the Hudson's Bay Company, Properly Called Rupert's Land* (Montreal: W. Gray, 1816).

Macdonell, Alexander Greenfield, *A Narrative of Transactions in the Red River Country; from the commencement of the Operations of the Earl of Selkirk, till the Summer of the Year 1816* (London: B. M'Millan for Egerton, 1819).

McKenzie, Daniel, *A Letter to the Rt. Hon the Earl of Selkirk in Answer to a Pamphlet entitled "A Postscript in Answer to the Statement respecting the Earl of Selkirk's Settlement on the Red River in North America"* (Sandwich, UC: n.p., 1818).

McTavish, Fraser, and Co., and Inglis, Ellice and Co., *To the Right Honorable Henry, Earl Bathurst, One of His Majesty's Principal Secretaries of State, . . . the Memorial of Messrs. M'Tavish, Fraser, and Co. and Messrs. Inglis, Ellice and Co.* (London, B. McMillan, 1816).

Narratives of John Pritchard, Pierre Chrysologue Pambrun, and Frederick Damien Heurter, Respecting the Aggressions of the North West Company, against the Earl of Selkirk's Settlement upon Red River (London: John Murray, 1819).

Observations upon the Papers Laid before the House of Commons, relating to the Red River Settlement (London: J. Brettell, 1820).

Papers Relating to the Red River Settlement (London: House of Commons, 1819).

Selkirk, Thomas Douglas, Fifth Earl of, *A Letter to the Earl of Liverpool from the Earl of Selkirk, Accompanied by a Correspondence with the Colonial Department (in the years 1817, 1818, 1819), on the Subject of the Red River Settlement in North America* (London, 1819).

Selkirk, Thomas Douglas, Fifth Earl of A, *Sketch of the British Fur-trade in North America, with Observations relative to the North-West Company of Montreal* (London: James Ridgeway, 1816).

Simpson, William S., *Report at Large of the Trial of Charles de Reinhard for Murder (Committed in the Indian Territories), at a Court of Oyer and Terminer Held at Quebec, May 1818, to Which is Annexed a Summary of Archibald M'Lellan's Indictment as an Accessory* (Montreal, 1819).

Substance of the Speech of Sir James Montgomery, bart., in the House of Commons, on the 24th of June, 1819, on Bringing Forward His Motion Relative to the Petition of Mr. John Pritchard, of Red River Settlement (London: 1819).

Strachan, John, *A Letter to the Right Hon. the Earl of Selkirk, on his Settlement at the Red River, Near Hudson's Bay* (London: Longman, Hurst, Rees, Orme, & Brown, 1816).

[Wilcocke, Samuel Hull], *A Narrative of Occurrences in the Indian Countries of North America, since the Connexion of the Right Hon. the Earl of Selkirk with the Hudson's Bay Company, and His Attempt to Establish a Colony on the Red River; with a Detailed Account of his Lordship's Military Expedition to, and Subsequent Proceedings at Fort William in Upper Canada* (London: B McMillan, 1817).

Wilcocke, Samuel Hull], ed., *Report of Proceedings at a Court of Oyer and Terminer Appointed for the Investigation of Cases from the Indian Territories, held . . . at Quebec . . . 21st October, 1819* (Montreal: William Gray, 1819).

[Wilcocke, Samuel Hull], ed., *Report of the Proceedings Connected with the Disputes between the Earl of Selkirk and the North West Company, at the Assizes, Held in York in Upper Canada, October, 1818* (Montreal: printed by James Lane and Nahum Mower, 1819).

[Wilcocke, Samuel Hull], ed., *Report of the Trials of Charles de Reinhard and Archibald McLellan for Murder, at a Court of Oyer and Terminer, Held at Quebec* (Montreal: James Lane and Nahum Mower, 1818.)

[Wilcocke, Samuel Hull], ed., *The Trial of John Cooper and Hugh Bennerman* (Montreal: Nahum Mower, 1819).

Other Primary Sources:

Bumsted, J. M., ed., *The Collected Writings of Lord Selkirk 1810-1820: Volume II in the Writings and Papers of Thomas Douglas, Fifth Earl of Selkirk* (Winnipeg: Manitoba Record Society, 1987).

Garry, Nicholas, "The Diary of Nicholas Garry, Deputy-Governor of the Hudson's Bay Company, from 1822-35," *Transactions of the Royal Society of Canada, 1900*.

Gates, C.M., ed., *Five Fur Traders of the North-West* (St. Paul: Minnesota Historical Society, 1933).

Glimpses of the Past on the Red River Settlement from the Letters of John Pritchard 1805-1836 (Middlechurch: Rupert's Land Indian Industrial School Press, 1936).

James, Edwin, ed., *A Narrative of the Captivity and Adventures of John Tanner (U.S. Interpreter at the Saut de Ste. Marie) during Thirty Years Residence among the Indians in the Interior of North America* (Minneapolis: Ross & Haines, 1956).

Lamb, W.K., ed., *Journal of a Voyage on the North West Coast of North America during the Years 1811, 1812, 1813 and 1814 by Gabriel Franchère* (Toronto: Champlain Society, 1969).

"Letter Book of Captain Miles Macdonell," *Report on the Canadian Archives 1886* (Ottawa, 1887).

Martin, Archer, ed., *The Hudson's Bay Company's Land Tenures and the Occupation of Assiniboia by Lord Selkirk's Settlers with a List of Grantees under the Earl and the Company* (London: W. Glowes,1898).

Masson, L. R., ed., *Les Bourgeois de la Companie du Nord-ouest* (Quebec, A. Coté. 1889).

Morrison, Jean, ed., *The North West Company in Rebellion: Simon McGillivray's Fort William Notebook, 1815* ([Thunder Bay], Thunder Bay Historical Museum, 1988).

Nute, Grace Lee, ed., *Documents relating to the North West Missions* (St. Paul: Minnesota Historical Society, 1942).

Oliver, E.M., ed., *The Canadian North West in its Early Development and Legislative Records* (Ottawa, 1914).

Rich, E. E., ed., *Colin Robertson's Correspondence Book, September 1817 to September 1822* (Toronto, Champlain Society for Hudson's Bay Record Society, 1939).

Rich, E. E., *Journal of Occurrences in the Athabasca Department by George Simpson, 1820-21 and Report* (Toronto: Hudson's Bay Record Society, 1938).

Ross, Alexander, *Adventures of the First Settlers on the Oregon or Columbia River: Being a Narrative of the Expedition Fitted out by John Jacob Astor, to Establish the "Pacific Fur Company"* (London: Smith, Elder and Co., 1849).

Spaulding, Kenneth A., ed., *Alexander Ross: The Fur Hunters of the Far West* (Norman: University of Oklahoma Press, 1956).

Stewart, Edgar I. and Jane R. Stewart, eds., *The Columbia River: Or scenes and adventures during a residence of six years on the western side of the Rocky Mountains among various tribes of Indians hitherto unknown; together with "A Journey across the American Continent"* by Ross Cox (Norman, Okla: University of Oklahoma Press, 1957).

Wallace, W. Stewart, ed., *Documents Relating to the North West Company* (Toronto: Champlain Society, 1934).

Secondary Printed:

Books:

Brode, Patrick, *Sir John Beverley Robinson: Bone and Sinew of the Compact* (Toronto: The Osgoode Society, 1984).

Brown, Jennifer, *Strangers in Blood: Fur Trade Families in Indian Country* (Vancouver and London: University of British Columbia Press, 1980).

Campbell, Marjorie Wilkins, *The North West Company* (rev. ed., Vancouver: Douglas & McIntyre, 1983).

Campbell, Marjorie Wilkins, *McGillivray Lord of the Northwest* (Toronto: Clark, Irwin, 1962).

Cole, Jean Murray, *Exile in the Wilderness: The Biography of Chief Factor Archibald McDonald, 1790-1853* (Don Mills: Burns & MacEachern Ltd., 1979).

Cookson, J. E., *Lord Liverpool's Administration 1815-1822* (Edinburgh: Scottish Academic Press, 1975).

Coutts, Robert and Richard Stuart, eds., *The Forks and the Battle of Seven Oaks in Manitoba History* (Winnipeg: Manitoba Historical Society, 1994).

Cruikshank, E. A., *Robert Dickson, the Indian Trader* (1892).

Davidson, G. C., *The North-West Company* (Berkeley: University of California Press, 1918).

David, Richard C., ed., *Rupert's Land: A Cultural Tapestry* (Waterloo: Wilfrid Laurier University Press, 1988).

Fisher, Robin, *Contact and Conflict: Indian-European Relations in British Columbia, 1774-1890* (Vancouver, UBC Press, 1977).

Gibson, Dale and Lee, *Substantial Justice: Law and Lawyers in Manitoba 1670-1870* (Winnipeg: Peguis 1970).

Gibson, James R., *The Lifeline of the Oregon Country: The Fraser-Columbia Brigade System, 1811-47* (Vancouver: UBC Press, 1997).

Gibson, James R., *Otter Skins, Boston Ships, and China Goods: The Maritime Fur Trade of the Northwest Coast, 1785-1841* (Montreal: McGill-Queen's UP, 1992).

Giraud, Marcel, *Le métis canadien; son vôle dans l'histoire des provinces de l'Ouest* (Paris: Institute d'Ethnologie, 1945).

Greer, Allan, *Peasant, Lord, and Merchant: Rural Society in Three Quebec Parishes 1740-1840* (Toronto: University of Toronto Press, 1985).

Gray, John Morgan, *Lord Selkirk of Red River* (Toronto: Macmillan of Canada, 1962).

Innis, Harold, *The Fur Trade in Canada: An Introduction to Canadian Economic History* (Toronto: University of Toronto Press, 1970).

Irving, Washington, *Astoria, or, Anecdotes of an Enterprise beyond the Rocky Mountains* (rev. ed., NY: G.P. Putnam's, 1868).

Karamanski, Theodore J., *Fur Trade and Exploration: Opening the Far Northwest 1821-1852* (London and Norman: University of Oklahoma Press, 1983).

MacEwan, Grant, *Cornerstone Colony: Selkirk's Contribution to the Canadian West* (Saskatoon: Western Producer Prairie Books, 1977).

Mackie, Richard Somerset, *Trading Beyond the Mountains: The British Fur Trade on the Pacific 1793-1843* (Vancouver: UBC Press, 1997).

MacLeod, Margaret Arnett and W. L. Morton, *Cuthbert Grant of Grantown* (Toronto: M & S, 1963).

Martin, Chester, *Lord Selkirk's Work in Canada* (Toronto: Oxford University Press, 1916).

Merk, Frederick, *The Oregon Question: Essays in Anglo-American Diplomacy and Politics* (Cambridge, Mass.: Harvard UP, 1967).

Milani, Lois Darroch, Robert Gourlay, Gadfly: *The Biography of Robert (Fleming) Gourlay, 1778-1863 Forerunner of the Rebellion in Upper Canada, 1837* (n.p.: Ampersand Press, 1971).

Morse, Eric W., *Fur Trade Canoe Routes of Canada/Then and Now* (Toronto, University of Toronto Press, 1969).

Morton, A.S., *History of the Canadian West to 1870-71* (Toronto: T. Nelson & Sons, 1939).

Ormsby, Margaret, *British Columbia: A History* (Toronto: Macmillan, 1971).

Parker, James, *Emporium of the North: Fort Chipewyan and the Fur Trade to 1835* (Regina, Alberta Culture and Heritage and Canadian Plains Research Centre, 1987).

Peterson, Jacqueline and Jennifer S. H. Brown, eds., *The New Peoples: Being and Becoming Métis in North America* (Winnipeg: University of Manitoba Press, 1985).

Porter, K. W., *John Jacob Astor, Business Man, 2 vol.* (Cambridge, Mass: Harvard UP, 1931).

Pritchett, John Perry, *The Red River Valley 1811-1849* (Toronto: Ryerson Press, 1942).

Ray, Arthur J., *Indians in the Fur Trade: their role as hunters, trappers and middlemen in the lands southwest of Hudson Bay 1660-1870* (Toronto and Buffalo: University of Toronto Press, 1978).

Ray, Arthur J., *I Have Lived Here since the World Began: An Illustrated History of Canada's Native People* (Toronto: Lester Publishing, 1996).

Rich, E. E., *The Fur Trade and the Northwest to 1857* (Toronto: McClelland and Stewart, 1967).

Rich, E. E., *The Hudson's Bay Company, 1660-1870, 3 vol.* (Toronto, McClelland and Stewart, 1960).

Riddell, William Renwick, *The Life of William Dummer Powell: First Judge at Detroit and Fifth Chief Justice of Upper Canada* (Lansing: Michigan Historical Commission, 1924).

Riddell, William Renwick, *Robert (Fleming) Gourlay as Shewn by His Own Records* (Toronto, Ontario Historical Society, 1916).

Roe, F. G., *The North American Buffalo: A Critical Study of the Species in its Wild State* (Toronto: University of Toronto Press, 1970).

Ronda, James P., *Astoria & Empire* (Lincoln & London: University of Nebraska Press, 1990).

Ross, Eric, *Beyond the River and the Bay: Some Observations on the State of the Canadian Northwest in 1811 with a View to Providing the Intending Settler with an Intimate Knowledge of That Country* (Toronto: University of Toronto Press, 1970).

Shilliday, Gregg, ed., *A History of Manitoba 125, Volume One Rupert's Land to Riel* (Winnipeg: Great Plains Publications, 1993).

Terrell, J. U., *Furs by Astor* (New York, 1963).

Wallace, J. N., *The Wintering Partners on the Peace River from the Earliest Records to the Union of 1821* (Ottawa: Thorburn and Abbott, 1929).

Articles:

Barron, F. L., "Victimizing his Lordship: Lord Selkirk and the Upper Canadian Courts," *Manitoba History* 7 (1984), 14-22.

Dick, Lyle, "The Seven Oaks Incident and the Construction of a Historical Tradition, 1816 to 1970," *Journal of the Canadian Historical Association,* new ser., 2 (1991) 91-114.

Dick, Lyle, "Historical Writing on "Seven Oaks": The Assertion of Anglo-Canadian Cultural Dominance in the West," in Robert Coutts and Richard Stuart, eds., *The Forks and the Battle of Seven Oaks in Manitoba History* (Winnipeg, 1994), 65-70.

Foster, Hamar, "Long-Distance Justice: The Criminal Jurisdiction of Canadian Courts West of the Canadas, 1763-1859," *American Journal of Legal History*, 34 (1990), 1-48. Glazebrook, G.P. de T., ed., "A Document Concerning the Union of the Hudson's Bay Company and the Northwest Company," *Canadian Historical Review*, 1932.

Gressley, Gene M., "Lord Selkirk and the Canadian Courts," in Bumsted, ed., *Canadian History before Confederation: Essays and Interpretations*, I (Georgetown: Irwin-Dorsey Ltd., 1972), 287-306.

Holland, Clive, "John Franklin and the Fur Trade, 1819-22," in Richard C. Davis, ed., *Rupert's Land: A Cultural Tapestry* (Waterloo: Wilfrid Laurier University Press, 1988), 97-111.

MacKay, C., "Kaministiquia, the Great Rendezvous," *Canadian Geographical Journal*, 36 (January 1948), 9-15.

MacLeod, M.A., "Cuthbert Grant of Grantown," *Canadian Historical Review*, March 1940.

Morton, A. S., "The Canada Jurisdiction Act and the North West," *Proceedings and Transactions of the Royal Society of Canada*, 3rd series, 1938, section II.

Morton, A.S., "The New Nation the Métis," Proceedings and Transactions of the Royal Society of Canada, 3rd series, 1939, section II.

Morton, A.S., "The North West Company's Columbian Enterprise and David Thompson," *Canadian Historical Review*, 17 (September 1936), 266-288.

Porter, K. W., "John Jacob Astor and Lord Selkirk," *North Dakota Historical Quarterly*, 1930.

Pratt, Julius W., "Fur Trade Strategy and the American Left Flank in the War of 1812," *American Historical Review*, January 1935, 246-273.

Stanley, G.F.G., ed., "Documents relating to the Swiss Migration to Red River, 1821," *Canadian Historical Review*, March 1941.

"The Appeal of the North West Company to the British Government to Forestall John Jacob Astor's Columbian Enterprise," *Canadian Historical Revew*, 17 (September 1936), 304-11.

Wallace, W. S., "The Literature Relating to the Selkirk Controversy," *Canadian Historical Review*, 13 (1932), 45-50.

Index